The characteristic form taken by English Ma~~~~~~~~~~~~~~~~~~~~~~~~~~~
history. No writer exemplifies its achieveme~~~~~~~~~~~~~~~~~~~~~~~~~~~
whose *Making of the English Working Class* is ~~~~~~~~ ~~~ ~~~~~ influential single
work of historical scholarship by a socialist today. An editor of *The New Reasoner*
in 1957-1959, a founder of the New Left in 1960, now an eloquent champion of
civil rights, Thompson has most recently aroused widespread interest with the
appearance of his *Poverty of Theory*, which combines philosophical and political
polemic with Louis Althusser, and powerful advocacy of the historian's craft.
Arguments Within English Marxism is an assessment of its central theses that
relates them to Thompson's major historical writings themselves. Thus the role
of human agency—the part of conscious choice and active will—in history is discussed through consideration of its treatment in *The Making of the English Working Class*. The problems of base and superstructure in historical materialism, and
of affiliation to values in the past, are reviewed in the light of *Whigs and Hunters*.
The claims of utopian imagination are illustrated from the findings of *William
Morris*. Questions of socialist strategy are broached in part through the articles
now collected in *Writing by Candlelight*. Exploring at once differences and
convergences between *New Left Review* and one of its founders, the essay
concludes by suggesting the virtues of diversity within a common socialist
culture.

V

Perry Anderson

Verso

Arguments Within
English Marxism

**British Library
Cataloguing in Publication Data**

Anderson, Perry
  Arguments Within English Marxism.
  1. Thompson, Edward Palmer
  I. Title
  907' .2'024   D15.T5/

© Perry Anderson, 1980
NLB and Verso Editions,
15 Greek Street, London W1

Photoset in Monophoto Plantin by
Red Lion Setters Ltd.,
Holborn, London

Printed in Great Britain by
Redwood Burn Ltd,
Trowbridge

ISBN 0 86091 727 4 (paper)
ISBN 86091 030 X (cloth)

Contents

The historian may tend to be a bit too generous because a historian has to learn to attend and listen to very disparate groups of people and try and understand their value-systems and their consciousness. Obviously in a very committed situation you can't always afford that kind of generosity. But if you afford it too little then you are impelled into the kind of sectarian position in which you are repeatedly making errors of judgement in your relations with other people. We have seen a lot of that recently. Historical consciousness ought to assist one to understand the possibilities of transformation and the possibilities within people.

EDWARD THOMPSON

Edward Thompson is our finest socialist writer today—certainly in England, possibly in Europe. Readers of *The Making of the English Working Class*, or indeed *Whigs and Hunters*, will always remember these as major works of literature. The wonderful variety of timbre and rhythm commanded by Thompson's writing at the height of its powers—alternately passionate and playful, caustic and delicate, colloquial and decorous—has no peer on the Left. Arguably, too, the strictly historical achievement of the series of studies that extends across the 19th and 18th centuries from *William Morris* to the rich group of recent essays whose collection is promised in *Customs in Common* is perhaps the most original product of the corpus of English Marxist historiography to which so many gifted scholars have contributed. Setting aside any other consideration, it is rare for any researcher to become equally at home in two such contrasted epochs. Whatever comparative estimate is made in this respect—where doubtless no final judgement is attainable—two distinctive characteristics of Thompson's practice as a historian stand out. Throughout, his has been the most declared political history of any of his generation. Every major, and nearly every minor, work he has written concludes with an avowed and direct reflection on its lessons for socialists of his own time. *William Morris* closes with a discussion of 'moral realism'; *The Making of the English Working Class* recalls our debt to the 'liberty tree' planted by the early English proletariat; *Whigs and Hunters* ends with a general revaluation of the 'rule of law'; an essay like 'Time, Work-Discipline and Industrial Capitalism'[1] speculates on the possible synthesis of 'old and new time-senses' in a communist society of the

1. *Past and Present*, No 38, 1967, pp. 56-97.

future that has surpassed the 'problem of leisure'. Each of these texts has been in its own way a militant intervention in the present, as well as a professional recovery of the past. The massive consistency of their direction, from the mid 50s to the late 70s, visibly attested in the long Postscript to the new edition of the study of Morris (1977) is profoundly impressive. At the same time, these works of history have also been deliberate and focused contributions to theory: no other Marxist historian has taken such pains to confront and explore, without insinuation or circumlocution, difficult conceptual questions in the pursuit of their research. The definitions of 'class' and 'class consciousness' in *The Making of the English Working Class*; the critique of 'base and superstructure' through the prism of law in *Whigs and Hunters*; the reinstatement as disciplined imagination of 'utopianism' in the new edition of *William Morris*—all these represent theoretical arguments that are not mere enclaves within the respective historical discourses, but form rather their natural culmination and resolution.

The claim on our critical respect and gratitude, then, is one of formidable magnitude and complexity. Some appraisal of Thompson's central ideas and concerns is, however, long overdue. The publication of *The Poverty of Theory* provides an occasion to begin such an assessment.[2] Released over a year ago, it has received a generally favourable press in England. But at the date of writing, no extended response to it has so far appeared. Given the challenge of the book, this seems like something of an anti-climax. In many ways, I cannot be regarded as the most apposite interlocutor. *The Poverty of Theory* contains four essays, three already published and one unpublished. The former include the famous critique of views of English society and history developed in *New Left Review*, entitled 'The Peculiarities of the English', to which I rejoined over a decade ago. The latter is an attack across two hundred pages on the thought of Louis Althusser, and by its scale and novelty inevitably dominates the book. The appropriate respondent to it would obviously be an Althusserian. However, in the absence for the moment of more indicated candidates, it seems worthwhile at this point to review the theses Thompson sets out in the book-length essay which gives its title—and manifesto—to the volume. For 'The Poverty of Theory—or an Orrery of Errors' is not only a polemic against Althusser: it is also the

2. London, 1978.

most sustained exposition of Thompson's own credo, as a historian and as a socialist, that he has given us to date. The purpose of the essay here, then, will be threefold. It will look at Thompson's criticisms of Althusser, and try to determine their justice. Simultaneously, and more importantly, it will seek to elicit some of the cruces of Thompson's substantive work, through the grill of the principles and procedures he recommends in *The Poverty of Theory*.[3] The treatment of Althusser, starting moderately and ending in a gale of fury, is unconventional in organization. Discussion of it will be facilitated by some regroupment of its themes, for a more compact comment on them. *The Poverty of Theory* is, in effect, dominated by four main problems: the character of historical inquiry, the role of human agency in history, the nature and fate of Marxism, and the phenomenon of Stalinism. I will consider each of these in turn, as they present themselves in Thompson's criticisms of Althusser and in his own practice as a historian; and in conclusion will try to put Thompson's work into a comparative context, capable of clarifying in some degree the differences which have arisen between him and *New Left Review*, a journal he took a central part in creating. Whatever our view of specific arguments in *The Poverty of Theory*, the enterprise itself must be welcomed. It represents the first full-scale engagement by an English historian with a major philosophical system from the continent, over the terrain of Marxism. A direct encounter between the two different discursive traditions represented by Thompson and Althusser has for some time now been much needed, for the development of historical materialism as a whole.[4] It is to Thompson's credit that he has undertaken the task, initiating a process of exchange that we must hope will eventually be many-sided.

---

3. References to the latter will henceforward be abbreviated to PT; *The Making of the English Working Class* (Penguin edition: 1963) to MEWC; *Whigs and Hunters* (1973) to WH; *William Morris—Romantic to Revolutionary* (1977 re-edition) to WM.
4. See the remarks in *Considerations on Western Marxism*, London 1976, pp. 111-112.

1
Historiography

The opening sections of *The Poverty of Theory* are addressed to certain general issues of historiography as a discipline. Three distinct problems are explored by Thompson, which can be formulated as follows: (i) what is the particular nature and place of *evidence* in any historical inquiry? (ii) what are the appropriate *concepts* for the understanding of historical processes? (iii) what is the distinctive *object* of historical knowledge? In each case, Thompson evokes and rejects what he takes to be Althusser's answer, and proposes his own solution. He begins his case with the charge that Althusser's epistemology exhibits a radical indifference towards the primary data which make up what it terms Generalities I: no explanation or attention is ever given to either the character of these data, or their origins—chief among which is 'experience'. Althusser's cavalier attitude towards empirical facts is confirmed by his account of Generalities II, or the process of cognition itself, which in effect assumes that any scientific theory can define and produce its own facts by self-validating protocols, without recourse to external appeals. Thompson argues that this is an abusive extension of the very limited and exceptional procedures of mathematics or logic, that is wholly illegitimate if applied to either the social or physical sciences, where the controls of evidence are always central. The result is that no genuine new knowledge can emerge in Althusser's Generalities III (its ostensible site), since Generalities II has already pre-packaged the data of Generalities I anyway—there is an epistemological circle. The result is *'exactly* what has commonly been designated, in the Marxist tradition, as idealism'[1]—that is, 'a self-generating conceptual universe which imposes its own identity upon the phenomena of material and social existence, rather than engaging in continual dialogue with them'.[2]

What is the justice of these charges? In my view, a great deal. Althusser's theory of knowledge—both of science and of ideology—is, as I have argued elsewhere, directly tributary to that of Spinoza.[3] It is not surprising that an epistemology with this metaphysical background should be incompatible with the canons of modern science. Lucio Colletti once remarked: 'One could say that there are two main traditions in Western philosophy in this respect: one that descends from Spinoza and Hegel, and the other from Hume and Kant. These two lines of development are profoundly divergent. For any theory that takes science as the sole form of real knowledge, there can be no question that the tradition of Hume-Kant must be given priority and preference over that of Spinoza-Hegel'.[4] The broad truth of this claim is incontrovertible. In the case in hand, there is no doubt whatever that Althusser displays no interest in the (diverse) origin and nature of Generalities I, within his schema. In one respect Thompson even goes too far towards him, when he casually supposes that 'sense-perception' is not 'knowledge'.[5] In fact, certain kinds of perceptual experience—the sense-data with which radical empiricism from Hume onwards has always been so preoccupied—do not need transformation by any Generalities II to yield knowledge: they constitute an elementary form of knowledge in themselves, without further ado (for example, what is the weather like?). Althusser's system wrongly assimilates knowledge to science *tout court*—an inaugural slip far from trivial in its consequences: the ultimate sources of his insensibility towards evidence lie here. Thompson is certainly right to indict this. On the other hand, his bracing attack on the notion that primary historical facts are in some sense typically 'rigged' or 'pre-selected' by the intention of those who left them behind[6] is germane to Popper, who has advanced

1. PT, p. 205.
2. PT, p. 205.
3. *Considerations on Western Marxism*, pp. 64-65.
4. 'A Political and Philosophical Interview', first published in *New Left Review* 86, p. 11, now in *Western Marxism—A Critical Reader*, London 1977, p. 325.
5. PT, p. 224.
6. PT, p. 218.

this absurd contention, but not to Althusser, who has never done so. An argument salutary in itself is here misused to suggest guilt by association. Similarly, Thompson condemns with every justification two English sociologists, Hirst and Hindess,[7] for their dictum that 'facts are never given, they are always produced', but fails to note that the work from which he quotes precisely attacks Althusser for 'empiricism', and hence can scarcely be regarded as a stand-in for the latter.

In constructing an eloquent and necessary general defence of the historian's craft, Thompson in effect too often proceeds to an amalgamation of individual positions, each of them deficient, but in significantly different degrees and ways. Thus Althusser does indeed reply improperly on logico-mathematical protocols of proof as models of scientific procedure. His theory of knowledge, dissociated from the controls of evidence, is untenably internalist: above all, it lacks any concept of falsification. *Vice versa*, however, the strength of Popper's philosophy of science—one is not sure whether Thompson realizes how strong it is—has always lain precisely in its insistence on falsifiability, a principle crucially qualified by Lakatos and others, but uncompromised by Popper's egregious illusions about historical records. The hostility which Thompson senses in the two philosophers to the practice of the historian has opposite origins—approximately, over-confidence in the paradigms of mathematics and of physics respectively; and opposite outcomes—denial of any laws of motion in the random course of history, and affirmation of them in the implacable machinery of the *Darstellung*. The familiar argument that extremes meet is not one that survives closer inspection. Far more pertinent and substantial is Thompson's analytic demolition of Althusser's maxim that 'the knowledge of history is no more historical than the knowledge of sugar is sweet'. In a spirited demonstration, he exposes the sophistry of the comparison, which he points out would have to read 'chemical' for 'sweet' to be sustained—and in so doing would cancel its own pretension.[8] The intention of Althusser's formula, of course, was to dramatize the distance between the 'real object' and the 'object of knowledge'. Ironically, the ambiguity of the word 'historical' in it produces exactly the confusion it is designed to avoid. For alone among the sciences, *history* as a term—unlike astronomy or sociology, linguistics or biology, physics or chemistry—designates at

7. PT, p. 218.
8. PT, p. 387.

once the process and the discipline that seeks to grasp it. Failing to locate the danger of conflation where it genuinely arises, in this ordinary usage, Althusser reproduces it in the very form of his gesture against it.

Thompson's own affirmation of the irreducible, independent reality of historical evidence, and of the various ways in which it can be interrogated, is in general a model of good sense. Some of the distinctions he draws—as between 'value-bearing' and 'value-free', or 'lateral' and 'structural', types of evidence—are perhaps less clear-cut than he suggests. But few writers, or reflective readers, of history would dissent from his description of the 'historian's workshop' here. The difficulties really begin on the other side of his enumeration of the different kinds of questionnaire that can be employed in looking at primary evidence. This is sharply brought home when Thompson recommends the 'reality rule' of J.H. Hexter, that the historian should seek out 'the most likely story that can be sustained by the relevant existing evidence', as 'helpful'— only to have to regret immediately afterwards that 'it has been put to work by its author in increasingly unhelpful ways, in support of a prior assumption that *any* Marxist story *must* be unlikely'.[9] But, of course, the banality of the formula is precisely the guarantee of its disutility: who is to determine what is relevant, or for that matter what constitutes a story? We are immediately referred back to the thornier problem of historical *concepts*. Thompson does not attempt to expound or justify the specific set of categories that defines historical materialism—an abstention with important consequences later in his essay. He suggests in passing, with perfect propriety, that 'there are other legitimate ways of interrogating the evidence'[10] than those which have formed the major patterns of inquiry for Marxist historians. Rather than dwell on the particular canons and procedures typical of Marxist historiography, he emphasizes the common 'test of historical logic'[11] to which they along with all others must submit. In a fine paragraph, he then represents the general verdict of the discipline thus: 'The court has been sitting in judgement upon historical materialism for one hundred years, and it is continually being adjourned. The adjournment is in effect a tribute to the robustness of the tradition; in that long interval the cases against a hundred other interpretive systems have been upheld, and the culprits have disappeared

9. PT, p. 387.
10. PT, p. 387.
11. PT, 236.

"downstairs". That the court has not yet found decisively in favour of historical materialism is not only because of the ideological *parti pris* of certain of the judges (although there is plenty of that) but also because of the provisional nature of the explanatory concepts, the *actual* silences (or absent mediations) within them, the primitive and unreconstructed character of some of the categories, and the inconclusive determinacy of the evidence.'[12]

The forms of appeal that the court of the historical discipline allows are dual: 'evidential' and 'theoretical'. Evidence, as Thompson notes, he has already sufficiently discussed. What of theory? Here appeal must be to 'the coherence, adequacy and consistency of the concepts, and to their congruence with the knowledge of adjacent disciplines'.[13] Wherein, then, does the force or fallibility of Marxist historical concepts lie? Thompson does not address himself directly to this issue. Instead, he poses a wider question: what is the distinctive nature of historical concepts *in general*—Marxist or non-Marxist? His answer is that they are 'expectations rather than rules', for they possess a 'particular flexibility', 'necessary generality and elasticity', a 'coefficient of mobility'[14] due to to the quicksilver nature of the historical process itself. The 'categories change as the object changes'.[15] Once this is understood, it can be seen that while historical materialism is distinguished 'by its stubborn consistency (alas, a stubbornness which has sometimes been doctrinaire) in elaborating such categories, and by its articulation of these within a conceptual totality',[16] for similar reasons it is also perpetually imperilled to a greater degree than non-Marxist historiography by the danger of a rigid and static conceptualization that is radically inappropriate to historical eventuation. 'It is the misfortune of Marxist historians (it is certainly our special misfortune today) that certain of our concepts are common currency in a wider intellectual universe, are adopted in other disciplines, which impose their own logic upon them and reduce them to static, ahistorical categories. No historical category has been more misunderstood, tormented, transfixed, and dehistoricized than the category of social class . . . It is not, and never has been, the business of history

12. PT, p. 237.
13. PT, p. 237.
14. PT, pp. 237, 249, 248.
15. PT, p. 248.
16. PT, p. 242.

to make up this kind of inelastic category.'[17]

Here, however, Thompson is under a misapprehension. His argument in effect amounts to a claim for a legitimate laxity of notions that would be the peculiar privilege of the historian. But the nature of the historical process warrants no such special licence. The fact that its object continually changes no more relieves the discipline of history of the duty of formulating clear and exact concepts for its comprehension than it does meteorology—a physical science whose data notoriously change rather more swiftly and mercurially than those of history itself. If the weather remains largely unpredictable (and uncontrollable), the meteorologist does not resign himself to professions of the inherent approximation of his study: he seeks to push back the limits of our knowledge by further scientific investigation, which will involve not less but more conceptualization, of wider ranges of evidence. So it is in every other science. History is no exception. Brecht once remarked that if human behaviour appears unpredictable, it is not because there are no determinations, but because there are too many.[18] The historian's necessary duty of attention to the particular event or the concrete custom is not to be discharged by bending or stretching general concepts around them. It can only be acquitted by reconstructing the complex manifold of their actual determinations, which will always demand further—*more rigorous*—conceptualization. Thompson tends to see concepts as models or diagrams of a reality that never quite behaves itself, in an alternation of the 'abstract' and the 'particular' which forgets this central injunction of Marx: 'The concrete is concrete because it is a synthesis of many determinations, hence unity of the diverse . . . the abstract determinations lead towards a reproduction of the concrete by way of thought'.[19] If categories are to be categories at all, they demand precise and unequivocal definition. To capture the processes of change which indeed characterize history, historical concepts have to be very carefully formulated and specified: but they will only *be* concepts if they fix some structure of invariance, however much internal variation such a structure may allow—in other words, however wide its morphology. Does this condition of intellectual cogency preclude an adequate grasp of any

17. PT, p. 242.
18. 'Die Unberechenbarkeit der kleinsten Körper', from *Me Ti—Buch der Wendungen*, in *Gesammelte Schriften*, Vol 12, Frankfurt 1967, p. 568.
19. *Grundrisse*, London 1974, p. 101.

diachronic history? In no way. On the contrary, far from being especially liable to a schedule of unduly static concepts, as Thompson contends, Marxism preeminently possesses concepts that both theorize the possibilities and limits of historical change as such (contradiction), and explore the dynamic of particular processes of development themselves (the laws of *motion* of capital). Its repertory remains, of course, partial and provisional—in a sense mere overtures to the composition of a plenary history. The absences and insufficiencies of its explanatory instrumentarium to date are not in doubt: Althusser emphasizes them as much as Thompson. But they are reason, not for retreating from theoretical endeavour, but for advancing towards fuller analysis. In other words, the realities of social diversity and historical flux oblige the historian to be more exacting and more productive of concepts, not less. For all his great distance from the practice of the historian, it must be said that Althusser has seen this exigency more clearly than Thompson. But it was Marx who originally inscribed it in the programme of historical materialism.

Thompson, however, contests that history is a science at all, and might therefore discount any comparison with other disciplines. 'The attempt to designate history as a "science",' he argues, 'has always been unhelpful and confusing',[20] because historical knowledge is of its nature provisional, incomplete and approximate. 'The older, "amateurish", notion of History as a disciplined "Humanity" was always more exact'.[21] Now, to quarrel over terms would in itself be idle. But Thompson's refusal of the title of a science to history in fact rests on a serious substantive misunderstanding of the nature of the sciences in general, which leads him to create a false extra-territoriality for history. For he goes on to assert: 'In this sense it is true (we may agree here with Popper) that while historical knowledge must always fall short of positive proof (of the kinds appropriate to experimental science), false historical knowledge is generally subject to *dis*proof.'[22] The contrast postulated here is an imaginary one, however, which suggests a rather limited acquaintance with contemporary philosophy of science. For Popper, of course, has always maintained that conclusive *verification* of scientific hypotheses— in physical or any other branches of knowledge—is axiomatically impossible: the cornerstone of *The Logic of Scientific Discovery* was

20. PT, p. 231.
21. PT, p. 387.
22. PT, p. 232.

precisely his rejection of the 'verification principle' of logical positivism.[23] In its stead, he put the falsification principle—that hypotheses were scientific only in so far as they could be falsified, by pertinent empirical testing. What Thompson thus takes to be the exceptional condition of history is, in fact, the normal status of all science. Provisionality, selectivity and falsifiability are constitutive of the nature of the scientific enterprise as such. Even lack of experimental controls is not confined to historiography: astronomy permits of no laboratory tests either. The most important recent philosophy of science, that of Lakatos, has shown the limits of even Popper's account by demonstrating that a scientific theory can survive a number of falsifications, and must be judged by the long-run development or deterioration of its 'research programme', rather than by its immediate pattern of disconfirmations or failures.[24] In other words, the prolonged 'adjournment' of the verdict on historical materialism, in Thompson's memorable metaphor, is very close to a description of the ordinary circumstances of any scientific theory.

Thompson's disclaimer of 'scientific' accuracy for history, on the other hand, proves to be a preamble to a much grander claim for it. For he goes on to write: ' "History" must be put back upon her throne as the Queen of the humanities, even if she has sometimes proved to be rather deaf to some of her subjects (notably anthropology), and gullible towards favourite courtiers (such as econometrics). But, second, and to curb her imperialist pretensions, we should also observe that "History", in so far as it is the most unitary and general of all human disciplines, must always be the *least* precise. Her knowledge will never be, in however many thousand years, anything more than approximate.'[25] This is certainly a pleasing image. But is it a persuasive one? The answer must surely be no. In what sense is history 'less precise' than aesthetics or

23. *The Logic of Scientific Discovery*, London 1960, p. 40: 'Theories are, therefore, *never* empirically verifiable. If we wish to avoid the positivist's mistake of eliminating, by our criterion of demarcation, the theoretical systems of natural science, then we must choose a criterion which allows us to admit to the domain of empirical science even statements which cannot be verified. These considerations suggest that not the *verifiability* but the *falsifiability* of a system is to be taken as a criterion of demarcation.' For Popper, of course, the problem of demarcation was that of the frontier between 'the empirical sciences on the one hand, and mathematics and logic as well as "metaphysical" systems on the other' (p. 34).
24. Imre Lakatos, *The Methodology of Scientific Research Programmes*, Cambridge 1978, especially pp. 31-47.
25. PT, p. 262.

literary criticism? It is obvious enough that, if we wish to keep these terms, it is far more so. Why should history be incapable of 'anything more than approximate' knowledge? Do we suppose that the date of the October Revolution is subject to alteration in the next century? Exact and positive knowledge has never been beyond the powers of history: its vocation, as with its sister disciplines, is to *extend* it—although the process, as Lenin noted, will always be asymptotic to its object. Any real scrutiny of Thompson's construction undoes it.

A central question remains, however. What defines the *content* of history's 'unitary and general' supremacy over all other human disciplines? We arrive here at the final issue of Thompson's opening discourse on method: what is the specific *object* of historical inquiry? The problem constitutes the classical conundrum of all theories of history. None has proved so intractable to generations of debate by historians and philosophers. Thompson's initial answer to it is surprisingly simple. He equates history with the past. ' "Historical" is a generic definition: it defines very generally a common property of its object—appertaining to the past and not to the present or future'.[26] At the same time, he contends that 'the human past is not an aggregation of discrete histories but a unitary sum of human behaviour'.[27] The logic of these propositions seems to be that history is the record of everything that has happened—a notoriously vacant conclusion to which virtually every previous thinker on the subject has given a *fin de non recevoir*. Carr's criticism of it is famous.[28] In fact, Thompson's slippage towards it is an unpremeditated movement of thought, not his due and deliberate answer to the question—although it is not without significance for another theme of *The Poverty of Theory*, as we shall see. When he consciously addresses the problem in a later section, in response to the very sharp formulation of it by Althusser, he concedes that 'if I get up from my desk (as I will do shortly), to take the darned dog for a walk, this is scarcely an "historical" event. So that what makes events historical must be defined in some other way.' But in what way? It is striking that Thompson scarcely attempts even the most cursory tour of the problem. He merely writes: 'Even when we have defined out innumerable events as of negligible interest to historical analysis, what we must analyze remains as a process of

26. PT, p. 223.
27. PT, p. 232.
28. *What is History?*, London 1961, pp. 5-6.

eventuation. Indeed, it is exactly the significance of the event to this process which affords the criterion for selection.'[29] In a text of two hundred pages, two lines. What do these yield us? A tautology. A historical event is one that is significant to the process of historical eventuation. How do we know whether an event has such significance or not? How do we delimit the eventuation to which it is significant? The two sentences form a single, empty circle.

The reason for Thompson's lapse here is probably that his polemical attention was so polarized by Althusser's solution to the problem that he failed to notice how scant was his own. Curiously, his dislike for Althusser's language is such that he here actually misreads what it is in fact saying. For Althusser does attempt a more substantive definition of the object of history: a historical fact is one 'which causes a mutation in the existing structural relations'.[30] Thompson's comment is indignant: 'Process turns out to be, not historical process at all (this wretched soul has been incarnated in the wrong body) but the structural articulation of social and economic formations . . . The soul of process must be arrested in its flight and thrust into the marble statue of structural immobilism.'[31] In his ire at the phrase 'structural relations', Thompson has overlooked what is the hinge of the definition he is attacking, the term 'mutation'. Althusser's formula puts an impeccable emphasis on *change*, rather than on stability as Thompson imagines it to do. This is not to say that it furnishes a satisfactory solution to the problem. On the contrary, it is undoubtedly too restrictive. Did Marx's death, for example, cause a mutation in existing structural relations? Scarcely. Yet it remains an eminently historical fact. The actual terrain tilled by the historian lies somewhere between a confinement to structural changes and an infinity of human behaviour. It is not a matter of reproach that neither Thompson nor Althusser should have resolved one of the oldest and most obdurate puzzles in the philosophy of history. But of the two, it must be said that it is the French philosopher rather than the English historian who on this occasion has given us the preferable reply—superior because sufficiently firm and definite to be falsifiable.

To sum up: Thompson's definition of the object of history is casual and circular; his prescription for historical concepts, in a traditional

29. PT, pp. 281-282.
30. *Reading Capital*, London 1970, p. 102.
31. PT, p. 281.

emphasis on the approximate character of the discipline, is finally uncompelling; but the opening sections of *The Poverty of Theory* eclipse these shortcomings in their superb vindication of historical evidence, and of its authority over historical materialism. The lack of empirical controls which Thompson rightly perceives in Althusser's work in fact forms part of a wider pattern within Western Marxism, as I have argued elsewhere, from whose speculative slide only Gramsci escaped. The period of that long proclivity is passing today, as a sounder and more inquisitive socialist culture has started to emerge in the 70s. The eloquence of Thompson's admonitions should henceforth stand between it and the temptation of any return to the past.

2
Agency

The second major theme of *The Poverty of Theory* is no longer procedural—what is the nature of historiography?—but substantive: what is the part of conscious human choice, value, action in history? Readers of *William Morris* or *The Making of the English Working Class* will be aware that this is the key organizing theme of Thompson's entire work. The passion he has brought to it over twenty-five years transpires from every page of what now takes its place as his most extended theoretical statement of the problem. His argument essentially runs as follows. Althusser's cardinal sin is his repeated assertion that 'history is a process without a subject',[1] in which individual men and women are 'supports of relations of production'.[2] Although presented as the last word in contemporary Marxism, 'this is a very ancient mode of thought: process is fate'.[3] Today, far from being a proposition of historical materialism, it is in tune with the most reified and decadent bourgeois ideology, which must be resisted by every committed socialist. For, on the contrary, both the genuine heritage of Marx's theory and the actual findings of historical research teach us that men and women are the 'ever-baffled and ever-resurgent agents of an unmastered history'.[4] No one saw this or expressed

1. *Politics and History*, London 1972, p. 183.
2. *Reading Capital*, pp. 112, 252.
3. PT, p. 281.
4. PT, p. 280.

it better than Morris, when he wrote: 'I pondered all these things, and how men fight and lose the battle, and the thing that they fought for comes about in spite of their defeat, and when it comes turns out not to be what they meant, and other men have to fight for what they meant under another name'.[5] History is not a process without a subject: it is 'unmastered human practice',[6] in which each hour is 'a moment of *becoming*, of alternative possibilities, of ascendant and descendant forces, of opposing (class) definitions and exertions, of "double-tongued" signs.'[7] The crucial medium in which men and women convert objective determinations into subjective initiatives is through their *experience*—the junction between 'being and consciousness', by which 'structure is transmuted into process, and the subject re-enters into history'.[8] It is through such experience, for example, that they make themselves into social classes—groups conscious of antagonistic values and interests, and struggling to realize them. 'Classes arise because men and women, in determinative productive relations, identify their antagonistic interests, and come to struggle, to think and to value in class ways: thus the process of class formation is a process of self-making, although under conditions which are "given".'[9] Engels's famous 'parallelogram of forces'—in which 'individual wills do not attain what they want' and yet 'each contributes to the resultant and is to this degree involved in it',[10] dismantled and dismissed by Althusser, can be reinstated once a substitution is made of class for individual volition: 'if the historical resultant is then seen as the outcome of a collision of contradictory class interests and forces, then we may see how human agency gives rise to an involuntary result and how we may say, at one and the same time, that "we make our own history" and "history makes itself".'[11] The real lesson of historical materialism is 'the crucial ambivalence of our human presence in our own history, part-subjects, part-objects, the voluntary agents of our own involuntary determinations'.[12]

The pivot of Thompson's construction, it will be seen, is the notion

5. PT, p. 280.
6. PT, p. 295.
7. PT, p. 295.
8. PT, p. 362.
9. PT, pp. 297-298.
10. PT, p. 279.
11. PT, p. 279.
12. PT, p. 280.

of agency—a dominant in his vocabulary since his earliest writings. Attractively, often movingly, as it is employed in *The Poverty of Theory*, it can come to seem virtually self-explanatory. But in fact it demands very careful and discriminating scrutiny. For its apparent simplicity is deceptive. Let us recall first of all that the term 'agent' reveals a curious ambiguity in ordinary usage, possessing two opposite connotations. It signifies at once active initiator and passive instrument. The word is intended by Thompson exclusively in the first sense: but phrases like 'agents of a foreign power' and 'agents for a merchant bank' remind us of the currency of the second sense. Ironically, Thompson without noticing uses it himself in just this way at a number of points in *The Poverty of Theory*, disparaging what he calls various 'import agencies' for foreign doctrines[13] (among them, *New Left Review*). The same capsizal of meaning, of course, occurs in the related term 'subject', signifying simultaneously 'sovereignty' and 'subordination': a striking coincidence. In the case of agency, however, we have a familiar way of distinguishing between the two senses of the word. Where necessary, speech customarily refers to '*free* agents' to make it clear that the former rather than the latter is intended. Is this what Thompson means by agency? The answer is of some interest. A very large philosophical issue is clearly at stake here. Yet throughout his long essay, the problem breaks surface only once, in a fleeting parenthesis. 'Whatever we may conclude, in the endlessly receding argument of pre-determination and free will', he notes at one point, 'it is profoundly important that we should *think* ourselves to be "free" (which Althusser will not allow us to think)'.[14] The avowal here approaches a pure pragmatism, akin to Nietzsche's doctrine of the 'useful illusion'.[15] In the midst of so many lengthy and unconditional arguments against Althusser, a short clause suddenly opens the gate to ultimate disarmament before him (what if truth belied comfort?). Then the dense press of refutation resumes its course again. We have been reminded, however, of a subterranean uncertainty beneath the confident ground on which agency is generally pitched in *The Poverty of Theory*.

Does Thompson's momentary equivocation disable his overall case?

13. PT, p. 366.
14. PT, p. 344.
15. 'The falseness of an opinion is not for us any objection to it . . . The question is, how far an opinion is life-furthering, life-preserving': *Beyond Good and Evil*, Edinburgh and London 1909, p. 8.

It need not. For the notion of agency can be retained, even on rigorously determinist premises, if we mean by it conscious, goal-directed activity. Sebastiano Timpanaro has proposed a definition close to this in his work *On Materialism*, from a standpoint faithful to the most stoical injunctions of the late Engels.[16] The problem of the ultimate sources of action can then be bracketed in a rational historical inquiry, for a study of its ends. But if agency is construed as conscious, goal-directed activity, everything turns on the nature of the 'goals'. For it is obvious that all historical subjects engage in actions all of the time, of which they are 'agents' in this strict sense. So long as it remains at this level of indeterminacy, the notion is an analytic void. To render it operative, at least three qualitatively different types of goal have to be clearly distinguished. Throughout history to date, the overwhelming majority of people for the overwhelmingly major part of their lives have pursued 'private' goals: cultivation of a plot, choice of a marriage, exercise of a skill, maintenance of a home, bestowal of a name. These personal projects are inscribed within existing social relations, and typically reproduce them. Yet they remain profoundly intentional enterprises, which have consumed the greater part of human energy and persistence throughout recorded time. The historian of any small community plunges directly into the milieu of this universal agency: Leroy Ladurie's study of a 14th century Albigensian village, Montaillou, is an archetypal instance. There have also, of course, been collective or individual projects whose goals were 'public' in character: quantitatively far fewer, involving lesser numbers in more fitful endeavours, but normally more interesting and important for the historian. Will and action here acquire an independent historical significance as causal sequences in their own right, rather than as molecular samples of social relations. The difference is typically inscribed in historical records themselves: to take two late medieval documents, say, between the Paston Letters and Froissart's Chronicles. Religious movements, political struggles, military conflicts, diplomatic transactions, commercial explorations, cultural creations, have been among the staple types of such public agendas. However, these too in their overwhelming majority have not aimed to transform *social relations as such*—to create new societies or master old ones: for the most part they were much more limited in their (voluntary) scope. The goals pursued have been

16. See, for example, *On Materialism*, London 1975, p. 105.

characteristically inserted within a known structural framework, taken for granted by the actors. The foundation of the Benedictine Order in the Dark Ages, the building of Notre Dame, the Habsburg-Valois wars in Italy, the Treaty of Westphalia or Utrecht, the competition between Hats and Caps in parliamentary Sweden, Commodore Perry's voyage to Japan—most familiar historical events or processes of this kind, whatever their misery or grandeur, have been marked by the pursuit of local objectives within an accepted order over-arching them. Large-scale military conquests themselves, which might appear an exception, have generally sought no more than to impose a new political and economic authority in otherwise unaltered lands: the Mongol Empire, the greatest of all, is a classic example. The *consequences* of foreign annexation could, of course, be far more drastic, in ways unimagined by the conquerors (the demographic collapse of the Mexican population after Cortes). But this is equally true of any of the forms of historical initiative just described. By definition, it is intentional reach rather than involuntary result that distinguishes one form of agency from another.

Finally, there are those collective projects which have sought to render their initiators authors of their collective mode of existence as a whole, in a conscious programme aimed at creating or remodelling whole social structures. There are isolated premonitions of this phenomenon, in political colonization, religious heterodoxy or literary utopia, in earlier centuries: but essentially this kind of agency is very recent indeed. On a major scale, the very notion of it scarcely predates the Enlightenment. The American and French Revolutions are the first historical figurations of collective agency in this, decisive sense. Originating as largely spontaneous explosions and ending with politico-juridical reconstructions, however, they still remain at a great distance from the manifestation of a full popular agency desiring and creating new social conditions of life for itself. It is the modern labour movement that has really given birth to this quite new conception of historical change; and it is with the advent of what its founders called scientific socialism that, in effect, for the first time collective projects of social transformation were married to systematic efforts to understand the processes of past and present, to produce a premeditated future. The Russian Revolution is in this respect the inaugural incarnation of a new kind of history, founded on an unprecedented form of agency. Notoriously, the results of the great cycle of upheavals it initiated have to date been far from those expected at their outset. But the alteration of the potential of historical action, in the course of the 20th century, remains irreversible.

Now the effect of Thompson's appeals to agency in his critique of Althusser is to permit a slide from sense one through sense two to sense three. Their rhetorical impact relies on the persuasive everyday evidence that people go about their lives making all sorts of choices, enacting values and pursuing ends, some of them realized, others not, others realized in ways not wanted. This kind of agency (choice of husband or lover, in Thompson's witty parable of the woman worker)[17] is then elided with the limited collective project, which is less frequent (the strike in her workshop), and that can then be tacitly equated with the form of agency indicated by Morris's dictum, which clearly refers to overall social trans- formations (its context is the Peasants' Revolt), which are very rare indeed as willed processes in history. The reductive phrase '*ever*-baffled, *ever*- resurgent human agents' provides the timeless linkage. The conceptual error involved is to amalgamate those actions which are indeed conscious volitions at a personal or local level, but whose social incidence is profoundly *in*voluntary (relation of marriage-age, say, to population growth), with *those actions which are conscious volitions at the level of their own social incidence*, under the single rubric of 'agency'. The paradoxical result of Thompson's critique of Althusser is thus actually to reproduce the fundamental failing of the latter, by a polemical inversion. For the two antagonistic formulae of a 'natural-human process without a subject' and 'ever-baffled, ever-resurgent agents of an unmastered practice' are both claims of an essentially apodictic and speculative character—eternal axioms that in no way help us to trace the actual, variable roles of different types of deliberate venture, personal or collective, in history. A *historical*, as opposed to an axiomatic, approach to the problem would seek to trace the *curve* of such enterprises, which has risen sharply—in terms of mass of participation and scale of objective—in the last two centuries, from previously low levels. Even so, however, it is important to recall that there are huge areas of existence which remain largely outside *any* form of concerted agency at all. Demographic patterns, to take the previous example, have traditionally fallen outside the domain of any conscious social choice. If they are now beginning for the first time to be the object of attempts at deliberate intervention, initial experiments in

17. PT, pp. 342-343.

population control still remain largely ineffective, as in India or China (as well as authoritarian), while inducements to population growth, as in the DDR or France, have so far yielded little results. Another zone of primordial human practice that remains even more unwilled is, of course, language: although even here the 20th century has seen partial exceptions, such as the revival of Hebrew in Israel. The area of self-determination, to use a more precise term than 'agency', has been widening in the past 150 years. But it is still very much less than its opposite. The whole purpose of historical materialism, after all, has precisely been to give men and women the means with which to exercise *a real popular self-determination for the first time in history*. This is, exactly, the objective of a socialist revolution, whose aim is to inaugurate the transition from what Marx called the realm of necessity to the realm of freedom.

The lack of any echo of this basic theme of Marxism in Thompson's essay on Althusser is very surprising. All the more so, perhaps, because it does find a place in the lengthy text addressed to Kolakowski, written earlier and now published in the same volume. There, Thompson singles out 'the human potential to act as rational and moral agents' as 'a concept coincident with that of the passage from the kingdom of necessity to that of freedom'.[18] Under communism, 'things are thrown from the saddle and cease to ride mankind. Men struggle free from their own machinery and subdue it to human needs and definitions. Man ceases to live in a defensive posture, warding off the assault of "circumstances", his furthest triumph in social engineering a system of checks and balances and countervailing powers against his own evil will. He commences to live from his own resources of creative possibility, liberated from the determinism of "process" within class-divided societies'.[19] From this account, however, Thompson draws an unexpected conclusion. 'Should this kingdom of freedom be attained, the argument entails no guarantee whatsoever that men will choose wisely nor be good.'[20] This contingency soon assumes a very tangible and immediate form. For 'it might be possible, hideously inapposite as the metaphor appears, that the "socialist" countries have already shuffled across Marx's frontier into the "kingdom of freedom". That is, whereas in previous history social being

18. PT, pp. 166-167.
19. PT, p. 167.
20. PT, pp. 167-168.

appeared, in the last analysis, to determine social consciousness, because the logic of process supervened over human intentions; in socialist societies there may be no such determining logic of process, and social consciousness may determine social being.'[21] Thompson then goes on to speculate as follows: 'Methods of historical analysis to which one had become habituated would cease to have the same validity in investigating socialist evolution. On the one hand, it opens up the perspective of a long protraction of tyranny. So long as any ruling group, perhaps fortuitously established in power at the moment of revolution, can reproduce itself and control or *manufacture* social consciousness there will be no inherent logic of process within the system which, as social being, will work powerfully enough to bring its overthrow.'[22] But at the same time, 'over and above any challenge emerging from "social being", the ruling group has *most* to fear from the challenge of rational "social consciousness". It is exactly rationality and an open, evaluative moral process which "ought" to be the logic of socialist process, expressed in democratic forms of self-management and in democratic institutions'.[23] The flight of this whole argument, hypothetically advanced as it is, must take aback anyone familiar with the theory of historical materialism or the reality of the USSR and associated countries. For the realm of necessity is founded, for Marx, on *scarcity*: the leap into freedom evoked in *Capital* only becomes possible with the advent of generalized abundance. While the ruling stratum in the USSR, far from enjoying a paramount mastery over the laws of historical development in the Soviet Union, has notoriously stumbled through a long series of unpredicted social crises and uncontrolled economic processes, from sudden grain shortages to wild epidemics of terror to creeping paralyses of productivity—all of them blind motions of a society dark to all its members.

How could Thompson have arrived at such a perverse construction? The answer lies in a twofold error. Firstly, he has implicitly identified historical agency with the expression of *will* or *aspiration*. Indeed, throughout *The Poverty of Theory*, the terms in which he conceives it tend to be existential in range—'choice', 'value', 'decision'. What is missing from them is any due complementary emphasis on the *cognitive* dimensions of agency. The sovereign practice of the associated producers

21. PT, p. 167.
22. PT, p. 155.
23. PT, p. 155.

envisaged by Marx as the attainment of communism was not only a product of will, but equally and indivisibly of *knowledge*. For any materialist study of the variable forms of social agency in history, this component of it is central. 'Mastery' of society in the mere sense of an instrumental political voluntarism has nothing new about it: it has been the ambition and activity of princes since the dawn of the division of labour. The very existence of the State, as a centralized apparatus of coercion and administration, guarantees the presence of this kind of power in every class society. From the earliest times, and in the most diverse social formations, it produced its own manuals—the *Mirror of Kings*, compilations of tactical adages and prescriptions for successful exercise of rule which can be found from ancient Egypt to mediaeval Tibet, and which flourished above all in the Islamic world. Modern political thought in the West owes its origins to these brittle guide-books of domination: what else is the form of Machiavelli's *Prince*? The limitations of this secular literature are those of its historical understanding: unable to grasp, often even to glimpse, the social mechanisms underlying political stability or change, it was confined to myopic maxims for regal conduct, sententious or cynical as the culture prompted. The conservative type of agency it codified survives to this day, but with an increasingly significant alteration. With the onset of industrial capitalism in the 19th century, the greatest statesmen of reaction were characteristically those who proved able to steer major transformations of State by calculated exploitation of social or economic forces beyond the purview of the traditional optic of politics. Cavour, Bismarck and Ito were the supreme exemplars of this major enlargement of the pattern of conscious superordination. But their lucidity remained operational rather than structural. None possessed any general vision of historical development, and the work of each ended in ulterior debacle, consummated by 20th century successors—Mussolini, Hitler and the Showa adventurers—who mistook their legacy as a lesson in the efficacy of a voluntarism without restraint. The cult of political will without social sight ended in near class suicide for German, Italian and Japanese capital in the Second World War. The record of this dementia is a reminder of how far a monopoly of political power is from a mastery of historical process. The same holds true for the Soviet or Chinese bureaucracies today, whose capacity to understand their own societies is inherently limited by the ideological necessities of their own usurpation and privilege. Indeed, it is safe to say that *no* social formation short of full socialist democracy is likely to generate accurate knowledge of its own deepest laws of motion.

In itself, however, even common aspiration fused with real cognition, in a post-revolutionary workers' democracy, would not suffice to cross the frontiers of necessity. Thompson's second mistake is to forget the irreducible material compulsions of scarcity. The USSR today, even delivered from bureaucratic misrule, would still remain at a vast distance from the perspective evoked by Thompson, of a 'primacy of social consciousness over social being'—a future first formulated in these terms sixty years ago by Lukács during the Hungarian Commune. Poverty and shortage still haunt Russian society, rural as well as urban, in an economy whose productivity of labour remains half that of West Germany. An inexplicable failure to register this familiar fact leads Thompson not only to attribute an imaginary liberty of manoeuvre to the Soviet leadership, but also to deprive its emergence of any rational historical causality. Thus he can tentatively wonder whether it or similar groups were not 'perhaps fortuitously established in power at the time of the revolution';[24] whereas in fact, as every serious Marxist study of the fate of the Russian Revolution has shown, it was the cruel inner environment of pervasive scarcity, allied with the external emergency of imperialist military encirclement, that produced the bureaucratization of party and state in the USSR. Trotsky's original analysis of this process remains unsurpassed to this day. The realm of necessity, far from having vanished in the Communist countries, still continues both to reproduce bureaucracy and to manacle it. Thompson's one conjectural admission of historical variation to his account of agency appears to confirm a tendency to make light of its objective circumscriptions.

We can explore this possibility further by turning back to *The Poverty of Theory* and looking at the central category which it deploys in support of its treatment of agency—the concept of 'experience'. Thompson tells us that it is 'through the missing term "experience" that structure is transmuted into process, and the subject re-enters into history'.[25] Repeatedly invoked as a veritable limbeck of social life, what is experience? Two somewhat different answers are given. Thompson initially writes that 'it

24. PT, p. 156.
25. PT, p. 362.

comprises the mental and emotional response, whether of an individual or a social group, to many inter-related events or to many repetitions of the same kind of event'.[26] Later, however, he suggests another definition: 'Experience is a necessary middle term between social being and social consciousness'. Thus if 'experience has, in the last instance, been generated in "material life", has been structured in class ways, and hence "social being" has determined "social consciousness" ', at the same time 'for any living generation, in any "now", the ways in which they "handle" experience defies prediction and escapes from any narrow definition of determination'.[27] The first of these formulations situates experience squarely 'within' consciousness, as a subjective reaction —'mental and emotional response'—to objective events. The second and third intercalate it 'between' being and consciousness, and introduce a further concept: instead of experience being a set of mental and emotional responses to events, it is itself 'handled' to yield the responses of (in particular) class and culture. The sense of a second order of subjectivity, so to speak, is reinforced by the unusual pleonasm to which Thompson has recourse in developing his account: 'People do not only experience their own experience as ideas, within thought and its procedures, or as proletarian instinct. They also experience their own experience as *feeling*'.[28]

What do these oscillations and uncertainties of usage signify? Essentially, they are reminders of the ambiguity of the term 'experience' in ordinary language itself.[29] On the one hand, the word denotes an occurrence or episode as it is lived by the participants, the subjective texture of objective actions, 'the passing through any event or course of events by which one is affected'.[30] On the other, it indicates a subsequent process of learning from such occurrences, a subjective alteration capable of modifying ensuing objective actions; hence, as the dictionary

26. PT, p. 199.
27. PT, p. 363.
28. PT, p. 363.
29. Oakeshott once remarked that: 'Experience, of all words in the philosophic vocabulary, is the most difficult to manage; and it must be the ambition of every writer reckless enough to use the word to escape the ambiguities it contains.' *Experience and its Modes*, Cambridge 1933, p. 9. Thompson refers once to Oakeshott, but does not seem to have registered his injunction—possibly because Oakeshott himself scarcely observed it, in his own pursuit of a single-minded neo-Hegelianism for which 'experience begins with ideas' and ends with them—'what is achieved in experience is a coherent world of ideas' (p. 28).
30. *Chambers Twentieth Century Dictionary.*

puts it, 'practical acquaintance with any matter gained by trial; long and varied observation, personal or general; wisdom derived from the changes or trials of life'.[31] These two distinct senses can be called here neutral and positive. The adjective 'experienced', of course, refers only to the latter. Now if we look at Thompson's usage of the term in his critique of Althusser, we can see that much of the time he is unconsciously transferring the virtues and powers of the (more restricted) second type to the (more general) first type of experience. The efficacy of the one is fused with the universality of the other, to suggest an alternative way of reading history as a whole. The generic category that results inevitably conflates very different problems. Thompson's most specific illustration of the force of the concept occurs at the very outset of his contest with Althusser. He writes: 'Experience is valid and effective but within determined limits: the farmer "knows" his seasons, the sailor "knows" his seas, but both may remain mystified about kingship and cosmology.'[32] Now, if followed through in one direction, this remark leads towards the kind of conclusion that *The Poverty of Theory* otherwise overlooks: that effective agency/knowledge has been hierarchically limited throughout human history, its reach typically not pertaining in any way to social relations as such. In other words, it permits at least a suggestion of the asymmetries, the *disparities*, between determination and self-determination in past epochs. But, of course, to register this point alone is not enough. For the problem posed by Thompson's argument is not just that of the spatial reach of a given experience, but of its relevant *type*. Farming and sailing, in the example he gives, are experimental practices, controlled by observable results. They certainly generate real knowledge. But they cannot be taken thereby as emblematic of experience in general. If we substitute, say, for Thompson's pair the 'parishioner' knows his 'prayers', the 'priest' his 'flock', what conclusion would we arrive at? Is religious experience 'valid and effective within determined limits'? Obviously not. One can scarcely suspect Thompson of concessions on this score. Indeed at one point he goes to the opposite extreme, committing himself to the boldly unhistorical view that 'the greater part of the history of ideas is a history of freaks'—'to any rational mind'.[33] We need not subscribe to this kind of rationalism to judge that

31. Ibid.
32. PT, p. 199.
33. PT, p. 195.

religious experience, while subjectively *very intense and real,* while enormously *effective* in moving great masses of men and women down the ages to routine duties and exceptional enterprises alike, is not 'valid' as knowledge, and never was.

How then do we distinguish valid from invalid experience? Thompson nowhere gives us any indications. Yet the problem is clearly a central one for his whole case in *The Poverty of Theory.* The examples just discussed are all regularly codified practices. But experience, of course, takes many other forms, and Thompson elsewhere alludes to some of them. A few pages later, he writes: 'Experience walks in without knocking at the door, and announces deaths, crises of subsistence, trench warfare, unemployment, inflation, genocide. People starve: their survivors think in new ways about the market. People are imprisoned: in prison they meditate in new ways about the law.'[34] The sense of 'experience' in this passage is clearly that of the *lesson* that unheralded processes —vicissitudes or calamities—can teach those who live through them. Thompson clearly assumes that the lessons taught will be correct ones, as can be seen from the comment which follows: 'Such imperative presentation of knowledge effects is not allowed for in Althusser's epistemology'.[35] The paradigm that is presumed here is, in fact, much more central to Thompson's work as a whole than the previous type. The emphasis of Thompson's 'experience' is in general closer to that of *Erlebnis* then *Erfahrung*—moral-existential more than practical-experimental. But the same problem recurs in this register as well. What ensures that a particular experience of distress or disaster will inspire a particular (cognitively or morally appropriate) conclusion? Did the famine of the 1840s lead the Irish peasantry to think in new ways about the market? Few countries in the West have remained so immune to the socialist critique of it, even in the most timorous social-democratic form, as the Republic founded on that class. Did the imprisonment of a generation of East European Communists before the War make them champions of a humane justice and legality after it? The longest single ordeal in a White gaol was endured by a prisoner whose name, an international legend of heroism in the 30s, became a byword for sadism in the 50s: Matyas Rakosi. Experience as such is a concept *tous azimuts*, which can point in any direction. The self-same events can be lived through by

34. PT, p. 201.
35. PT, p. 195.

agents who draw diametrically opposite conclusions from them. Another of the transformative upheavals cited by Thompson is war, which provides some of the most spectacular illustrations of this polyvalence. Just as few collective experiences were probably as intense as religion to the majority of producers at particular times in their lives (very unevenly) in pre-industrial epochs, so in modern times few popular experiences have been as strong and as widespread to many millions as national sentiment—materially rooted in locality, language, customs. What did this experience tell the exploited masses of Europe in 1914? That it was right and natural, even if unfortunate, that they should fight each other on an unprecedented scale. Did the four years of bitter massacre which followed undo this illusion, teaching them to reflect in new ways on the nation? In some cases—most of the Russian working class and peasantry, much of the Italian and a minority of the German working class—it did: the Third International grew precisely out of this matrix. In other cases, it did not: the traditional patriotism of the English and French masses was tempered by a certain post-war pacifism, but not fundamentally modified. In yet other cases, nationalism on the contrary underwent a hellish exacerbation: among the German and Italian petty-bourgeoisie, the Austrian peasantry, the Hungarian lumpenproletariat, defeat tightened the springs of revenge into fascism. The mass experience of death and destruction itself brought with it no necessary illumination. A forest of interpretations grew over the deserted battlefields.

In other words, the tacit first version of experience to be found in *The Poverty of Theory*—a set of mental and emotional responses as it were 'given with' a set of lived events to which they correspond [36]—cannot be sustained. However, as we have seen, Thompson also sketches a second definition, which seems to allow for divergences and variations of response much better. Here, experience itself remains an objective sector of 'social being', which is then processed or handled by the subject

36. Interestingly, this fallacy was the object of a classical critique by Sartre, in his polemic with Lefort in the early 50s, in which he attacked what he called the portmanteau notion of *l'expérience-qui-comporte-sa-propre-interprétation*. See 'Réponse à Claude Lefort', *Les Temps Modernes*, April 1953, pp. 1577-1579, 1588-1589. Sartre's own theoretical positions in this series of articles, *Les Communistes et la Paix*, were by no means free from errors: of the extensive literature that they provoked the best rejoinder was the work of Ernest Mandel: 'Lettre à Jean-Paul Sartre', now reprinted in *La longue marche de la révolution*, Paris 1976, pp. 83-123. But Sartre's discussion of this point is of lasting merit.

to yield a particular 'social consciousness'. The possibility of different ways of 'handling' the same experience is epistemologically secured. This schema represents, in fact, the more recurrent and important of the two accounts advanced by Thompson, although there is a significant degree of oscillation between them. To see it worked through on a grand scale, we must turn to *The Making of the English Working Class*. In doing so, we will immediately rejoin the problem of historical agency at the deepest levels of Thompson's intellectual engagement with it. This great work opens with the famous declaration: 'The working class did not rise like the sun at an appointed time. It was present at its own making'.[37] For this making was an active process, 'which owes as much to agency as to conditioning'.[38] The early English proletariat was not the mere product of the advent of the factory system. On the contrary, 'the working class made itself as much as it was made'.[39] The fundamental form this agency took was the conversion of a collective experience into a social consciousness which thereby defined and created the class itself. 'Class happens when some men, as a result of common experiences (inherited or shared), feel and articulate the identity of their interests as between themselves, and as against other men whose interests are different from (and usually opposed to) theirs. The class experience is largely determined by the productive relations into which men are born—or enter involuntarily. Class consciousness is the way in which the experiences are handled in cultural terms: embodied in traditions, value-systems, ideas and institutional forms. If the experience appears as determined, class consciousness does not . . . class is defined by men as they live their own history, and, in the end, this is its only definition.'[40] The process of this formative definition is studied in three consecutive movements. The first part of the book reconstructs the political and cultural traditions of English radicalism in the 18th century: religious dissent, popular tumult, and constitutional conviction—the latter eventually culminating in Paine's rupture with constitutionalism, followed by the brief episode of English Jacobinism in the 1790s. The second part deals with the catastrophic social experience of the Industrial Revolution, as it was lived by successive groups of primary producers—field labourers, artisans,

37. MEWC, p. 9.
38. MEWC, p. 9.
39. MEWC, p. 213.
40. MEWC, pp. 9-10, 11. Similar, later formulations by Thompson always include women.

weavers—and discusses the standard of living, proselytization, work discipline and community institutions of the working people in these grim years. The third part traces the growth of working class consciousness in successive political and industrial struggles against the new order during and after the Napoleonic epoch—the parliamentary campaigns in London, the outbreak of Luddism in the North and Midlands, the national radicalism led by Cobbett and Hunt, the massacre at Peterloo, the spread of Owenism. By the time of the crisis of 1832, Thompson concludes, 'the working class presence was the most significant factor in British political life'.[41] By now, indeed, 'there is a sense in which the working class is no longer in the making, but has been made'.[42]

It will soon enough be twenty years since *The Making of the English Working Class* was published. Yet there has been surprisingly little historiographic discussion of the book on the Left; its extraordinary power seems to have inhibited the ordinary flow of critical reflection and assimilation which normally attends work of such magnitude. There are two main avenues along which a contemporary revaluation of *The Making of the English Working Class* could proceed. The first is a detailed empirical review of the evidence that has since come to light on the early years of the English proletariat, to see how far the panorama presented by Thompson needs local or general retouching. There is, of course, neither space nor competence for that here. The second is a closer look at the logical structure of the argument in this classic of English Marxist history. A few remarks will be attempted on this. From the brief summary given above, it will be seen that three fundamental theses sustain the architecture of *The Making of the English Working Class*. The first we shall call the claim of *co-determination*: that is, the thesis that the English working class 'made itself as much as it was made', in a causal parity of 'agency and conditioning'.[43] The second is the criterion of *consciousness* as the touchstone of class: namely, the contention that 'class happens when some men, as a result of common experiences, feel and articulate the identity of their interests as between themselves, and as against other men whose interests are different from (and usually opposed to) theirs'.[44] The formulation here is closely echoed in *The*

41. MEWC, p. 12.
42. MEWC, p. 887.
43. MEWC, pp. 213, 9.
44. MEWC, pp. 9-10.

Poverty of Theory: 'Classes arise because men and women, in determinative productive relations, identify their antagonistic interests, and come to struggle, think and value in class ways'.[45] Classes exist in and through the process of collective self-identification that is class consciousness: 'Class is defined by men as they live their own history, and, in the end, this is its only definition'.[46] The third thesis might be termed the implication of *closure*: in other words, the assertion that the identity of the English working-class was in some sense completed by the early 1830s, such that we can speak of it as 'no longer in the making' but 'made'. The title of the work lends a decisive force of suggestion to this notion. Let us consider each of these themes.

The peculiar interest of the first is that we are presented with a practical test of the theoretical declarations of *The Poverty of Theory*. The 'proportions' of agency and necessity are specified, in a particular historical process—the formation of the English working class. Thompson judges them equal. The clarity and seriousness with which he poses the problem is beyond praise: it has no precedent in Marxist or other historiography. At the end of his study, however, if we are to be faithful to the issue he has raised at the outset, we must ask ourselves a number of questions. The first is this. Has Thompson *demonstrated* that the English working class made itself as much as it was made—not in a false, scientistic sense, but in terms of plausible balance of evidence? Few of the professional historians who have reviewed *The Making of the English Working Class* have tarried over this issue, although it looms over the whole book: no doubt it has generally appeared too 'meta-historical' for them. But is it incapable of empirical control or arbitration? To ask this is to realize that *The Making of the English Working Class* does not, contrary to appearances, give us the means by which we could settle the question. For if the claim for co-determination of agency and necessity was to be substantiated, we would need to have at a minimum a conjoint exploration of the objective assemblage and transformation of a labour-force by the Industrial Revolution, and of the subjective germination of a class culture in response to it. That alone could furnish the initial—not conclusive—elements for a judgement of their relative historical weight. The former, however, is essentially missing from *The Making of the English Working Class*. The second part of the book, where one would

45. PT, pp. 298-299.
46. MEWC, p. 11.

expect to find it, in fact concentrates largely on the immediate experience of the producers rather than on the mode of production itself. The advent of industrial capitalism in England is a dreadful backcloth to the book rather than a direct object of analysis in its own right. The result is a disconcerting lack of objective coordinates as the narrative of class formation unfolds.[47] It comes as something of a shock to realize, at the end of 900 pages, that one has never learnt such an elementary fact as the approximate size of the English working class, or its proportion within the population as a whole, at any date in the history of its 'making'.

A lacuna like this cannot be dismissed by mere disdainful reference to 'the endless stupidities of quantitative measurement of classes', if only because Thompson does provide one or two numerical estimates of specific occupational categories himself.[48] More generally, what the omission symbolizes is the absence from *The Making of the English Working Class* of any real treatment of the whole historical process whereby heterogeneous groups of artisans, small holders, agricultural labourers, domestic workers and casual poor were gradually assembled, distributed and reduced to the condition of labour subsumed to capital, first in the formal dependence of the wage-contract, ultimately in the real dependence of integration into mechanized means of production. The jagged temporal rhythms and breaks, and the uneven spatial

47. In some ways, a more satisfactory treatment of the basic problem at issue here can be found in Barrington Moore's account of the evolution of the German working class in his book *Injustice: The Social Roots of Obedience and Revolt* (London 1978, pp. 126-353), which moves between objective determinants and subjective constellations with greater purpose and consistency. Moore's study is of particular interest, because it is partly inspired by Thompson's example, as the author explains. On the other hand, unlike Thompson, Moore is uninformed and uninterested in the actual political ideology (or organization) of the German socialist movement proper, perhaps especially in the development of revolutionary Marxism within in it. The contrast with *The Making of the English Working Class* is in this respect very great.

48. The phrase is from 'Eighteenth-Century English Society: Class Struggle without Class?', *Social History*, vol. 3, no. 2, May 1978, p. 149. Examples of such quantification in *The Making of the English Working Class* include agricultural labourers and weavers. It is not the redundancy but the deficiency of accurate statistical information that is the real problem in this period. The 1831 Census, the first to provide any breakdown of occupations, confined its inquiries into them to 'trades and handicrafts', ignoring any provision of comparable data for 'manufactures'. These lacunae render difficult, but not altogether impossible, assessments of the size and structure of different classes in the English society of the time. For the kind of retrospective projections that can be made from later and more useful data, see J.A. Banks, 'The Social Structure of 19th Century England as Seen through the Census', in Richard Lawton, ed, *The Census and Social Structure*, London 1978, pp. 179-223.

distributions and displacements, of capital accumulation between 1790 and 1830 inevitably marked the composition and character of the nascent English proletariat. Yet they find no place in this account of its formation. Towards the end of the book, Thompson remarks that: 'the British working class of 1832' was 'perhaps a unique formation', because 'the slow, piecemeal accretions of capital accumulation had meant that the preliminaries to the Industrial Revolution stretched backwards for hundreds of years. From Tudor times onwards this artisan culture had grown more complex with each phase of technical and social change. Delaney, Dekker and Nashe: Winstanley and Lilburne: Bunyan and Defoe—all had at times addressed themselves to it. Enriched by the experiences of the 17th century, carrying through the 18th century the intellectual and libertarian traditions we have described, forming their own traditions of mutuality in the friendly society and trades club, these men did not pass, in one generation, from the peasantry to the new industrial town. They suffered the experience of the Industrial Revolution as articulate, free-born Englishmen . . . This was, perhaps, the most distinguished popular culture England has known'.[49] Exceptionally, here, the objective pattern of capital accumulation is formally accorded an original primacy of determination. But the secular scale on which it is evoked—back to Tudor times—allows the brief period under study to appear in the guise of a codicil. The real centre of gravity of the passage is the survival and continuity of so many popular values and traditions of resistance—of which the slow tempo of capitalist development in England is little more than the enabling condition. Yet the speed and extent of industrialization should surely be woven into the very texture of any materialist study of a working class. If it is not taken as 'external' to the making of the Russian or Italian proletariat—as any glance at the labour history of Petrograd or Turin suffices to remind us—why should it be to the English proletariat? Thompson rightly emphasizes that 'factory hands, so far from being the "eldest children of the industrial revolution", were late arrivals'[50] in England, and that out-workers anticipated many of their ideas and forms of organization. But does this justify a survey of the making of the English working class which omits any direct account of them altogether? Cotton, iron and coal together form virtually the sum of the first phase of industrialization in Britain: yet the

49. MEWC, pp. 913-914.
50. MEWC, p. 211.

direct labour-force of not one of them is treated in *The Making of the English Working Class*.[51] In the absence of any objective framework laying down the overall pattern of capital accumulation in these years, there is little way of assessing the relative importance of one area of subjective experience within the English working class against another. Proportions are wanting. Selectivity of focus is combined with sweep of conclusion, typically with such passion and skill that the former can easily be forgotten by the reader.

Nor is it only a question of the weighting of different groups of producers within the developing process of the Industrial Revolution. The inter-relations are obviously of even greater importance. Thompson devotes a number of very perceptive pages to the different popular cultures of London and of the North, what he calls the dialectic of 'intellect and enthusiasm', commenting that 'each tradition seems enfeebled without the complement of the other'.[52] This division, which extends down to the SDF and the ILP and beyond, has surely been a key trait of the English labour movement. But it is not adequately anchored in *The Making of the English Working Class*, for all its consequences as the narrative develops, because there is no spatial map of British capitalism that would reveal its measure of importance. In effect, the cold economic fact that London remained throughout the 19th century largely a rentier, commercial and bureaucratic capital, dominated by court and city—closer in some ways to Vienna or Madrid than to Paris, Berlin or Saint Petersburg—was to be a major obstacle to the emergence of a politically aggressive labour movement in England. A capital without heavy industry helped to separate a factory proletariat from an instinct for power. Once artisan radicalism broke down, with the decline of the skilled trades on which it was based, the inherent weaknesses of the division between metropolitan and provincial traditions, founded on

---

51. Booth's calculations indicate that some 210,000 workers were employed in mining in England and Wales in 1841, and 188,000 in metallurgy, as against 604,000 in textiles, of whom by then some 300,000 would have been operatives in cotton mills: Charles Booth, 'Occupations of the People of the United Kingdom 1801-1881', *Journal of the Statistical Society*, June 1886, pp. 314-435. A decade earlier (1832), cotton operatives numbered just over 200,000: N.J. Smelser, *Social Change in the Industrial Revolution*, London 1959, p. 194. Growth was, of course, much less rapid in mining or siderurgy. In his 1968 postscript, Thompson himself concedes that his account omits large areas of the working class: MEWC, p. 916.
52. MEWC, p. 58.

such separate types of accumulation, became evident.[53] The growing influence of Benthamism in the work of Place and his associates after 1815, described by Thompson, foreshadowed much later developments. It might be said that London ended by bureaucratizing Northern moderation into a municipal-national system, in the age of Morrison.

The peculiar complexion of the world's largest city in the epoch of the Industrial Revolution was, of course, intimately related not only to its court and parliamentary establishments, but also and above all to its imperial functions. Here too, however, it is difficult to feel that Thompson gives the kind of attention and weight to the objective coordinates of his subject that the title of his work leads one to expect. This is perhaps most obvious at the political level itself, where there is little sustained acknowledgement of the international dimensions of English working-class history. In the first part of his study, Thompson emphasizes that despite the ideological strength of the complex of beliefs summed up in the notion of the 'Free-Born Englishman', radical demands remained imprisoned within the terms of an imaginary constitutionalism down to the 1790s. The decisive break, which shifted the parameters of radical politics, came with the publication of Paine's *Rights of Man*, which for the first time rejected the constitutional monarchy and attacked the Bill of Rights. He also notes the unremarkable tenor of Paine's own life and thought as a customs official in England, down to the early 1770s, and the sudden change precipitated by his emigration to America. Likewise, the circumstance that *The Rights of Man* was written in response to Burke's *Reflections on the French Revolution* is of course registered. But nowhere does the combined shock of the American and French Revolutions, of which Paine's work is the *direct* political product in England, find any space in *The Making of the English Working Class* commensurate with its real historical importance. The fact is that the whole ideological universe of the West was transformed by these two great upheavals. The pattern of their international impact is the theme of a work like Palmer's major study, *The Age of the Democratic Revolution*. Their significance—especially that of the French Revolution—is incomparably greater for the political formation of the English working class than, say, popular attitudes towards crime. Yet the latter receives careful

53. See the pertinent comments by Victor Kiernan, 'Working Class and Nation in Nineteenth Century Britain', in Maurice Cornforth, ed., *Rebels and Their Causes. Essays in Honour of A.L. Morton*, London 1978, p. 126.

treatment, while the former is relegated off-stage. Despite their central importance over two decades, the reader learns little or nothing of the complicated attitudes and debates within English radicalism over events in France. An apparent procedural bias excludes them: since social revolutions abroad cannot be entered as self-activity of the working class in England, they fall outside the historical accounting given of these years.

Their sequel is also largely omitted from the later parts of the book. For while Thompson invokes in principle the coincidence of industrial revolution and political counter-revolution during the Napoleonic Wars, with its simultaneous 'intensification of two intolerable forms of relationship: those of economic exploitation and of political repression',[54] in practice the impact of two decades of *war* on English popular culture is virtually ignored. Like the pattern of capital accumulation itself, the reality of military conflict figures only gesturally in the narrative. One inevitable result is a minimization of the *nationalist* mobilization of the whole English population by the ruling class, in its tremendous struggle for supremacy with France. Yet no full picture of English popular culture after 1815 can be gained without due notice of the depth of the ideological capture of the 'nation' for conservative ends in Britain. The result is a serious over-simplification of the legacy of the wars. Thus in a memorable conclusion to the second part of the book, Thompson writes of 'the loss of any felt cohesion in the community, save that which the working people, in antagonism to their labour and to their masters, built for themselves'.[55] Eloquence here is not necessarily accuracy, however. The sense of *national* community, systematically orchestrated and instilled by the State, may well have been a greater reality in the Napoleonic epoch than at any time in the previous century. By overlooking it, Thompson can argue that whereas in 1792 the ruling class had governed by means of consent and deference, 'in 1816 the English people were held down by force'.[56] Hated though the Liverpool government was by wide sectors of the masses, this judgement must be deemed an exaggeration. An army of 25,000—the total troop-force available for domestic repression—was scarcely sufficient to pin down a society of

54. MEWC, p. 217.
55. MEWC, p. 488.
56. MEWC, p. 663.

12,000,000.[57] The power of the English *ancien régime* rested on a combination of culture and coercion, after no less than before the Wars. The prime weapon in its ideological arsenal, after twenty years of victorious fighting against the French Revolution and its successor regimes, was a counter-revolutionary nationalism. The structural importance of the latter, general and durable, was certainly greater than that of the more local and limited phenomenon of Methodism, however hysterical its manifestations—to which Thompson devotes one of the most unforgettable chapters of his book. England was, in fact, probably the first country in Europe in which nation overtook religion as the dominant form of ideological discourse—a change already, of course, under way in the 18th century. It would be difficult to guess this from *The Making of the English Working Class*, where few or none of the ideological bonds subordinating the immediate producers—not to their employers (Methodism or Utilitarianism are certainly present)—but to their rulers materialize.

How far do these omissions affect Thompson's achievement? After all, no book can say everything. In face of the profusion of riches in *The Making of the English Working Class*, is it reasonable to ask for anything more? By ordinary standards, no. But the theme of the work is no ordinary historical one either, as we have seen. The pertinence of the gaps suggested above—the spearhead sectors of the Industrial Revolution, the commercial-rentier configuration of London, the impact of the American and French Revolutions, the galvanization of wartime chauvinism—is that they render a judgement of the issue posed at the beginning of the book unnegotiable. In the absence of any direct treatment of these

57. The pattern of military deployment by the English ruling class on the conclusion of the Napoleonic Wars is revealing. In 1816, the Army of Occupation in France itself numbered 35,000. Another 35,000 troops were stationed in India, 10,000 in Canada and the Bahamas, 13,000 in the West Indies, 3,000 each in the Cape, Mauritius and Ceylon, and 11,000 in the Mediterranean. While the garrison in England was 25,000, Ireland—with a third of the population—needed one of 35,000: there Thompson's remarks would be more applicable. See J.W. Fortescue, *A History of the British Army*, London 1923, vol. XI, p. 50. By 1817, Castlereagh was lamenting that the government disposed of a force of no more than 16,000 soldiers at home. In the crisis of 1819, some 11,000 pensioners had to be called up, and the yeomanry augmented. The permanent military apparatus of the English State at home remained sketchy throughout this period. At the end of it, in the national crisis of 1832, Halévy could still write of 'a mere handful of aristocrats supported by 11,000 mercenaries whose fidelity was by no means above suspicion' confronting the Reform movement: *A History of the English People 1830-1841*, London 1927, p. 57.

massive moulds of the early history of the English working class, we have no way of adjudicating the part of collective self-determination in its making. The parity between agency and conditioning asserted at the outset remains a postulate that is never really tested through the relevant range of evidence for both sides of the process. For all their power, the descriptions of mass immiseration and alienation etched in the second part of the book are in no sense equivalent to a survey of the objective determinants of the formation of the English working class. It is not the structural transformations—economic, political and demographic—which Thompson invokes at the head of this part of the book which are the objects of his inquiry, but rather their precipitates in the subjective experience of those who lived through these 'terrible years'. The result is to resolve the complex manifold of objective-subjective determinations whose totalization actually generated the English working class into a simple dialectic between suffering and resistance whose whole movement is internal to the subjectivity of the class. This is the force of the celebrated ending of the book. 'Such men met Utilitarianism in their daily lives, and they sought to throw it back, not blindly, but with intelligence and moral passion . . . These years appear at times to display, not a revolutionary challenge, but a resistance movement, in which both the Romantics and the Radical Craftsmen opposed the annunciation of Acquisitive Man'.[58] Inscribed in the moving clauses of its conclusion, the claim of parity between agency and necessity recurs, but within the form of the work it is not justiciable.

We may now look at the second major theme of *The Making of the English Working Class*, that 'class happens when some men, as a result of common experiences (inherited or shared), feel and articulate the identity of their interests as between themselves, and as against other men whose interests are different from (and usually opposed to) theirs'.[59] We have called this the criterion of consciousness, because the effect of Thompson's definition is to make the existence of a class depend on the presence of collective expression (feeling/articulation) of common interests in opposition to those of an antagonistic class (or classes). In *The Poverty of Theory*, as we have seen, Thompson restates this position even more sharply and unequivocally: 'Classes arise because men and women,

58. MEWC, p. 915.
59. MEWC, p. 9.

in determinative productive relations, identify their antagonistic interests, and come to struggle, to think, and to value in class ways'.[60] Class consciousness here becomes the very hallmark of class formation. How plausible is this definition, empirically? The answer is surely that it is impossible to reconcile with the plain record of historical evidence. Classes have frequently existed whose members did not 'identify their antagonistic interests' in any process of common clarification or struggle. Indeed it is probable that for most of historical time this was the rule rather than the exception. The very term class, in the modern sense, is after all a coinage of the 19th century. Did Athenian slaves in ancient Greece, or caste-ridden villagers in mediaeval India, or Meiji workers in modern Japan 'come to struggle, think in class ways'? There is every evidence to the contrary. Yet did they thereby cease to compose classes? Thompson's error is to make an abusive generalization from the English experience he has studied himself: the remarkable class-consciousness of the first industrial working class in world history is projected universally onto classes as such. The result is a definition of class that is far too voluntarist and subjectivist—closer to an ethical-rhetorical *parti pris* than to a conclusion from empirical investigation. In his fundamental work *Karl Marx's Theory of History*, Cohen has rightly criticized the logic of Thompson's description of class, vindicating the traditional Marxist thesis that 'a person's class is established by nothing but his objective place in the network of ownership relations...His consciousness, culture and politics do not enter the *definition* of his class position. Indeed these exclusions are required to protect the substantive character of the Marxian thesis that class position strongly conditions consciousness, culture and politics.'[61] Cohen's own account of the structural position of the proletarian in a capitalist economy, and of the gamut of possible relations of production that generate classes, is of exemplary clarity and subtlety. The concept of class as an objective relation to means of production, independent of will or attitude, is unlikely to need further reinstatement.

The untenability of Thompson's definition of class in *The Making of the English Working Class*, if taken literally, can be seen from the later development of his own writing. As the field of his historical research has moved back into 18th century England, a period in which class consciousness among the primary producers is obviously far less visible, his

60. PT, pp. 298-299.
61. G.A. Cohen, *Karl Marx's Theory of History—A Defence*, Oxford 1979, p. 73.

positions have undergone an interesting change. In a brilliant recent essay on 'Eighteenth-Century English Society', Thompson advances a set of new propositions. He now concedes that 'class, as it eventuated within 19th century industrial capitalist societies, and as it then left its imprint upon the heuristic category of class, has in fact no claim to universality. Class in that sense is no more than a special case of the historical formations which arise out of class struggle.'[62] For in the 19th century, 'class in its modern usage became available to the cognitive system of the people then living at the time . . . Hence the concept not only enables us to organize and analyze the evidence; it is also, in a new sense, *present in the evidence itself*. We can observe, in industrial Britain or France or Germany, class institutions, class parties, class cultures'.[63] Prior to the 19th century, however, historians are still obliged to use the concept of class, not because of its perfection as a notion, but because 'no alternative category is available to analyze a manifest and universal historical process'—namely 'class struggle'.[64] These arguments lead to the concise conclusion: 'Class struggle is the prior, as well as the more universal, concept'—for 'people find themselves in a society structured in determined ways (crucially, but not exclusively, in productive relations), they experience exploitation (or the need to maintain power over those whom they exploit), they identify points of antagonistic interest, they commence to struggle around these issues and in the process of struggling they discover themselves as classes, they come to know this discovery as class-consciousness. Class and class consciousness are always the last, not the first, stage in the real historical process'.[65] Hence the paradox that across England in the 18th century lay a 'societal field of force' of class struggle between 'the crowd at one pole, the aristocracy and gentry at the other',[66] yet without the former truly constituting a class.

Does this comprehensive redefinition solve the difficulties of Thompson's view of class? At first sight, it appears a major step beyond the formulations of *The Making of the English Working Class*. On closer

---

62. 'Eighteenth-Century English Society: Class Struggle without Class?', p. 149.
63. 'Eighteenth-Century English Society', p. 149.
64. 'Eighteenth-Century English Society', p. 149.
65. 'Eighteenth-Century English Society', p. 151.
66. 'Eighteenth-Century English Society', p. 151. Contradictorily, he elsewhere speaks of the 'agrarian bourgeoisie' (p. 162) and reproaches myself, among others, for not seeing the ruling class of 18th century England in this light—a quarrel that his own normal usage shows to be a false one.

inspection, however, the same theoretical inspiration can be seen, and with it some of the same logical and empirical problems recur. What Thompson has in effect done is to *retain* the equation: class = class consciousness, but to postulate behind it—at once conceptually and historically—an anterior stage of class struggle, when groups conflict without achieving that collective self-awareness that defines class itself. But why in that case use the term 'class' for such 'struggle' at all? The answer appears to be an essentially pragmatic one—no better word has so far turned up. A liberal historian would no doubt retort that 'social conflict' is therefore preferable, precisely because it begs no questions. It is not easy to see what reply Thompson could make, for the whole thrust of his argument is still to detach class from its objective anchorage in determinate relations of production, and identify it with subjective consciousness or culture. Once this is done, the absence of a class 'culture' automatically puts in question the very existence of class itself—as in 18th century England. In perverse logic, it is then possible to suggest that there was 'class struggle without class'—in the title of the essay. To which there are two straightforward answers. Firstly, the *ruling class*—the 'aristocracy and gentry' as he here rightly designates it—was certainly possessed of the necessary sense of identity and combativity to constitute a class, even on Thompson's own criteria, which would leave us with the curiosity of 'class struggle with a single class'—a *koan* of one hand clapping. Secondly, absence of class consciousness in the 19th century sense in no way means that the plebs of the 18th century was therefore an a-class phenomenon. It was not, of course, a homogeneous social bloc, but a changeable coalition composed of different categories of urban or rural wage-earners, small producers, petty traders, and unemployed, whose frontiers would vary according to the successive conjunctures that crystallized it—very much as Thompson so ably describes. Each of these categories, however, can be rationally ordered in a materialist class analysis, by their respective structural positions within the several modes of production of Hanoverian society. To disaggregate the social or political affrays of the time into their component class units, in other words, is not to do violence to their intelligibility but to help to elucidate it. No economism need be implied in such a procedure, which does not render study of the process of *congregation* that formed 18th century crowds (dissident-radical or clerical-monarchist, spontaneous or manipulated, as the case might be) unnecessary, but rather more precise and pointed.

Thompson's dictum that 'we know about class because people have repeatedly behaved in class ways'[67] disallows its presence where behaviour appears so coalescent and contradictory as to be 'unclasslike'. Whether the accent is put on behaviour or consciousness[68]—struggling or valuing—such definitions of class remain fatally circular. It is better to say, with Marx, that social classes may not become conscious of themselves, may fail to act or behave in common, but they still remain—materially, historically—classes.

The third major claim contained in *The Making of the English Working Class* brings us back to the 19th century. The title of the book promises to trace a process with a finite end: the English working class, as such inexistent in the 1790s, is made by the mid-1830s, when its presence is the most significant factor in national politics, felt in 'every county in England, and in most fields of life'.[69] The term *making* here has an unmistakable force: it suggests that the character of the English working class was in its most essential traits formed by the time of the Reform Bill. What are the arguments Thompson adduces for this periodization? The first and most salient is that the English proletariat had achieved a new consciousness of its own unity by the 1830s. An identity of interest was felt by workers across the most diverse occupations, where before traditional divisions of trade or region had prevailed. First expressed in the growing 'ethos of mutuality' of local friendly societies, it emerged on a national scale with the General Unionism of 1830-1834. Politically, the course of the whole parliamentary crisis of 1831-1832 revealed the stamp of its initiative and independence. Thus it was a peculiarity of English development that 'where we would expect to find a growing middle-class

67. 'Eighteenth-Century English Society', p. 147.
68. Interpretation of class predominantly through the prism of consciousness is by no means, of course, exclusive to Thompson. In different variants, it has represented a recurrent temptation in the history of Western Marxism. Lukács's most famous work provides a salient example. Writing of the peasantry or petty bourgeoisie, he remarks: 'we cannot really speak of class consciousness in the case of these classes (if, indeed, we can even speak of them as classes in the strict Marxist sense of the term)'—*History and Class Consciousness*, London 1971, p. 61. Sartre adopted a more extreme version of the same stance in *Les Communistes et la Paix*, in which he argued that the French proletariat itself lacked any 'class-being' till endowed with consciousness and unity by its party: a position later retracted in the more complex radiography of class attempted in *Critique of Dialectical Reason*, which assumes full unity and consciousness to be incompatible on principle with the objective coordinates of any social class.
69. MEWC, p. 887.

reform movement, with a working-class tail, only later succeeded by an independent agitation of the working class, in fact this process was reversed'.[70] Thereafter, middle-class reformers succeeded in utilizing popular agitation to force from the landowning classes an enfranchisement that was carefully demarcated to exclude the masses who had rendered it possible. In these years, too, 'something was lost' in the failure of the tradition of working-class Radicalism to achieve a junction with the Romantic critique of utilitarianism that was contemporary with it. Yet it is the collective achievement of this time that is finally remarkable. 'The working people should not be seen only as the lost myriads of eternity. They had also nourished, for fifty years, and with incomparable fortitude, the Liberty Tree. We may thank them for these years of heroic culture'.[71]

The grandeur of these concluding pages has been unanimously acknowledged. In a sense, it is their very power that forces on us their major problem. For as Tom Nairn wrote fifteen years ago, in what remains the most serious reflection on the book to date, one of the most central facts about the English working class is that 'its development as a class is divided into two great phases, and there appears at first sight to be hardly any connection between them.' For 'the early history of the English working class is a history of revolt, covering more than half a century, from the period of the French Revolution to the climax of Chartism in the 1840s'.[72] Yet 'what became of this revolt? The great English working class, this titanic social force which seemed to be unchained by the rapid development of English capitalism in the first half of the century, did not finally emerge to dominate and remake English society. It could not break the mould and fashion another. Instead, after the 1840s it quickly turned into an apparently docile class. It embraced one species of moderate reformism after another, and has remained wedded to the narrowest and greyest of bourgeois ideologies in its principal movements'.[73] Discounting the undoubted element of exaggeration in the final clause, which overstates the degree of later Fabian domination, the general truth of this description is hard to deny. Victor Kiernan has recently pronounced the same verdict: 'with

70. MEWC, p. 888.
71. MEWC, p. 915.
72. 'The English Working Class', *New Left Review* 24, March-April 1964, p. 43.
73. Ibid, p. 44.

Chartism by 1850 virtually at an end, the failure of the new working class
to enter and remould the national life left it shut up in the "labourism",
the self-absorption and political apathy, from which it has never really
recovered.'[74] The question it immediately poses is: how could the
English working class have been 'made' in the 1830s if it later underwent
this 'astonishing transformation'—one whose main outlines have now
lasted nearly a century? The answer is surely that the connotations of the
term are wrong. In the first place, the English working class was not
'made' by the 1830s in the simple sociological sense that it was still far
from being predominantly a labour-force operating genuinely industrial
means of production, whether in factories or other technical complexes.
'Machinofacture', in fact, was much slower to spread even in the
Victorian economy than has traditionally been thought.[75] Its gradual
advent, however, betokened a radical long-term *recomposition* of the class,
profoundly altering its structures at every level, as the figure of the
collective labourer in an integrated work-process was generalized. The
protracted hiatus in the development of the labour movement between
the 1840s and the 1880s may be partly explained by the length and
hesitancy of the transition between workshop and factory as modal types
of industrial organization in England. At all events, it is *discontinuity, not
continuity*, that is the keynote of 19th century working-class history. The
sociological evolution from artisanate to proletariat, an objective transformation induced by the process of capital accumulation, was accompanied by so deep a dislocation of political, ideological and cultural
traditions that the new patterns which emerged in the 1880s have been
dubbed by Gareth Stedman Jones, in an outstanding essay, an effective
're-making' of the English working class.[76]

The most important change was, of course, at the political level itself.
The main ideological influences and spokesmen in the world of the early
English working class were themselves external to it. Paine, Cobbett and
Owen—customs officer, journalist, manufacturer—were all from
propertied backgrounds. The English working class in this period

---

74. 'Working Class and Nation in Nineteenth Century Britain', p. 125.
75. See the magisterial demonstration by Raphael Samuel, 'Workshop of the World:
Steam Power and Hand Technology in mid-Victorian Britain', *History Workshop*, no. 3,
Spring 1977, pp. 6-72.
76. 'Working-Class Culture and Working-Class Politics in London, 1870-1890: Notes on
the Remaking of a Working Class', *Journal of Social History*, Summer 1974, pp. 460-508.

produced no Weitling or Proudhon. Of these three, Owen alone anticipated the characteristic outlook of the modern proletariat with his
cooperative socialism, but the impact of his ideas was the most transient.
As Thompson remarks: 'The main tradition of 19th century working-
class Radicalism took its cast from Paine. There were times, at the
Owenite and Chartist climaxes, when other traditions became dominant.
But after each relapse, the substratum of Painite assumptions remained
intact. The aristocracy were the main target ... but, however hard trade
unionists might fight against their employers—industrial capital was
assumed to be the fruit of enterprise and beyond the reach of political
intrusion. Until the 1880s, it was, by and large, within this framework
that working-class Radicalism remained transfixed'.[77] This judgement
needs some nuancing, since by the trough of the 1860s the positive
heritage of Painism was largely in abeyance. For *The Making of the
English Working Class* also correctly stresses its anti-constitutionalism,
republicanism and internationalism, together with the associated Jacobin
virtues of *egalité*, and notes that later labour traditions in England
typically lacked precisely these qualities.[78] The main tradition of late
19th and 20th century Labourism took *its* cast from anti-capitalist ideas
beyond those of Paine, yet remained 'transfixed' in a parliamentarist
framework in regression behind him. The class Thompson describes was
revolutionary in temper and ideology, but not socialist. After the mid-
century metamorphosis, as sections of it became socialist, it ceased to be
revolutionary. Therein lies the whole tragedy of English labour history to
date, as Tom Nairn was perfectly right to call it.

Thus if we take what are probably the two most fundamental dimensions of any working class—its objective composition as a social force and
its subjective outlook as a political force—we are obliged to conclude that
the English proletariat was in no way essentially made by 1832: or if it
was, its first 'incarnation' was to be strangely, systematically inverted by
its second. Thompson, of course, is not unaware of the problem. It is not
addressed in *The Making of the English Working Class* itself, but he has
subsequently spoken of the work of class unification that produced
Chartism, in a sense the culmination of the period of 'making', as having
been undone in a later phase.[79] But if the same class could be made by the

77. MEWC, p. 105.
78. MEWC, pp. 200-201.
79. Postscript (1968) to MEWC, p. 937.

30s, unmade after the 40s, and remade during the 80s, how ultimately satisfactory is the whole vocabulary of making itself? In a different context, Thompson has indirectly pinpointed some of its difficulties himself. Writing his essay 'The Peculiarities of the English', he was concerned not so much to vindicate the insurgent agency of the early working class, as to reject what he judged to be the shallow and dismissive treatment of the moderate reformism of the later working class by Tom Nairn and myself. In doing so, he advanced two arguments which are of great interest for the light they shed on *The Making of the English Working Class* itself. Firstly, he argued that in our account of English history, 'class is clothed throughout in anthropomorphic imagery. Classes have attributes of personal identity, with volition, conscious goals, and moral qualities'.[80] Conceding that this was 'in part a matter of metaphor', he went on: 'But one must never forget that it remains a metaphorical description of a more complex process, which happens *without* volition or identity'.[81] To illustrate this criticism, Thompson then selected precisely the watershed we have been discussing—what we had called the 'profound caesura in English working-class history' from the 1850s through to the 1870s. Rebuking this phrase, he argued that the period between Chartism and the New Unionism was in fact characterized by new sociological divisions within the working class, a psychological adjustment to the factory system, and the building up of the typical institutions of the Labour movement—trade unions, trades councils, cooperatives. 'The workers, having failed to overthrow capitalist society, proceeded to warren it from end to end . . . It was part of the logic of this new direction that each advance within the framework of capitalism simultaneously involved the working class far more deeply in the *status quo*. As they improved their position by organization within the workshop, so they became more reluctant to engage in quixotic outbreaks which might jeopardize gains accumulated at such cost'.[82] From this description, he drew the following conclusion: 'This is the direction that was taken, and, beneath all differences in ideological expression, much the same kind of imbrication in the *status quo* will be found in all advanced capitalist nations. We need not necessarily agree with Wright Mills that this indicates that the working class can be a revolutionary class only in its

80. PT, p. 69.
81. PT, p. 69.
82. PT, p. 71.

formative years; but we must, I think, recognize that once a certain climacteric moment is passed, the opportunity for a certain *kind* of revolutionary movement passes irrevocably—not so much because of "exhaustion" but because more limited, reformist pressures, from secure organizational bases, bring evident returns.'[83]

Now what is surely striking about this argument is that it runs against the whole grain of *The Making of the English Working Class*. The emphases are suddenly reversed here. Less a celebration of agency than a dwelling on necessity; rather than a projection of identity, an emphasis on mutability of class; no longer a national process, but an international pattern. The polemical thrust points in an unwonted direction. For if it is misleading to ascribe 'volition and identity' to classes, how can we speak of the working class 'making itself'—a verb that seems to combine the two errors in a single phrase? Where *The Making of the English Working Class* claimed that this making 'owed as much to agency as to conditioning', 'The Peculiarities of the English' warns its readers: 'Let us look at history *as* history—men placed in actual contexts which they have not chosen, and confronted by indivertible forces, with an overwhelming immediacy of relations and duties and with only a *scanty opportunity* for inserting their own agency'.[84] Co-determination has dwindled to a much more modest claim here. The differing polemical contexts, of course, explain much of the contrast. In *The Making of the English Working Class*, Thompson sought to uphold the creative activity and autonomy of English Radicalism against economic historians or sociologists bent on reducing the early working class to a passive object of industrialization. In 'The Peculiarities of the English', he is concerned to defend the record of Left Labourism, by appealing for greater understanding of the ungovernable weight of circumstances compressing its capacity for action. The political intention is honourable in both cases. But when allowance has been made for it, the theoretical discrepancy remains insurmountable. The part of agency in history cannot be adjusted *ad hoc* to fit particular forensic purposes. There is no reason to think that the line from Lansbury to Benn has confronted forces that were more indivertible than those which loomed over Jacobin or Luddite. The contrary would be more plausible.

The variance of the evaluations in the two texts, however, goes further.

83. PT, p. 71.
84. PT, p. 69. My italics.

For in the latter, Thompson in effect sketches a general theory of the evolution of the working class, good for all industrialized countries. A 'certain kind of revolutionary movement' is characteristic of the early years of a working class: but a 'climacteric moment' once passed, it disappears, and a more 'limited, reformist' phase sets in. This schema bears some resemblance to a widespread view within conventional sociology that the working class is rebellious in its youth because it has not yet accepted the irreversible advent of industrialism, unwillingly adjusts to the reality of the capitalist order in middle-age, and becomes reconciled to it through new levels of consumption towards retirement—before passing away altogether in a post-industrial society. The large difference, of course, is that Thompson—while willing to concede the possibility of a 'break-up of the old class institutions and value-system', and 'far-reaching changes in the sociological composition of the groups making up the historical class'[85]—holds firmly to the hope of a transition to socialism, if necessary after such a transmutation. There is nothing discreditable about these hypotheses. But what leaps to the eye is that this *type* of perspective is quite incongruent with that of *The Making of the English Working Class*. For if such a universal sequence is ordained, what remains of the claim for particular invention in the case of England? Collective agency must inevitably seem to shrink in scope, once 'much the same' kind of outcome ultimately results from its exercise in 'all advanced capitalist countries'. We are led to wonder: could the English working class *not* have made itself? The *reductio ad absurdum* involved in such a question casts a sharp final shadow over the claim for co-determination. The role of agency in history, just because it is so unremittingly pursued in *The Making of the English Working Class*, remains the more unmistakably elusive at the end of it.

Thompson's major substantive work of history is concerned with the making of classes themselves. We can trace the recurrence of the same intellectual movement, and its limits, when he turns to the question of the making of history *by* classes, in *The Poverty of Theory*. There he cites Engels's famous paradigm of the historical process: 'History makes itself in such a way that the final result always arises from conflicts between many individual wills, of which each again has been made what it is by a

85. PT, p. 72.

host of particular conditions of life. Thus there are innumerable inter-
secting forces, an infinite parallelogram of forces which give rise to one
resultant—the historical event. This again may be viewed as the product
of a power which, taken as a whole, works *unconsciously* and without
volition. For what each individual wills is obstructed by everyone else,
and what emerges is something no one willed.'[86] Thompson concedes
part of the force of Althusser's criticism of this construction. In
particular, 'Engels has not offered a solution to the problem, but re-stated
it in new terms. He has commenced with the proposition that economic
presuppositions are 'finally decisive', and this is where he concludes. On
the way he has gathered in an infinitude of "individual wills" whose
agency, in the result, is cancelled out'.[87] But Thompson nevertheless
sharply diverges from Althusser in his overall assessment of the passage,
considering that 'Engels has proposed a very critical problem (agency and
process) and that, despite deficiencies, the general tendency of his
meditation is helpful'.[88] He argues, in effect, that with an amendment
Engel's formula can be retained. All is well if we substitute class wills for
individual wills. Thus 'the historical "resultant" cannot usefully be
conceived as the involuntary product of the sum of an infinity of
mutually-contradictory individual volitions', for 'these "individual
wills", however "particular" their "conditions of life", have been
conditioned in class ways; and if the historical resultant is then seen as the
outcome of a collision of contradictory class interests and forces, then we
may see how human agency gives rise to an involuntary result—"the
economic movement finally asserts itself as necessary"—and how we may
say, at one and the same time, that "we make our own history" and
"history makes itself".'[89]

Does this emendation resolve the aporia of Engels's solution?
Thompson, of course, is right to emphasize that 'individual wills are not
de-structured atoms in collision but act with, upon and against each other
as *grouped* wills'. But what he has forgotten is that he himself redefines
class in such a way as in effect to make *it* dependent on a sum of individual
wills. For 'classes arise because men and women, in determinative
productive relations, identify their antagonistic interests, and come to

86. PT, p. 279.
87. PT, p. 279.
88. PT, p. 280.
89. PT, p. 279.

struggle, to think and to value in class ways: thus the process of class formation is a process of self-making, although under conditions which are "given" '.[90] In other words, the same regression towards infinity occurs within Thompson's construction as in Engels's: the only difference is that whereas for Engels the immediate building-blocks of history are individual men and women, for Thompson they are classes that are themselves built in turn by individual men and women. The convergence of end-results can be seen in Thompson's dictum elsewhere: '*agency* lies, not in class but in men'.[91] The central theoretical difficulty in either case remains intact. It concerns not the *appropriate type*—personal or collective—but the *pertinent place* of will in history. For the intractable question posed by any construction like that of Thompson is this: if fundamental historical processes, the structure and evolution of whole societies, are the involuntary resultant of a duality or plurality of voluntary class forces clashing with each other, what explains their *ordered nature*? Why should the intersection of rival collective wills not produce the random chaos of an arbitrary, destructured log-jam? Two of the greatest works of modern social thought have addressed themselves to precisely this problem—Parsons's *The Structure of Social Action* and Sartre's *Critique of Dialectical Reason*. Parsons's statement of the problem remains unsurpassed in clarity and cogency. How could the utilitarian model of conflicting rational interests ever found a coherent social order?[92] What prevented it from dissolving into a relentless war of all against all? Himself deeply committed to a 'voluntarist theory of action', Parsons sought to provide a superior answer to the conundrum of how a multitude of individual 'unit-acts' could ultimately constitute a 'social system'. His solution, as is well known, was to postulate common norms and values as the integrative framework of any society, informing individual acts and annealing divisive interests to ensure a stable and cohesive social whole. The idealist stamp of this escape from the Hobbesian problem of order, unable to explain either the generation or conflict of values themselves, has been criticized many times and need not detain us here. What is of greater interest is the close parallelism of

90. PT, pp. 298-299.
91. PT, p. 86.
92. Talcott Parsons, *The Structure of Social Action*, New York 1961, pp. 87-125. For Parsons, Marxism itself was a variant of 'individualistic positivism' within the same field.

problem and divergence of solution in Sartre's *Critique of Dialectical Reason*.

Sartre's basic question was how historical processes could be rationally intelligible if they were composed of a multiplicity of individual 'projects' colliding, clashing and thwarting each other to produce the deadened and alienated inverse of human agency—the practico-inert in all its myriad figures. His aim was to explore how the 'different practices which can be found and located at a given moment of the historical temporalization finally appear as partially totalizing and as connected and merged in their very oppositions and diversities by an intelligible totalization from which there is no appeal'.[93] Thereby he hoped to establish the nature of history as a 'totalization without a totalizer', and of its 'motive forces and its non-circular direction'.[94] Unlike Parsons, Sartre as a Marxist naturally refused to invoke 'hyper-organicist' values as a totalizing principle of social or historical ensembles. He also proceeded beyond individual 'praxes' to the level of class practices and projects as such, while attempting to preserve the epistemological continuity between the two in a way that is not dissimilar to that of Thompson. In fact, it might be said that Thompson's conclusion (substitute class for individual wills, which themselves compose classes) rehearses Sartre's point of departure. For what it lacks is Sartre's tormented awareness of the logic and empirical difficulties of constructing an ordered set of social structures from a multiplicity of antagonistic unit-acts. The remarkable unpublished second volume of the *Critique* is precisely devoted to the question: how can 'a plurality of epicentres of action have a single intelligibility', such that class *struggles* can be described as *contradictions*—in other words 'particularizations of a unitary totalization beyond them'?[95] The bulk of the work is taken up with an intricate series of analyses of social and political conflicts rending Soviet society after the Russian Revolution—within the Bolshevik Party itself, between proletariat and bureaucracy, between working class and peasantry—designed to show the history of the USSR up to the death of Stalin as the unitary process of a single 'enveloping totalization'. The series of concrete investigations finally moves to a theoretical meditation on the personality and role of Stalin himself, of great brilliance—and then abruptly breaks off, the

93. *Critique of Dialectical Reason*, London 1976, p. 817.
94. Ibid., p. 817.
95. *Critique*, vol. II, mss. pp. 3-5.

rest of the manuscript swerving away into an ontological discourse of impenetrable abstraction and obscurity, concerned with quite other questions. The reason for this final loss of direction, which perhaps prevented publication of the study, is clear enough. For all the ambition and ingenuity of his exploration of the successive contradictions of Soviet society, Sartre was unable actually to demonstrate how the ravaging struggles of the time generated an ultimate structural unity. In the absence of any extended principle of explanation, the needle of his account swings back to the shortest and simplest answer: Soviet society was held together by the dictatorial force wielded by Stalin, a monocentric sovereignty imposing a repressive unification of all the conflicting praxes within it. Hence the logic of the *Critique*'s terminus in the figure of the despot himself. The effective upshot is thus paradoxically a totalization *with* a totalizer—undermining that very complexity of the historical process which it was Sartre's express purpose to establish. Nowhere spelt out as such, the unhappy silence that suddenly falls across the work bespeaks Sartre's unease with the conclusion his argument had arrived at. He had lucidly emphasized, indeed, at the outset that the case of a dictatorial society was easier for his task—the more demanding test for Marxist theory being posed by bourgeois democracies, whose class struggles were not compacted together by a police regime.[96] But much as Engels had done before him, in confining himself to the USSR he thereby ended by finding in the historical 'resultant' what he had put into it in the first place. The general tendency of his response to the problem of order, however, can be discerned in this specialized exploration of it. Confronted with the direct question as to what prevented history from being 'an arbitrary chaos of inter-blocking projects' within his conceptual framework, his essential answer was: *power*.[97] In lieu of Parsons's consensus of moral values, Sartre's centre of integration was the command of a coercive State.

Althusser, it will be recalled, in criticizing Engels's paradigm extended his attack to Sartre's attempt to rework the problem on a much vaster scale in the *Critique*, linking the two directly: 'It is only possible to bar Sartre from his path by closing the one Engels opened for him'.[98] But

96. *Critique*, vol. II, mss. pp. 392-393, 396.
97. Interview, 'The Itinerary of a Thought', *New Left Review* 58, November-December 1969, p. 60, now collected in *Between Existentialism and Marxism*, London 1974, p. 55.
98. *For Marx*, p. 127.

the radical rejection in *For Marx* and *Reading Capital* of any form of volition, individual or collective, as an epistemological starting-point did not at the same stroke lift the issue of social order. Althusser subsequently found himself confronted with it too, and it is of interest that his initial answer to the question was in effect a hybrid of the positions of Parsons and of Sartre. His vocabulary for posing the problem was, of course, significantly different. Citing Marx's dictum that 'a social formation which did not reproduce the conditions of production at the same time as it produced would not last a year', he asked: '*how is the reproduction of the relations of production secured?*'[99] His reply was that the ongoing reproduction of any social formation was essentially assured by the combined operation of the coercive and cultural machinery of the State (the latter interpreted *in senso latu*). 'For the most part it is secured by the exercise of State power in the State Apparatuses, on the one hand the (Repressive) State Apparatus, on the other hand the Ideological State Apparatuses'.[100] The former are directed by 'the leadership of the representatives of the classes in power executing the politics of the class struggle of the classes in power', while the latter effect a 'massive inculcation of the ideology of the ruling class' in the oppressed classes.[101] Ironically, these formulations veer close to the voluntarist schema of historical explanation that Althusser had sought to renounce. Perhaps sensing this, in a postscript he stipulated two qualifications: the 'total process' of reproduction was 'realized' within the processes of production and circulation, through a 'class struggle' counterposing ruling to ruled classes.[102] Some years later, he proffered a further amendment: 'The class struggle does not go on in the air, or on something like a football pitch. It is rooted in the mode of production and exploitation in a given class society.'[103] Thus 'the *material* basis' of the class struggle was 'the unity of the relations of production and the productive forces *under* the relations of a given mode of production, in a concrete historical social formation'.[104] Here the emphasis reverts sharply back towards the 'base', in the traditional Marxist topography, which possesses and enforces its own 'unity'.

What view should be taken of these successive adjustments? The logic

99. *Lenin and Philosophy and Other Essays*, London 1971, p. 141.
100. *Lenin and Philosophy*, p. 141.
101. *Lenin and Philosophy*, pp. 142, 148.
102. *Lenin and Philosophy*, pp. 170-171.
103. *Essays in Self-Criticism*, London 1976, p. 50.
104. Ibid., p. 50.

of historical materialism precludes either the Parsonian or the Sartrean solutions. To contend that social formations typically derive their unity from the diffusion of values, or the exercise of violence, across a plurality of individual or group wills is to reject the Marxist insistence on the ultimate primacy of economic determinations in history. In fact, Marx and Engels directly polemicized in their own time with 19th century versions of precisely these two positions—in the work of Hegel and of Dühring, respectively. The problem of *social order* is irresoluble so long as the answer to it is sought at the level of intention (or valuation), however complex or entangled the skein of volition, however class-defined the struggle of wills, however alienated the final resultant from all of the imputed actors. It is, and must be, the dominant *mode of production* that confers fundamental unity on a social formation, allocating their objective positions to the classes within it, and distributing the agents within each class. The result is, typically, an objective process of class struggle. To stabilize and regulate *this* conflict, the complementary modalities of political power, which include repression and ideology, exercised *inside* and *outside* the State, are thereafter indispensable. But class struggle itself is not a causal prius in the sustentation of order, for *classes are constituted by modes of production, and not vice versa.* The one mode of production of which this will not be true is communism—which, precisely, will abolish classes.

At the same time, of course, the question of order is not exhaustive of the nature of the historical process. Upheaval and disorder equally require explanation. The temptation is to say that these form the peculiar province of the class struggle that is set in motion by the mode of production. This, however, would be facile. For among the most fundamental of all mechanisms of social change, according to historical materialism, are the systemic contradictions between *forces and relations of production*, not just social conflicts between classes generated by antagonistic relations of production alone. The former *overlap* with the latter, because one of the major forces of production is always labour, which simultaneously figures as a class specified by the relations of production. But they do not coincide. Crises within modes of production are not identical with confrontations between classes. The two may or may not fuse, according to the historical occasion. The *onset* of major economic crises, whether under feudalism or capitalism, has typically taken all social classes unawares, deriving from structural depths below those of direct conflict between them. The resolution of such crises, on the other hand, has no less typically been the outcome of prolonged war between classes. In general, *revolutionary* transformations—from one mode of production to another—are indeed the privileged terrain of class struggle. Here too, however, it is essential to remember the great distance between the relatively blind clashes of the immemorial past, and the recent—very uneven and imperfect—conversion of them into conscious contests in the 19th and 20th centuries. Thus in both reproduction and transformation—maintenance and subversion—of social order, mode of production and class struggle are always at work. But the second must be activated by the first for it to achieve its determinate effects, which on either ground will find their maximum point of concentration in the political structure of the *State*.

Towards the end of *The Poverty of Theory*, Thompson approaches for the first time an acknowledgment of this basic duality of the forms of historical determination, which stops all volitional constructions. He does so by way of an analogy. 'Societies', he argues, 'may be seen as very complex "games"', governed by visible and invisible rules, which 'assign to each player his role or function in the game'.[105] But within these rules, the players confront each other as creative agents. We should thus envisage a 'rule-governed structuration of historical eventuation, within which men and women remain as subjects of their history'.[106] This image seems to allow for the double determinacy just indicated. But the appearance is misleading, because Thompson's analogy conceals a central *petitio principii*. For games, precisely, are deliberate constructs—new ones are invented every day, as commodities, under capitalism—whose rules are consciously learnt by players from positions of parity, and which contain goals homogeneous to the rules. But no one 'learns' the rules of social relations of production in this sense; there is no equality of initial position among the players; and there is no common goal, specified by the rules, for which they compete. Indeed, the only players who hypothetically could master the rules, revolutionary socialists in knowledge of capitalist relations of production, are those whose aim is to break them. At every point, in other words, the analogy breaks down. Its suggestive function is to conjure up an orderly system, that is nevertheless one of conflict—squaring the circle of Engels's paradigm. Such a metaphor only

105. PT, p. 344.
106. PT, p. 345.

works—even then, rather partially—where the conflicts are strictly local and partial. Eric Hobsbawm's application of it to describe the beginnings of wage-bargaining in Victorian England, its original use, was in context not inappropriate.[107] But it is inoperable as a general analogy for large-scale or long-term historical processes, which are not consciously learnt systems—or where they exceptionally become so, are fought not *within* but *over* rules. Developing his imagery of games, in other words, Thompson concludes his long discussions of agency with a figurative reprise of the bias inflecting them throughout: a tendency to overpitch the share of conscious choice and action within social formations of the past, and to under-record the historical rupture represented by the advent of the enterprise of socialism itself.

We have seen how this tincture insistently colours the axiomatic reflections on agency in *The Poverty of Theory*, the deployment of the category of experience, the architecture of *The Making of the English Working Class* itself, the amendment of Engels's paradigm, and now the final ludic metaphor for society. The best way of assessing Thompson's overall position, and contribution, in this intractable domain is to compare it with that of his elective antagonist Althusser. The symmetry of their opposition is virtually complete. For Althusser immediate experience is the universe of illusion—Spinoza's *vaga experientia*, which induces only error. Science alone, founded on a work of conceptual transformation, yields knowledge. The incompatibility of this view with any materialist account of physical sensation or practice, as ineliminable bases of the natural sciences themselves, let alone as valid sources of truth in their own right, is plain. For Thompson, on the other hand, experience is the privileged medium in which consciousness of reality awakens and creative response to it stirs. Index of authenticity and spontaneity, it links being to thought, and checks the flights of theory towards artificiality and unreason. This account, in turn, is irreconcilable with the blinkering from reality and the depth of disaster which such salient experiences as religious faith or national loyalty have brought upon those in their grip. Althusser wrongly identifies experience only with such illusions: Thompson inverts this error, identifying experience essentially with insight and learning. What is needed, beyond the

107. 'Custom, Wages and Work-Load in Nineteenth Century Industry', in *Labouring Men*, London 1964, pp. 344-370.

abstract counterposition of these two poles, is *conceptual* clarification of the very different senses and forms of 'experience', and *empirical* study of the respective historical variations encompassed by each. The term is no talisman, of either truth or falsity, advance or regression, in itself. So too the treatment of the problem of agency by these rival theorists, diametrically contrasted in their emphases, suffers from a common indiscriminacy. The very *form* of their encapsulations of history—'process without a subject', 'unmastered human practice'—is latently unhistorical. Neither, of course, can be unaware of the possibility of curvature in the field of inquiry, but each definitionally ignores it. The result is once again an absence of necessary historical differentiation. The consequences of the two axiomatics are, however, quite distinct. They might be put like this. Althusser's unilateral and remorseless stress on the overpowering weight of structural necessity in history corresponds more faithfully to the central tenets of historical materialism, and to the actual lessons of scientific study of the past—but at the price of obscuring the novelty of the modern labour movement and attenuating the vocation of revolutionary socialism. Thompson's passionate sense of the potential of human agency to shape collective conditions of life, on the other hand, is much closer to the political temper of Marx and Engels themselves in their own time—but tends to be projected backwards as a uniform weft of the past, in defiance of the millennial negations of self-determination in the kingdom of necessity. Strangely, of two unbalanced sets of generalizations, Althusser's inclines better towards history, Thompson's towards politics. The classical equipoise of the founders of historical materialism is some distance from both.

3
Marxism

Thompson, however, has his own critical reflections on the work of the founders. In the course of *The Poverty of Theory* he proposes a complete new account of Marx and of Marxism, which contains some of his most interesting and original arguments. Approximately, his thesis goes like this. The true object of historical materialism is a 'unitary knowledge of society',[1] whose charter was set out by Marx in the 1840s, especially in the *1844 Manuscripts*, *The German Ideology*, *The Poverty of Philosophy*, and *The Communist Manifesto*. Marx, however, did not keep to his own programme sufficiently. In the 1850s, he unfortunately became so hypnotized by the intricacies of bourgeois political economy that, in his effort to master and criticize it, he for a time forgot all else and, abandoning the quest for a unitary social knowledge, started to produce a socialist version of its narrow theory of economic man—setting aside the 'many activities and relations (of power, of consciousness, sexual, cultural, normative) which are not the concern of Political Economy, which have been *defined out of* Political Economy, and for which it has no terms.'[2] The results can be seen in the 'static, anti-historical structure'[3] of the *Grundrisse*. Later, in the 1860s, under the influence of the revival of political activity in the ranks of European labour and of the intellectual

1. PT, p. 252.
2. PT, p. 254.
3. PT, p. 253.

revelation of Darwin's method in *The Origin of Species*, he corrected himself to a certain extent in *Capital*, which lets some real history in to the airless abstractions of Political Economy. But the book remains a 'mountainous inconsistency'[4] by and large still imprisoned in the struggle to produce an internal answer to Political Economy, and compromised by a rococo Hegelianism of exposition. Its extrapolation of the purely economic categories of capital from the full social process led to a closed system of 'too obsequiously ahistorical economic laws',[5] which had a disastrous effect on later Marxism. Engels ultimately saw this, in the 1890s, and devoted many letters to trying to rectify Marx's emphasis, by stressing the relative autonomy of superstructures, the importance of the non-economic elements in history, and the necessity of studying these in their own right. Althusser, however, has absolutized the errors of Marx in the *Grundrisse* and *Capital*, seeking 'to thrust historical materialism back into the prison of Political Economy',[6] by making Marxism into a theory of modes of production. The key blunder that results, which Marx himself prepared, is a systematic confusion of the capitalist mode of production with actual social formations, capital with capital*ism*. This mistake is aided and abetted by the whole mechanical metaphor of 'base' and 'superstructure'. The arctic structuralism and idealist reductionism of *Reading Capital* are the misbegotten consequences.

If the original Marx gave us the charter of genuine historical materialism, but then strayed away from it himself, in this century Marxist historians have sought to restore it. The quest for a unitary knowledge of society has taken them to 'the drama of Aeschylus, ancient Greek science, the origins of Buddhism, the city-state, Cistercian monasteries, utopian thought, Puritan doctrines, feudal tenures, the poetry of Marvell, Methodist revivalism, the symbolism of Tyburn, *grands peurs* and riots, Behmenist sects, primitive rebels, economic and imperialist ideologies, and every type of class confrontation, negotiation and refraction'.[7] In the course of their explorations, they have discovered that Marx's work suffered from a central absence as deep as Darwin's. Where the theory of evolution lacked an explanation of the means of the transmission and mutation of

4. PT, p. 257.
5. PT, p. 257.
6. PT, p. 260.
7. PT, p. 362.

species, the theory of historical materialism lacked an explanation of the means of the (partial) correspondence between modes of production and historical process. The genetics of Mendel provided the first. The task of Marxist historians has been to furnish the second. What they have discovered? 'Human experience'.[8] This genetics is not so rationalist as that sketched in philosophical language by Marx: it gives much greater weight to culture, and within culture to 'affective and moral consciousness'.[9] Here there is a real and complete silence in Marx himself—who never had a proper sense of the force of morality and affectivity, as opposed to interest and ideology, in history. Even at his best, he was too rationalist. In this respect, Engels was no improvement. His brusque dismissal of Morris, a great and sensitive communist moralist, is revealing of a common blindness. The locust desolation of Althusserianism has been the ultimate product of a heritage of default here. Consequently, Marx*ism* as a theory must be renounced. Its pretension to be a science is and always was obscurantist. There is, however, a *tradition* that derives from Marx that is at the antipodes of such theory, and should be honoured. The former has nothing further to tell us of the world: the latter is exploratory and positive. To this genuine historical materialism—'the tradition of open, empirical inquiry, originating in the work of Marx, and employing, developing and revising his concepts'[10]—affiliation is still eminently worthwhile.

In many ways, this case represents the most coherent and novel development within *The Poverty of Theory*. It amounts, in effect, to a quite new reading of Marx's intellectual trajectory, which privileges neither the early philosophical writings nor the late economic works, but instead accords central importance to the polemical texts of the mid 40s. In this perspective, *The German Ideology* would probably be the nearest, not only to an enunciation, but to an outline embodiment of the programme of a materialist reconstruction of the full history of humanity, as a unitary social process. Marx's major works thereafter subtly changed direction, in a movement away from history. The later writings of Engels, *Anti-Dühring* and *The Origin of The Family*, can then be seen as unsatisfactory attempts to remedy the 'great omission' of any sustained exposition or demonstration of historical materialism itself in the legacy

8. PT, p. 356.
9. PT, p. 363.
10. PT, p. 361.

of Marx. In this light, *Capital* becomes a kind of diversion, a narrowing lapse into mere 'political economy'.

How far can this reinterpretation of Marx's life-work be accepted? The key to it, as may be seen, is the claim that the itinerary from *The German Ideology* or *The Communist Manifesto* to the *Grundrisse* or *Capital*, was a false step, a 'turning aside'[11] from the global historical project first set out in the *1844 Manuscripts*. The best way of assessing this suggestion is to try to imagine for a moment what Marx would have written, had he accepted Thompson's formula of 'unitary social knowledge'[12] as his goal in the 50s and 60s. What would the probable result have been? Surely the answer is: something like Kautsky's *Die Materialistische Geschichtsauf-fassung*—a superficial, universal compendium of evolution, from the picanthrope to Palmerston. In other words, it is scarcely conceivable, for reasons that Thompson as a historian should know especially well, that Marx could really have produced new knowledge on a 'unitary' scale, given the exigencies—of time and energy—of mastering even one limited field of inquiry, at a time when no such thing as a cumulative corpus of reliable research into the past yet existed. Historical scholarship, as a modern discipline, was only just beginning to emerge in his own life-time—numbering among its first pioneers Niebuhr and Mommsen. What Marx did do was to select the domain that the theory of historical materialism had indicated as determinant in the final resort—namely, economic production—and to devote all his passion and industry to exploring and reconstructing that, in the *one* historical epoch of capital-ism. What other *scientific* path was open to him? His procedure was, in fact, the classical démarche of the real scientist. If *Capital* is to be faulted, it is in terms of its internal cogency, not its external limits. Would Thompson really have preferred Marx to be Buckle or Dühring, encyclo-paedizing the received illusions of his age—dealing with 'all things under the sun and some others as well', as Engels put it of the latter?[13] It must be said that here Althusser's formula is much more precise and telling in catching the nature of Marx's enterprise: he *started* an exploration of the vast continent of History, which still today remains in many respects largely unknown, but which he could never have overflown at the outset. The condition of later advances was precisely the limit of his initial

11. PT, p. 355.
12. PT, p. 257.
13. *Anti-Dühring*, Moscow 1954, p. 10.

investigation to a single region, which rendered it capable of ascertaining real processes in history, not mythic ones.

For the *Grundrisse* and *Capital* are in no sense mere works of an 'anti-political-economy'. Thompson is able to treat them as such only by ignoring the fact the writings of the 1840s he foregrounds, which Althusser calls the Works of the Break, do not yet possess the basic *historical* concepts that were to constitute the cornerstone of the theory of historical materialism as such—the 'forces and relations of production'. Göran Therborn has shown in detail the process of their crystallization in Marx's intellectual development. The key innovation of 'social relations of production', which can be found nowhere in classical political economy, does not occur before *The Poverty of Philosophy*, and does not acquire its full sense before the *Grundrisse*; the *couplet* of the two terms is first formalized in the *Preface* of 1859.[14] It was this progressive theoretical discovery which finally made possible the full-scale exploration of a *new historical object* in *Capital*: the capitalist mode of production. Marx's essential movement after 1848, in other words, was not 'away' from history, but deeper into it. We can now see the consequence of Thompson's omission in his otherwise lengthy dissertation on historical concepts of any account of *Marxist* categories as such. The silence is a remarkable one. In two hundred pages, there is scarcely even one mention of the forces/relations of production. Possibly Thompson took the pair so much for granted that he thought he could dispense with reference to them. But the failure at any point to pause over the *specificity* of the concepts of historical materialism, as opposed to the generic elasticity of all historical notions, radically disables an understanding of the real achievement of *Capital*. The term 'mode of production' does figure with some frequency in Thompson's text. At the conclusion of his criticisms of *Capital*, he writes indeed: 'These reservations do not in any way go to show that Marx's project was not legitimate. It was an epoch-making advance in knowledge to construct, by arduous theoretical engagement, by hypothesis and by equally arduous empirical investigation, the concept of a structured mode of production in this way'.[15] It would appear, then, that there are no grounds for quarrel here.

14. See the meticulous tracing in Göran Therborn, *Science, Class and Society*, London 1976, pp. 365-377—much the best discussion of the subject.
15. PT, p. 346.

Thompson himself asks the question: 'Is this not to give back to Althusser with my left hand all that I have taken away with my right?' His answer is a swift and aggressive negative. The reason is illuminating. The concept of a mode of production is for him essentially a category proper to *economic theory*, not to history, which cannot be extended to the characterization of societies whose study is the object of the historian. 'A capitalist mode of production is not capital*ism*. We pass on one letter from the adjectival characterization of a mode of production (a concept within Political Economy, albeit within Marxist "anti" Political Economy) to a noun descriptive of a social formation in the totality of its relations'.[16] Moreover, while 'the theory of a mode of production belongs, very properly, within [the] conceptual system' of 'Marxist economists', it suffers only an '*actively* misleading and diversionary'[17] maltreatment at the hands of Marxist philosophers like Althusser.

How should we judge this set of arguments? It ought, first of all, to be clear enough that Marx did not develop the concept of mode of production as a category within political economy, even an adversary version of it. For what, after all, is the primordial function of the concept? To think the *diversity* of socio-economic forms and epochs—to give us the means of *differentiating* one major type of historical structure from another, in the evolution of mankind. Political economy, on the contrary, was a system of thought which ultimately tended to deny and suppress the historicity of economic relationships and institutions, eternalizing the particular patterns of capitalism as perennial traits of civil society as such. It is thus no accident that the very first extended exposition of the elements comprised within the complex of a mode of production to be found in Marx should be, not an analysis of capitalism itself, but a comparative survey of *pre-capitalist* societies: the famous chapter of the *Grundrisse* (a work Thompson finds 'unreconstructed Hegelianism' in the abstraction of its 'whole mode of presentation')[18] which sweeps from ancient Greece and Rome to German tribes and Asian tyrants, through to mediaeval seigneurs and Renaissance merchants. Genetically and functionally, Marx's discovery of the concept of a mode of production marks a decisive exit from the world of political economy; with it, he embarked on a new kind of history.

16. PT, p. 346.
17. PT, p. 348.
18. PT, p. 253.

The notion, however, for all its centrality in his later writings, was never systematically articulated by him. Thompson seems insensitive to this obvious point. For he writes: 'Historians within the Marxist tradition have for many decades employed the concept of a mode of production, have examined the labour process and the relations of production',[19] and then dismisses the discussions of the concept by Althusser and Balibar on the grounds that they are innocent of any reference to the empirical findings of these historians and others. Hence 'it is not a question of disagreement about this or that, but one of total incompatibility in the way in which a historian and such a "theorist" situates himself before a mode of production'.[20] This pronouncement allows Thompson, in his turn, to ignore the analytic findings of philosophers within the Marxist tradition no less completely. In his entire essay, for all his many fulminations against the usage of 'modes of production' by Althusser and Balibar, Thompson never stops to discuss, even for a paragraph, their actual account of the combination of three elements (producer, nonproducer, means of production) and two relations (appropriation, property) which they argue make up any mode of production. None of this is written in the letter of Marx. Nor was it to be found in the writings of Marxist historians. There is no doubt that it can be, indeed has been, improved upon: Cohen's recent re-examination of the components of 'forces' and 'relations' of production alike represents a significant advance. But what is quite undeniable is that the *kind* of systematic conceptual clarification attempted by Althusser and Balibar was an original and fruitful enterprise, which yielded an account far more specific and precise than any prior Marxist discussion, whether among historians or anthropologists, that Thompson can adduce. The legitimacy and productivity of their contribution can be seen in at least two fields. On the one hand, it has pioneered closer theoretical scrutiny of the canons of historical materialism, of a type whose most lucid and critical example is Cohen's philosophical work. On the other, it has informed major works of empirical research, by both historians and anthropologists: Guy Bois's great study of Norman feudalism and Pierre-Philippe Rey's reconstruction of the impact of French colonialism in the Congo are cases in point. Thompson's belief that Althusser's influence excludes disciplined investigation of the real world is quite unfounded.

19. PT, p. 346.
20. PT, p. 347.

There is no doubt that *Reading Capital* would have been a better—much better—book if its authors had possessed a greater historical culture and shown more respect for the craft of historians. But *The Poverty of Theory* would also have benefited if its author had taken a more patient and scrupulous interest in the theoretical elucidations of Balibar. Thompson assumes that the concept of mode of production was a ready-made tool available for 'employment' by historians: this is demonstrably not the case. Althusser and Balibar sought to construct it as an articulated concept, without relation to historical materials other than those of Marx: undoubtedly a fault. But what these insufficiencies really teach us is not the 'total incompatibility' of the two perspectives decreed by Thompson, but the very opposite: their *mutual indispensability*. Marxist history is impossible without the formal construction of theoretical concepts, which are not those of 'historiography in general': but these concepts will only produce real knowledge if they derive from and return to controllable historical research. Thompson complains of the lack of historical referents in the discussion of modes of production by Althusser and Balibar, with some justice. But since he himself fails to engage intellectually with it, he is paradoxically unable to make an actual *historical* criticism of *Reading Capital*. Defeating his own intention, his pages remain more abstract and declaratory than those he is attacking.

The source of Thompson's distrust of *Capital* and aversion to contemporary debate over its concepts is not far to seek. They are inspired by the fear that a regional theory of a 'mode of production' must lead to economic reductionism, deforming or neglecting every other domain of social life, where 'many of the most cherished of human concerns are sited'.[21] Associated with this suspicion is a rejection of the traditional Marxist distinction between base and superstructure, as at once mechanical and chimerical. Yet Thompson does not deny the general hypothesis of the primacy of economic determinations in history. But how could that hypothesis be grounded other than by the exploration of determinate modes of production? To establish a secure notion of the 'economic structure' of society is not thereafter to preclude or compromise historical study of its cultural or political 'superstructures', but to facilitate it. *Without* the construction of a theory of the mode of production in the first instance, any attempt to produce a 'unitary knowledge' of

21. PT, p. 353.

society' could only have yielded an eclectic interactionism. Thompson, however, charges that Marx in the *Grundrisse* tended to collapse the one into the other—taking his regional theory of the circuits of capital for a total map of the structures of society. 'Capital is an operative category which laws its own development, and capital*ism* is the effect, in social formations, of these laws.'[22] Althusser, he contends, has systematized this gross identification of 'a mode of production' with a 'social formation in the totality of its relations',[23] which ultimately derives from the one-eyed vision of Political Economy. Thus Thompson writes that Althusser 'wishes to return us to the conceptual prison (mode of production = social formation) that had been imposed upon Marx by his bourgeois antagonist'.[24] In the lengthy bill of indictment of Althusser in *The Poverty of Theory*, it must be said that this refrain is one of the more astonishing accusations. For it was Althusser and Balibar themselves who *invented* the very distinction between mode of production and social formation which Thompson now brings against them. The notion of social formation itself had little or no currency within Marxism prior to Althusser. Why did he start to introduce it in *For Marx*, in lieu of 'society'? Because the familiar term suggested a deceptive simplicity and unity, which he sought to challenge—the Hegelian notion of a circular, expressive totality. By contrast, the term 'social formation', taken from the 1859 Introduction (*Gesellschaftsformation*) was utilized to underline the complexity and overdetermination of any social whole. In *Reading Capital*, Balibar went a decisive step further, by stressing that any given social formation is likely to contain not just one, but a *plurality* of modes of production—a lesson learnt, not from Marx, but from Lenin. '*Capital*, which expounds the abstract theory of the capitalist mode of production, does not undertake to analyze concrete social formations which generally contain *several* different modes of production, whose laws of coexistence and hierarchy must therefore be studied.'[25] With this the standard form of the distinction between the two concepts passed into general usage. Balibar, on the very occasion of coining it, was at pains to point out the dangers of the 'constant confusion in Marxist literature between the *social formation* and its economic infrastructure (which is itself often

22. PT, p. 253.
23. PT, p. 346.
24. PT, p. 355.
25. *Reading Capital*, p. 207.

related to *one* mode of production).'[26] Thompson, in other words, has contrived to convict his opponents of an error which they were the first to name.

The result is ironic. For the authors of *Reading Capital* long ago went *further* in emphasizing the distance between 'capital' and any given (say) Western social formation, than does *The Poverty of Theory* itself—which never broaches the problem of a combination of modes of production within a single society.[27] The concept of social formation was initially introduced as a forcible reminder that the diversity of human practices in any society is irreducible to economic practice alone. The issue it addressed was precisely that which gives rise to Thompson's anxieties about base and superstructure: the difference between the bare economic structures of 'capital' and the intricate fabric of social, political, cultural and moral life of (French or English or American) capitalism. Its stress was then further radicalized, to widen the discrepancy between 'capital' and 'capitalism' by recalling the existence of non-capitalist forms even within the economy itself. Preoccupied with the former problem, Thompson appears to have failed to notice the latter, and ended by forgetting where the terms in which either are formulable come from. Yet what is notable in the Althusserian concept of social formation is the *historiographic* advance—towards greater discrimination and complexity in the investigation of concrete societies—that it demonstrably permits. Far from imprisoning Marxists in a rigid equation between mode of production and social formation, the effect of Althusser's work has been to emancipate them from it.

Thompson's reservations about *Capital*, and its consequences for a later Marxist tradition, have a further motivation. The very procedure of treating the 'mode of production in abstraction', he seems to feel, tends towards a fatal laceration of the real historical process. 'Marxism was marked, at a critical stage in its development, by the categories of Political Economy: the chief of which was the notion of the "economic", as a first-order activity, capable of isolation in this way, as the object of a science giving rise to laws whose operation would over-ride second-order activities.'[28] But, Thompson asserts, 'a unitary knowledge of society

26. Ibid., p. 207.
27. There is a passing mention of the existence of 'overlapping modes of production' in India, in the context of another topic: PT, p. 353. This is the only allusion to the problem in the essay.
28. PT, pp. 252-253.

(which is always in motion, hence a historical knowledge) cannot be won from a "science" which, as a presupposition of its discipline, isolates certain kinds of activity only for study, and provides no categories for others.'[29] It might be thought that Althusser was not culpable of this error, since it is well known that he devotes much energy to emphasizing the difference between the various practices in a social formation, and the need for specific historical accounts of each. *For Marx* distinguishes three fundamental levels in every society—economic, political and ideological—and insists at length on the irreducibility of each to the other. The most famous concept of the book, 'overdetermination', was precisely designed to bring this *constitutive* complexity of any social formation home with maximum force. The subsequent development of Althusserian Marxism in no way lingered on the economic region alone: if anything, the latter was for some time relatively neglected. The major application of Althusser's concepts was to be in the political field, with the extensive theoretical work of Poulantzas on the State. Althusser's own later interests were mainly in the area of ideology. It would thus be difficult to claim that this tradition has 'isolated certain kinds of activity for study' and 'provided no categories for others'.

For Thompson, nevertheless, it represents no improvement on the abstractionist legacy of the *Grundrisse* or the bulk of *Capital*, since its very separation of plural instances is a violation of the imperative of unitary knowledge of society, no less than isolated concentration on one instance alone. To illustrate his objection to Althusser's formulations, he cites his own work on the role of law in 18th century England, which he argues shows that law operated at every rung of Hanoverian society, not just one. 'I found that law did not keep politely to a "level" but was at *every* bloody level; it was imbricated within the mode of production and productive relations themselves (as property rights, definitions of agrarian practice) and it was simultaneously present in the philosophy of Locke; it intruded brusquely within alien categories, reappearing bewigged and gowned in the guise of ideology; it danced a cotillion with religion, moralizing over the theatre of Tyburn; it was an arm of politics and politics was one of its arms; it was an academic discipline, subjected to the rigour of its own autonomous logic; it contributed to the definition of the self-identity both of rulers and of ruled; above all, it afforded an

29. PT, p. 257.

arena for class struggle, within which alternative notions of law were fought out'.[30] This splendid enumeration should send every reader to that memorable work *Whigs and Hunters*. There they will find the most remarkable explorations of the multiple meanings and functions of law ever written by a Marxist or any other historian. But do its findings actually annul the notion of different instances or levels within a social formation? If we look at Thompson's list, it will be seen that it breaks down quite naturally into three regions, traversed by a force common to them all:

economy	'mode of production'/'property rights'	
polity	'arm of politics'	'class struggle'
culture	'philosophy' 'ideology' 'religion' 'self-identity' 'academic discipline'	

What does this tell us? Something which is perfectly compatible with the most orthodox Althusserian account: namely that in a capitalist social formation law is essentially an *ideological* system (five entries), whose specificity is at the same time to be by definition materialized through the *political* institution of the State (one entry), where its primary function is the regulation and protection of *economic* property (one entry). The formal protocols of *Reading Capital*, in point of fact, spell out just such a complexity of terrain: 'The knowledge of one instance of the social formation through its structure includes the theoretical possibility of knowing *its articulation* with other instances. This problem then emerges as the problem of the mode of *intervention* of the other instances in the history of the instance analyzed ... The forms of intervention of law in economic practice are not the same as the interventions of economic practice in legal practice, i.e., as the *effects* which a transformation dictated by economic practice may have on the legal system, precisely by virtue of its systematicity (which also constitutes a system of internal "limits")'.[31] The ubiquity of law in Hanoverian England after the Revolution of 1688, demonstrated so eloquently by Thompson, tallies very closely with the description given by Poulantzas, when he argues

30. PT, p. 288.
31. *Reading Capital*, pp. 250, 306.

that 'ideology slides into every level of the social structure'[32] as a kind of 'cement' of social cohesion and that 'capitalist law is preeminently able' to perform this 'unifying' function.[33] Indeed, the parallelism between 'Thompsonian' and 'Althusserian' accounts of modern law goes even further. Douglas Hay, in an outstanding essay whose themes are taken up by Thompson, argues that law replaced religion as the central legitimating ideology in 18th century England.[34] Poulantzas maintains precisely the same thesis: 'The centre of legitimacy shifts away from the sacred towards legality. Law itself, which is now the embodiment of the people-nation, becomes the fundamental category of state sovereignty; and juridical-political ideology supplants religious ideology as the predominant form.'[35]

There are, of course, differences between the two expositions, apart from the far greater empirical wealth of the former. Thompson's concluding reflections on law in *Whigs and Hunters* are much more sensitive to the progressive dimensions of bourgeois legal ideology in the epoch of the Enlightenment, and to the points of defence it could afford to popular resistance against economic marauding by the ruling class, as well as the bulwarks it constituted against arbitrary political authority within the propertied classes themselves—in other words, its historical contradictions as a movable field of class struggle. Poulantzas, on the other hand, shows greater acuity towards the lure of the notion of the 'rule of law', uncritically accepted—even exalted—by Thompson as a gain of the Hanoverian epoch. As he rightly points out, even the most despotic states have typically had comprehensive legal codes and ruled by laws.[36] One of the most advanced such codes in history, enforcing rigorous equality before the law, was the Mongol *yasa* of Genghis Khan. We shall return to this question; for our purposes here, it is enough to note that Poulantzas, from within the very topography of instances denounced as metaphysical in *The Poverty of Theory*, is capable of making a valid *historical* criticism of Thompson, verifiable on ordinary empirical grounds.

The fear that lies behind Thompson's rejection of the notion of

32. *Political Power and Social Classes*, London 1974, p. 207.
33. *State, Power, Socialism*, London 1978, p. 88.
34. 'Property, Authority and the Criminal Law' in Hay et al., *Albion's Fatal Tree*, London 1973, pp. 7-63.
35. *State, Power, Socialism*, p. 87.
36. *State, Power, Socialism*, p. 76.

different levels in a society is, of course, a widespread one. Raymond Williams has expressed it with greatest force in *Marxism and Literature*. It is the misgiving that to distinguish analytically between various instances in a social formation tends to induce the belief that these exist substantively as separate objects, physically divisible from each other in the real world.[37] It would be wrong to deny that such a confusion of epistemological procedures with ontological categories can occur. But the cause of it is precisely the failure to keep sufficiently in mind the distinction between the object of knowledge and the real object which Althusser above all has emphasized. Hence the supererogation of objecting to him that in reality all social activities are mixed and interfused with each other, something he less than anyone would think of contesting. The strictly metaphorical nature of the base/superstructure distinction itself, repeatedly adverted to by Thompson and others, has likewise been pointed out by Althusser too.[38] The difference is that the one would reject it outright, while the other would retain and improve on it. Once, however, the long-run primacy of economic processes in history is conceded—as Thompson does concede it—any figuration of it, whether mechanical, vitalist or mathematical, must inevitably be *asymmetrical*. Dismissing base/superstructure as too 'constructional', Thompson toyed with the alternative of kernel/nut, before judging it too 'vegetative', and concluding that 'it may well be that no metaphor can be devised which is not in specifically human terms'.[39] It would seem that so far he has hit upon no substitute to propose. In the interim, we have no reason not to continue to employ the traditional image. It so happens, in fact, that we now possess a stringent and persuasive vindication of its role within Marxist theory, in Cohen's work, whose intellectual force supersedes virtually all previous discussion. It is thus of particular interest here that Cohen's demonstration of its utility should focus exactly on the case of law—which, he argues, must always be distinguished as a superstructure from the economic base. Among sources that have mistakenly assimilated the two, he singles out a discussion by myself of pre-capitalist societies.[40] His arguments are equally pertinent to Thompson's account of law in early capitalist society. They seem compelling to me: perhaps they may

37. *Marxism and Literature*, Oxford 1977, pp. 80-81.
38. *Lenin and Philosophy*, pp. 129-130.
39. PT, p. 121.
40. *Karl Marx's Theory of History—A Defence*, pp. 217-248.

persuade Thompson too, as a model of the kind of reasoning for which he pleads. Law can be empirically omnipresent in a society, as he has shown, yet remain analytically a level of it, as Poulantzas maintains: and that level can indeed be elevated as a superstructure above an economic base, even while being indispensable to it, as Cohen demonstrates. There is no incompatibility between these successive propositions.

After developing the thesis of the necessary regional complexity of any social formation in *For Marx*, Althusser went on to argue in *Reading Capital* that each region possessed its own temporality, which could only be captured after constructing the concept of the instance concerned. This notion, of differential historical times, is rejected no less categorically by Thompson. Essentially his claim is that to speak of either discrete levels or differential temporalities is to break the *unitary texture of experience*, in which all instances are simultaneously lived by the subject. Thus 'Althusser's constructions are actively *wrong* and thoroughly misleading', because 'all these "instances" and "levels" are in fact human activities, institutions and ideas. We are talking about men and women, in their material life, in their determinate relationships, in their experience of these, and in their self-consciousness of this experience. By "determinate relationships" we indicate relationships structured within particular social formations in class ways and that the class experience will find simultaneous expression in all these "instances", "levels", institutions and activities'.[41] It follows, therefore, that Althusser's 'notion of "levels" motoring around in history at different speeds and on different schedules is an academic fiction.'[42] Here, it would seem, *furor polemicus* has driven Thompson to a denial that his professional common sense would ordinarily have warned him against. For who, after all, were the original authors of the idea of differential historical temporality? His fellow historians Braudel and Labrousse. The very architecture of *The Mediterranean and the Mediterranean World in the Age of Philip II* is layered in descending levels: structural, conjunctural, eventual—denoting distinct regions of history: geographic, socioeconomic, political—each of which is accorded a different pattern of duration: long, medium, short. Is this whole construction to be contemptuously waved aside as a mere academic fiction? Obviously not. Would Thompson really contest that the temporality of Saharan transhumance

41. PT, p. 289.
42. PT, p. 289.

was distinct from that of the gold traffic out of the Sudan into the Mediterranean, and both from that of Spanish military probes in the Maghreb? With greater precision, Labrousse already before the War had demonstrated the existence of different historical schedules within a single region itself, tracing superimposed price-waves—secular, cyclical and seasonal—in the agrarian economy of 18th century France.[43] Further concrete examples could be multiplied at will. To take only one of the nearest: who would deny that the rate of change evinced by the population has been slower than that of the polity in 20th century England? Such considerations are so elementary that it is baffling that a historian could appear to scout them.

In his next paragraph, Thompson provides a counter-example to illustrate his own claim that the 'same unitary experience' can find a circular 'expression' in a synchronized cluster of disparate social processes. In 18th century England, 'fear of the crowd in "politics" reappearing as contempt for manual labour among the genteel reappearing as contempt for *praxis* in the academy reappearing as Black Acts in the "law" reappearing as doctrines of subordination in "religion"—will be *the same unitary experience* or determining pressure, eventuating in the *same* historical time, and moving to the *same* rhythm'.[44] But it is not difficult to reply to this. For hasn't contempt for manual labour *outlived* the Black Acts (as well as long *preceding* them)? Hasn't fear of the crowd persisted long after doctrines of religious subordination have withered away? Weren't the academies themselves more recent than either, yet more durable than Hanoverian capital statutes? Each of these different attitudes or codes has its own tempo and span of evolution. In this one sentence there swarms a plurality of historical times. Thompson should have no problem in seeing them, but he seems to feel that to admit them is to rend the seamless cloth of experience beyond repair. Yet the subjective sensation of 'simultaneity' is no guarantee of the objective co-temporality in a deeper sense of the processes experienced.

Thompson is on much sounder ground when he goes on to remark: 'All these distinct "histories" must be convened within the same real historical time, the time within which process eventuates.'[45] This is very

43. Ernest Labrousse, *Esquisse du mouvement des prix et des revenus en France au XVIIIe siècle*, Paris 1933.
44. PT, p. 289.
45. PT, p. 289.

well said. Here is the true weakness of Althusser's discussions of history: not his emphasis on the existence of different sectoral times, which was salutary, but his failure to stress the necessity of reconvening them within a plenary societal time. It is not that Althusser ignores the issue entirely: referring to 'the different temporalities produced by the different levels of the structure', he writes that 'their complex combination . . . constitutes the peculiar time'[46] of the development of a social formation. But the memory of this discreet allusion is soon effaced in the thick of the subsequent denunciations of the 'ideology of time' in *Reading Capital*. 'There can be no question of relating the diversity of the different temporalities to a single ideological base time, or of measuring their *dislocation* against the line of a single continuous reference time.'[47] Althusser here entertains, rather than dispels, a central conceptual ambiguity: the result is a grave confusion. Time as *chronology* is a single, homogeneous continuum. There is nothing in the least 'ideological' about this concept of temporality, which forms the scientific object of such institutions as the Greenwich Observatory. Time as *development* is differential, heteroclite, discontinuous. The two senses of the word are engraved in every-day language as, approximately, 'clock-time' and 'musical time'. The latter, however, connotes only *rhythm*, whereas the technical sense above also includes *duration*. 'What is the time of Bach's *Prelude in C Major*?' The three different possible answers (say: 2 o'clock; 4/4; 5 minutes) indicate the range of daily meanings of the term. All discussions of *historical time* refer to the combination of the last two senses, as anyone acquainted with the emergence of the theme from Labrousse and Braudel onwards will realize. Such historical temporalities, however differential, are always convertible into chronological time, which remains identical. Althusser's fustigation of a 'single continuous reference time' is in truth 'thoroughly misleading', because it fails to make any clear distinction between the indisputable (indeed indispensable—think of dating) existence of such time, as the medium of all history, and its lack of pertinence as a common organizing principle of the diverse scansions of historical development. The *relevant* time in which all regional histories should be convened is not an empty grid of dates, but the full movement of the social formation as a whole. At a minimum. Claiming that 'it is only possible to give a content to the

46. *Reading Capital*, p. 104.
47. *Reading Capital*, pp. 104-105.

concept of historical time by defining historical time as the specific form of existence of the social totality under consideration', Althusser characteristically assumes that the 'social totality' in question is equivalent to a 'social formation', in other words that national ensembles form the natural boundaries of historical investigation. But in fact historical materialism above all insists on the *international* character of modes of production, and the need to integrate the times of each particular social formation into the much more complex general history of the mode of production dominant in them.

The theoretical and technical problems involved in the reconvening of differential historical temporalities into a single social time are formidable. It is scarcely an accident that Braudel's monumental work itself has been faulted by critics ever since its first publication on precisely the grounds that it fails in this task—its three strata never achieving any significant synthesis.[48] The absence of adequate emphasis on the problem, let alone the elements of a satisfactory solution to it, is thus not wholly surprising in Althusser's work. By contrast with Braudel, however, Labrousse did succeed in integrating different sectoral times into a single historical movement, by concentrating on conjunctures of *crisis*. The classic text in this respect is his succinct essay on the patterned intertwining of plural economic cycles (agricultural/industrial) with financial and political fissures inside the governing bloc and State apparatus, which detonated the great revolutionary explosions of 1789, 1830 and 1848 in France.[49] Probably this study provided the remote model for the reflections on the question of revolutionary situations in *For Marx*. For Althusser's work does not altogether lack concepts for convoking differential temporalities into a common history: the notions of 'displacement', 'fusion' and 'condensation' of contradictions are designed to serve this purpose in his early work. In fact, *For Marx* contains one express category of overall integration—that of the 'ruptural unity'. Althusser coined this phrase to describe the paradigm of October 1917. In such crises, 'a vast accumulation of "contradictions" comes into play *in the same court*, some of which are radically heterogeneous—of different origins, different sense, different *levels* and *points* of

48. For a representative sample of opinion, see J.H. Hexter, *On Historians*, London 1979, pp. 134-138.
49. 'Comment Naissent les Révolutions', in *Actes du Congrès du Centenaire de la Révolution de 1848*, Paris 1948.

application—but which nevertheless "merge" into a ruptural unity'—
'the *unity* they *constitute* in this "fusion" [is] a revolutionary rupture'.[50]
The limitation of this set of terms is that they are essentially concerned
with conjunctures of revolutionary upheaval, (when 'the immense
majority of the popular masses' are '*grouped* in an assault on a regime
which its ruling classes are *unable to defend*'),[51] which are very rare
historically. More usual is not a 'unity of rupture', but a 'unity of contain-
ment' or 'reinforcement' or 'blockage'. The conjunctural unity which
Thompson evokes in Walpole's time is a vivid example. Although he is
aware of the problem (he mentions the case of Wilhelmine Germany),[52]
Althusser's vocabulary has no effective concepts for negotiating this type.
In that sense, Thompson's complaint against it is justified and the
example he musters is well chosen. But the quantitative predominance of
'blocked unities', or more accurately 'adaptive unities', is itself a
reminder of the lesser incidence of collective agency ever operating at the
level of the social formation as such, to mould or remould it.

There remains one final, and fundamental criticism made by Thompson
of Althusser's writing on history. The master concept which won him his
initial fame was over-determination. Its central role in *For Marx* is never
in doubt: the very ruptural unity just discussed is only a specification of
the universal mechanism of the over-determination of contradictions in
the complex social whole which Althusser held to be peculiar to
Marxism. Yet Thompson rightly notes that '*determination*, which is still
at the centre of his whole revolving gravitational field, does not merit one
sentence of theoretical scrutiny.'[53] The result, in Althusser's keynote
account of the causes of the Russian Revolution, is a curious slippage
towards a mere empirical pluralism: a variegated host of 'circumstances'
and 'currents' responsible for the ruptural unity of October is conjured
up, but their material *hierarchy* and *interconnection* are nowhere established. We are left with an indiscriminate list, rather than a genuine
explanatory structure. The reason is in part to be found in the authority
on which Althusser based himself—Lenin. For Lenin never produced a
comprehensive historical analysis of the Russian Revolution as such:

50. *For Marx*, p. 100.
51. *For Marx*, p. 99.
52. *For Marx*, p. 106.
53. PT, p. 288.

his views on its causality must be reconstructed from a scatter of occasional articles and speeches during and after the event, which never found a point of integration. Althusser's theorization of them mimes this original dispersal. The failure here was political as much as intellectual. For historical materialism actually possessed an account of October of incomparably greater depth and relevance—Trotsky's *History of the Russian Revolution*, which precisely advances an overall Marxist *theory* of it, worked through a detailed narrative reconstruction of the events themselves. Althusser's organizational allegiances at the time of *For Marx* foreclosed even the possibility of allusion to it. The consequence is a drastic weakening of the force of his exposition of over-determination itself, which remains more a sobriquet for the multiform surface of the revolutionary process in Russia than an explanation of its inner unity and intelligibility.

The question remains: could the concept of over-determination *develop* a more adequate causal range, at the theoretical level proper? Thompson, pointing out the deficiency of Althusser's unexamined uses of the term 'determination', cites his own and Raymond Williams's discussions of it in favourable contrast. He would probably agree that of the two Williams's have been more sustained. The merit of the reflections in *Marxism and Literature* on 'determination' is unquestionable:[54] characteristically, Williams focused earlier and more clear-sightedly on the ambiguities of the term than any other thinker. In doing so he set out his preference for the reading of it as 'setting of limits' or 'exerting of pressures', rather than as 'control'—one that Thompson shares—yet also expressed a view of 'over-determination' rather more appreciative than that of Thompson.[55] It is of particular interest, therefore, that in the first *systematic* exploration to have been made of the different types of causal determination at work in society and history, the initial mode distinguished is precisely Williams's first sense of the term, while the intellectual filiation of the enterprise as a whole is derived from Althusser's original concept of over-determination. Erik Olin Wright's *Class, Crisis and the State* constructs a theoretical range of six different types of determination, headed but far from concluded by 'structural limitation', which offers empirical historical examples of each, and seeks to trace out their complex social interconnections in the ongoing

54. *Marxism and Literature*, pp. 83-89; *Keywords*, London 1976, pp. 87-91.
55. *Marxism and Literature*, p. 88.

relationships between modes of production, class struggle and states.[56] As a first venture into uncharted terrain, it will certainly be susceptible to improvement and correction—from historians, sociologists or philosophers. But it is clear that the *direction* of this pioneering discussion is the right one: long overdue among all Marxists. If Thompson's reproaches to Althusser on the score of determination are warranted, a work written within the Althusserian tradition has—contrary to his confident inferences—produced far the most developed and discriminating account of its modalities to date.

In sum, Thompson's attack on the historical concepts to be found in Althusser's work lacks depth or nuance. Taking Marx's notion of a mode of production as effectively given, it fails to register either the novelty or the necessity of systematic analysis of it; mistakes the provenance and purpose of the concept of social formation; exaggerates the dangers of an analytic topography of regions; and forgets the general origin and gain of the notion of differential time for historians. But this series of dismissals is in a sense no more than the negative concomitant of the positive proposals that Thompson advances in *The Poverty of Theory*. For if he rejects the itinerary—mode of production > social formation > topography of practices > differential temporality—it is because he has another and shorter route to recommend. The missing link between the abstract 'mode of production' and the concrete 'historical process' is 'human experience'. With their discovery of it, modern Marxist historians have, he argues, started to remedy the Darwinian limits of Marx himself with a boldly new Mendelian genetics. 'For just as Darwin proposed and demonstrated an evolutionary process which proceeded by means of a hypothetical transmutation of the species—species which had hitherto been hypostatized as immutable and fixed—and yet remained wholly in the dark as to the actual genetic means of this transmission and transmutation—so, in an analogous way, historical materialism, as a hypothesis, was left unprovided with its own "genetics". If a correspondence could be proposed—and, in some part, demonstrated—between a mode of production and historical process, how, and in what ways, did this come about?'[57] The answer, Thompson tells us, 'lies within a missing term: "human experience"', where 'men and women

56. *Class, Crisis and the State*, London 1978, pp. 14-27.
57. PT, p. 356.

also return as subjects'—'persons experiencing their determinate productive situations and relationships, as needs and interests and as antagonisms, and then "handling" this experience within their *consciousness* and their *culture* in the most complex ways, and then acting upon their determinate situation in their turn.'[58]

Are we shown here a preferable road to historical understanding? The force of Mendelian genetics, in the account above, was to provide the *causal mechanism* that *explained* the evolution of species that Darwin had merely observed. If 'experience' is really the genetic code of history, it presumably likewise constitutes the explanation of the development of all societies. Can the concept possibly bear such weight? We have already seen the central difficulty internal to it. Where does experience lead? What consciousness does it generate? What action does it inspire? No reply comes packaged together with it—alone, the word remains dumb before these questions. For explanatory purposes, the term is an ambiguous void. Hence the necessity of filling it with a further term—the meta-experience already encountered, and predictably present here again: the 'handling' of experience. The mystery of this notion is paradoxically reminiscent of that of some of Althusser's own concepts (ideology defined not as an imaginary relation of men to their conditions of existence, but as an imaginary relation to the way in which they live their conditions of existence). Its function is to supply a bridge between an imponderable cause and an incalculable effect. But if there is no readily univocal passage from 'experience' to 'action', the interpolation of 'handling' to convert the one into the other does not advance our comprehension of either. It merely reproduces the indeterminacy of the connection between the two, within a yet more secluded sanctum of the subject. The way to a better materialist understanding of historical action is not to be found in a regression to ever more intangible sources of motivation, but in progressing towards an ever more specific and concrete grasp of the manifold of its social determinations.

The appeal to experience in *The Poverty of Theory*, however, involves two further corollaries of importance. For it will be remembered that experience is not only the lived fabric of society, it is the solution in which 'structure is transmuted into process' and the 'subject re-enters history'. But if it is to be at the same time the Mendelian code of the human

58. PT, pp. 362, 356.

adventure on earth, this medium in which 'men and women return as subjects in their own history' becomes nothing less than the *causal secret* of the whole 'historical process'. The logic of the comparison is another way of over-writing, of inflating to plainly untenable dimensions, the actual role of agency in historical change till now. An increasingly idealist and voluntarist drift emerges in the argument here. The impression is reinforced if we look at the—rather sparse—specifications Thompson gives of the new genetics. Suggesting that human experience can explain why societies undergo transitions and modifications in a way unavailable to Marx, Thompson writes: 'At "experience" we were led on to re-examine all those dense, complex and elaborated systems by which familial and social life is structured and social consciousness finds realization and expression (systems which the very rigour of the discipline in Ricardo or in the Marx of *Capital* is designed to exclude): kinship, custom, the invisible and visible rules of social regulation, hegemony and deference, symbolic forms of domination and of resistance, religious faith and millenarian impulses, manners, law, institutions and ideologies—all of which, in their sum, comprise the "genetics" of the whole historical process, all of them joined, at a certain point, in common human experience'.[59]

How should we assess this claim? The first thing to be said is that Thompson has simply forgotten the central tenet of historical materialism. For far from lacking any explanatory principle of a 'genetic' type, Marx's theory conspicuously possesses one—set out with singular clarity and force in the 1859 *Preface*: the thesis that the contradiction between forces of production and relations of production is the deepest spring of long-term historical change. Thompson, perhaps averse to the objectivism of its terms, ignores the idea altogether. No argument is even adduced against it in *The Poverty of Theory*: it is abandoned in silence. What does the inventory of Thompson's genetics afford us instead? In contrast to Marx, it provides us with a catalogue of systems, not a causal hypothesis about them. A listing is not an explanation. However, it is not thereby merely neutral. The elements selected for inclusion intimate a definite pattern:

---

59. PT, pp. 362-363.

kinship	visible rules
custom	law
hegemony	institutions
deference	
symbols	
religious faith	
millenarial impulse	
manners	
ideologies	
invisible rules	

The ten items on the left all pertain approximately to the area of culture, taken in the wider sense adopted by Thompson in his historical work. The three items on the right are more vaguely, potentially political in character. The balance between the two, and the distribution of interest and specificity (compare 'religious faith and millenarial impulses' with 'institutions') is scarcely in doubt. Involuntarily, a creeping culturalism appears to be at work. On the next page, Thompson tells us that 'with "experience" and "culture" we are at a junction-point of another kind'—for 'people do not only experience their own experience as ideas, within thought and its procedures, or (as some theoretical practitioners suppose) as proletarian instinct. They also experience their own experience as *feeling*, and they handle their feelings within their culture, as norms, familial and kinship obligations and reciprocities, as values or (through more elaborated forms) within art or religious beliefs.'[60] He goes on: 'This half of culture (and it is a full one-half) may be described as affective and moral consciousness.'[61] Marx and Engels exhibited a particular blindness towards it, transmitting a repression of this whole domain to later Marxism with dire intellectual and political consequences. The effect of these successive definitions is a surreptitious set of equations: mode of production = lacking in 'experience' to explain historical process; experience = lived out in culture and consciousness, with complex systems Marx excluded; half of culture = non-ideational elements, above all affectivity and morality; Marx precisely and most systematically ignored these. Construed strictly, these pages come near to saying that morality and affectivity provide a moiety of the experience

60. PT, p. 363.
61. PT, p. 363.

that genetically propels the transformations of history. Such a position has a respectable liberal pedigree, but it is not—plainly not—a Marxist one. In fact, of course, Thompson does not in practice subscribe to it. He remains far more materialist as a historian. In *The Poverty of Theory* itself, he subsequently insists that values must be situated in 'culture's material abode: the people's way of life, and, above all, their productive and familial relationships'.[62] But the tendency of his reflections always reverts to a circular simultaneity between 'values' and 'interests', 'want' and 'ought', 'class struggle' and 'moral conflict', rooted in the expressive totality of experience. An explanatory *dynamic* remains unprocurable from them.

As if in part aware of this himself, Thompson elsewhere in *The Poverty of Theory* presents another account of the relations between values and history, which suggests a deeper position. For there he argues, not so much that morality or affectivity are half of the hidden causes of historical change, as that the values they express constitute the imperishable links between individuals in the overall course of history. Historical processes as such cannot be deemed 'progressive' or 'reactionary'. But 'while we may not attribute value to process, the same objections do not arise with the same force when we are considering the choices of individuals'.[63] For particular individuals in the past may exhibit values with which we can identify, or by which we may be inspired today, that we in turn can transmit by the quality of our judgement or lives to future individuals. Such moral affiliation, beyond the task of causal explanation, is an inherent and saving dignity of the discipline of history itself. 'For "progress" is a concept either meaningless or worse, when imputed as an attribute *to* the past, which can only acquire a meaning from a particular position in the present, a position of value in search of its own genealogy'.[64] Thus we may 'identify with certain values which past actors have upheld, and reject others. We may give our vote for Winstanley and for Swift; we may vote against Walpole and Sir Edwin Chadwick. Our vote will change nothing. And yet, in another sense, it may change everything. For we are saying that these values, and not those other values, are the ones which make this history meaningful *to us*, and that these are the values which we intend to

62. PT, p. 368.
63. PT, p. 234.
64. PT, pp. 234-235.

enlarge and sustain in our own present. If we succeed, then we reach back into the past and endow it with our own meanings: we shake Swift by the hand. We endorse in our present the values of Winstanley, and ensure that the low and ruthless kind of opportunism which distinguished the politics of Walpole is abhorred.'[65]

The power of this vision is not to be gainsaid. It constitutes the core of Thompson's own practice, and much of the reason of his greatness, as a historian. But at the same time, it is also impossible not to note its distance from historical materialism as understood by Marx or Engels. One early symptom of a dissociation between the two in *The Poverty of Theory* is the pattern of Thompson's definitions of history and of historical materialism themselves. Repeatedly, he spontaneously equates 'history' with the 'past'. Thus 'historical is a generic definition: it defines very generally a common property of its object (appertaining to the past and not to the present or the future).'[66] Again, 'the real object remains unitary. The human past is not an aggregation of discrete histories'.[67] These are unwary formulations, of whose pitfalls Thompson would elsewhere be conscious. Their significance lies in their alliance with another set of identifications. In these historical materialism is assimilated to historiography *tout court*—the practice of writing history. Thus in the very first line of *The Poverty of Theory*, 'historical materialism' as a 'mature practice' is the 'strongest discipline deriving from the Marxist tradition'—which during the life-time of Thompson 'as a historian' has made considerable advances.[68] Later, 'historical materialism' is distinguished from 'Marxist practitioners in other disciplines' and straightforwardly equated with 'Marxist historiography'.[69] Thereafter the equivalence of the two is by and large taken for granted. Yet if we recollect the work of Marx and Engels themselves, we can see immediately that Thompson's constant assimilation of history to the past, historical materialism to historiography, was entirely alien to them. For historical materialism to its founders was also 'scientific socialism', in other words the enterprise of understanding the *present* and mastering the *future*—a political project at one with the idea of proletarian revolution. In this perspective, historical materialism is not confined to,

65. PT, p. 234.
66. PT, p. 223.
67. PT, p. 232.
68. PT, p. 153.
69. PT, p. 236.

or even overwhelmingly concentrated on, the past. The history with which it is concerned is at least equally the present. Indeed, what else is *Capital* actually oriented towards? Its essential 'empirical' reference-point is the English economy of the 1860s. This seems like a supremely obvious and elementary point. What is surprising is how completely Thompson fails to engage with it, in his lengthy commentary on the differences between *Capital* and historical materialism as he interprets it.

Now in the annals of 20th century Marxism, it is the opposite error which has been widespread—the reduction of historical materialism to a sociology of revolution, and the compression of its principles of inquiry to the norms of political struggle. Against this instrumental narrowing, it is necessary to stress firmly and clearly that the *past*, which lies beyond any material alteration by the activities of the present, remains nonetheless a perpetual and essential object of knowledge for Marxism, a zone of cognition unimpaired—contrary to the theses on Feuerbach—by absence of transformation. In an essay on the forms and limits of Western Marxism, I have discussed the dangerous impoverishment involved in any confinement of historical materialism to contemporary horizons alone.[70] Thompson, on the other hand, tends to commit a reduction in the other direction, a much more unusual deviance. For what his whole account of historical materialism in *The Poverty of Theory* lacks is any real sense that one of the central purposes of understanding the past is to provide a *causal knowledge* of historical processes capable of furnishing the basis for an adequate political practice in the present, aimed at transforming the existing social order into a prepared, popular future—for the first time in history. This is the ambition of *The Communist Manifesto*. Yet in Thompson's account of the original charter of historical materialism, from which he alleges Marx turned away into the labyrinths of political economy, the slightest allusion to it is wanting. Something else takes its place in *The Poverty of Theory*. For Thompson, in effect, history becomes essentially a pattern-book of moral examples, to be learnt and handed on for ethical imitation. The continuity of past and present is th reby snapped at the basic level where it is materially effective—in the objective processes of social development and change, which till now have *not*—precisely—been the arena of a celebration of free collective agency.

70. *Considerations on Western Marxism*, pp. 109-111.

Aware of the political difficulty of presenting it as such, Thompson falls back on salvaging individual moral values from an amoral, direction-neutral process. The echoes of the more classical Marxist tradition are not entirely absent from *The Poverty of Theory*,[71] but they are increasingly weak and distant. The main score of the text is in another key. It is one which is fundamentally at variance with the mainstream of historical materialism. Neither Marx nor Engels—as Thompson notes—were in any way reluctant to express social-moral judgements. They did not, however, ever systematize these into a separate discourse. In a certain sense, Thompson is right to tax their legacy with this relative silence—whose most serious result in their own life-time was, he justly points out, Engels's impatience and insensibility towards the peculiar genius of Morris. But what he fails to see is that the reason why the founders of historical materialism were so chary of ethical discussions of socialism—a reason which has not lost its relevance to his own present championship of them—is their tendency to become *substitutes* for explanatory accounts of history. Aggressively claiming to reinstate 'moralism' as an integral part of any contemporary culture of the Left, Thompson has forgotten the distinction which the term itself is designed to indicate in ordinary usage. Moral consciousness is certainly indispensable to the very idea of socialism: Engels himself emphasized that 'a really human morality'[72] would be one of the hallmarks of communism, the finest product of its conquest of the age-old social divisions and antagonisms rooted in scarcity. Moral*ism*, on the other hand, denotes the vain intrusion of moral judgements in lieu of causal understanding—typically, in everyday life and in political evaluations alike, leading to an 'inflation' of ethical terms themselves into a false rhetoric, which lacks the exacting sense of material care and measure that is inseparable from true moral awareness. This process is all too evident and familiar in contemporary politics outside the socialist movement, and against it. Solzhenitsyn since his exile is a signal example. Its end-result is to devalue the writ of moral judgement altogether.

Thompson can be exempted from this logic. In other moods, different

71. See, for example, the remark that knowledge of the past 'helps us to know who we are, why we are here, what human possibilities have been disclosed, and as much as we can know of the logic and forms of social process': PT, p. 239. It is the marginalization of reflections such as these, however, which is striking in the argument of the essay as a whole.
72. *Anti-Dühring*, p. 133.

circumstances, he has shown himself critical of these dangers. In *The Making of the English Working Class*, Cobbett's 'moralizing' is treated as a weakness which diminished his appeal to the emergent working class;[73] in the revised edition of *William Morris*, he writes of his original version of the book: 'I intruded far too often upon the text with moralistic comments'.[74] The usage of history which he advocates in *The Poverty of Theory* is not moralistic in this, deteriorated, sense. But the notion of history as an album of values to be bequeathed from individual to individual is nevertheless not a Marxist or even a specifically socialist one. Roll-calls of past lives, as moral exemplars for present struggles or aspirations, are a feature of very many political movements of the most opposing character—conservative or liberal as much as radical. Their original source is the romantic nationalism of mid-19th century, which very early patented resonant recollection of a ceremonial line of dead heroes: to take a standard example, the speeches of Kossuth were customarily filled with evocations of Zrinyi, Dobozy, Bethlen, Tökölli, Rakoczy, as cynosures of the fight for Hungarian independence. The rhetorical force of these lists was fully consonant with the nationalist ideology of the epoch, which possessed a very uncomplicated—indeed largely mythical—conception of historical time. Transposition of similar procedures into the outlook of modern socialism is much more problematic. We can see this immediately if we look at the prime illustration given by Thompson of the relationship to history he recommends. In the passage cited above, four names occur as prototypical objects for admiration or abhorrence. Two of these, Winstanley and Chadwick, are separated by over 200 years from each other—an epoch of social transformation so vast as to deprive the contrast between them of real tension: if the difference is dramatic, so too is the discrepancy of context. It is the other two names, which recur twice, that supply the crux of the argument. Swift and Walpole were contemporaries, and adversaries. If a retrospective 'vote', as Thompson would have it, is to be staged, the only common polling-station would be situated in the early 18th century.

It is no accident, then, that precisely the same pair figure as symbolic contrasts in *Whigs and Hunters*. Walpole is there characterized as 'England's

73. MEWC, p. 707.
74. WM, p. x. See the further disavowal of 'hectoring political moralisms', p. 769.

first and least lovely Prime Minister':[75] the preface informs the reader at
the outset that Thompson is at a loss to know who benefited from his
administration—'beyond the circle of Walpole's own creatures'.[76]
Stigmatizing Walpole's rule as an unprecedented morass of corruption,
repression and manipulation, he argues that 'the most gifted writers,
almost to a man, took refuge from these standards of Whig politicians in
Tory humanism'.[77] For them 'the ascendant Hanoverian Whigs
appeared as no more than a sort of State banditry'[78]—a view authorita-
tively endorsed by Thompson himself. Preeminent among the Tory
assailants of Walpole's regime was Swift, whose *Gulliver's Travels*
illuminates the age, and whose 'accurate and morally poised comment'[79]
on the preferment of one of its minions is given the last word in the book.
The importance of Swift for Thompson's present stance is underlined by
the physical accolade he receives in *The Poverty of Theory*: across the
centuries 'we shake Swift by the hand'—a homage that stirs uncomfortable images, as we read, beneath the complaisant portrait of the author,
the official plaudit on the back of *The Poverty of Theory* for its 'Swiftian
irony', of the writer shaking hands with himself.

Setting this aside, however, what reasons are furnished for the antithetical evaluations to which we are invited, in *The Poverty of Theory* and
Whigs and Hunters alike? Thompson demonstrates, powerfully and originally, the brutality of the legal repression visited by Walpole's
government on the smallest infractions against agrarian property. The
main bulk of *Whigs and Hunters* is devoted to an exposure of the springs
of the Black Acts of 1723, as grandee interests encroached on popular
rights and traditional customs in the forests of Berkshire and Hampshire.
The reconstruction of these deadly, muffled conflicts is a magnificent
feat of historical retrieval. Thompson, however, does not confine his
judgement to them: he brings back a general verdict on the nature of
Walpole's government that extends well beyond the issues studied in
detail in his book. The burden of this wider characterization is
the claim that Whig rule in the 1720s represented an abrupt degradation
of the political standards of the dominant class in England. 'It is not true,

75. WH, p. 198.
76. WH, p. 17.
77. WH, p. 216.
78. WH, p. 294.
79. WH, p. 294.

unless in the eye of the mystic, that the political morality of one age is much the same as any other; precedents of corruption do not add up to a system of corruption. It is not true that the Walpole and Newcastle system—of nepotism, of the brutal imposition on every branch of public service of the Whig interest, of the purchase and intimidation of electors, of diverting public money into private pockets, of bribes and pensions, of death bills, press prosecutions and taxes on the means of life, of the Riot Act and the Black Act, and of religious cynicism combined with the subordination of the Church to factional interest—was identical to that of twenty or fifty years before, even if it is true that the system was to be inherited, with little modification, by George III and the Tories. Somewhere between the Puritan gentry and officers of the Commonwealth and the great Whig managers of the 1720s some lapse had taken place.'[80]

   There are three charges that can be separated out here. Firstly, there is the suggestion that the Walpole system was exceptional in the ferocity of its proscription and repression ('death bills'/'press prosecutions'). Yet Thompson himself concedes elsewhere in *Whigs and Hunters* that political executions were now fewer than in the previous century—'cashiered politicians did not mount the scaffold.'[81] Against this, however, he points to the escalation of penalties against economic 'crimes' committed by the poor: 'in every decade more intrusions upon property were defined as capital matters'.[82] But the evidence for an actual increase in ruling class ruthlessness is lacking, since Thompson provides no figures on the overall operation of the capital statutes in the late 17th or 18th centuries. His omission here is all the more surprising, since his colleague Douglas Hay does so, reaching conclusions directly relevant to the issue. Hay reports that the number of executions in London and Middlesex in the early 17th century was about four times the level towards 1750. Despite the proliferation of new capital statutes, which had risen from fifty to 200 by the time of Waterloo, the actual incidence of criminal executions seems, in fact, to have been largely stable in the 18th century.[83] The obvious hypothesis suggests itself—and it is strange Thompson does not explore it in *Whigs and Hunters*—that the legislation

80. WH, p. 216.
81. WH, p. 197.
82. WH, p. 197.
83. *Albion's Fatal Tree*, pp. 22-23.

of the Black Acts and their like should be seen more as part of that stylized 'theatre' of class hegemony which he analyses so imaginatively elsewhere,[84] a legislative show designed to impress and intimidate, more than an executive instrument of day-to-day retribution. At all events, it is quite clear that the record of Walpole's government contains no episode comparable to the wholesale massacres and deportations conducted by the 'puritan gentry and officers of the Commonwealth' in Ireland in the 1650s. Windsor and Waltham bear no comparison with Wexford or Drogheda, let alone what succeeded them.[85] Secondly, there is the complaint of 'religious cynicism combined with subordination of the Church to factional interest'—which would, it seems, have 'sickened Archbishop Laud'.[86] This is a peculiar grievance for a socialist historian. Was the fanaticism that was still widespread in the previous century so preferable to scepticism? Did not the laicization of the Established Church contribute precisely to cultural and intellectual emancipation from it? Whig rule in the 1720s meant religious toleration—a major human gain where Tory 'humanism' stood for return to bigotry and inhumanity. The gravamen of Thompson's prosecution of Walpole's methods of rule thus comes down, in effect, to the third article in his address, and by far the lengthiest ('imposition of the Whig interest/ purchase and intimidation of electors/diverting public money into private pockets/bribes and pensions'). It is here that his polemic with other historians is sharpest. Significantly, this is also the basis for the conceptualization he proposes of Walpole's regime. Thus he writes: 'Political life in England in the 1720s had something of the sick quality of a "banana republic". This is a recognized phase of commercial capitalism where predators fight for the spoils of power and have not yet agreed to submit to rational or bureaucratic rules and forms. Each politician, by nepotism, interest or purchase, gathered around him a following of loyal dependents. The aim was to reward them by giving them some post in which they could milk some part of the public revenue: army finances, the Church, excise. Every post carried its perquisites, percentages,

---

84. 'Patrician Society, Plebeian Culture', *Journal of Social History*, Summer 1974, pp. 389-390; 'Eighteenth-Century English Society', p. 158.
85. Between 1641 and 1652, perhaps 600,000 Irish perished out of a total population of some 1,500,000: such was the scale of the Cromwellian devastation. See Patrick Corish, 'The Cromwellian Regime, 1650-1660', in T.W. Moody et al., *A New History of Ireland*, vol. III, Oxford, p. 357.
86. PT, p. 198.

commissions, receipt of bribes, its hidden spoils.'[87] Elsewhere, he radicalizes the argument yet further: 'The State was less an effective organ of any class than a parasitism upon the backs of that very class (the gentry) who had gained the day in 1688'.[88] Hence 'Old Corruption is a more serious term of political analysis than is often supposed; for political power throughout the 18th century may best be understood, not as a direct organ of any class or interest, but as a secondary political formation, a purchasing-point from which other kinds of economic and social power were gained or enhanced; in its primary functions it was costly, grossly inefficient, and it survived the century only because it did not seriously inhibit the actions of those with de facto economic or (local) political power.'[89]

With this, we return to the picture of Walpole's administration benefiting no one 'beyond the circle of Walpole's own creatures', and—logically—of Walpole himself as the embodiment of a 'low and ruthless opportunism', an object of 'abhorrence', our 'least lovely Prime Minister'. Can this be regarded as an accurate characterization of the rule of the Hanoverian Whigs, or an adequate portrait of their most durable leader? The answer is surely no. The key error, on which the whole edifice of typification rests, is to be seen in the initial formula, equating English society in the early 18th century with a 'banana republic'. The phrase is the sort of calculated anachronism sported by academic historians keen to avoid the reproach of antiquarian solemnity or irrelevance. What it overlooks is the simple fact—which should be obvious enough—that the term 'banana republic' was coined to designate a state that is a small and weak *semi-colonial dependency*, and whose politics are therefore the plaything of *foreign* commercial interests. Central American societies, which gave rise to the term, are the classic instances: an area where the plantation economy of Honduras remains a reserve of United Brands to this day. Hanoverian England, on the other hand, exhibited a State that was the exact opposite in its basic determinations: in other words, an *ascendant colonial power*, rapidly rising towards international hegemony across five continents. The mistake here is no trivial one. Its consequences can be seen in Thompson's reduction of the functions of Whig rule to a mere 'parasitism', answerable to no class

87. PT, pp. 197-198.
88. 'Eighteenth-Century English Society', p. 139.
89. 'Eighteenth-Century English Society', p. 141.

interest, battening on English society through the medium of a State that was 'weak', 'costly' and 'grossly inefficient in its primary functions'. Yet it was this State which encompassed the downfall of French ascendancy in the continent of Europe, seized commercial advantage in South America, and was about to expand in Canada, India and the Antilles. Its *overseas* role was in no sense a 'secondary' function.[90] Military expenditure accounted for between 75% and 90% of all State outlays during the 18th century. The formative years of Walpole's political career were precisely those in which this supremely successful machinery of imperial dominion was being constructed. The War of the Spanish Succession marks the advent of historically new levels of permanent armaments: after 1705, Britain possessed for the first time a professional standing army, and a military budget that never seriously fell back to pre-war levels again. By 1725, after a decade of peace, civil expenses had risen to no more than 23% of total public expenditure—the peak for the century.[91] Like its absolutist counterparts on the continent, the English state in the 18th century was built for war—albeit different, and far more profitable, types of aggression. To qualify the Whig regimes of the times as mere parasitic rackets is to substitute the invective of Tory lampoons for the categories of materialist analysis. Under the Hanoverian Whigs, the English State served the interests of the dominant agrarian and mercantile bloc in England, and served them extremely well. By the 1760s colossal wealth was pouring into the country from the colonial tribute of an Empire that now eclipsed all others. At home, the same regime proved its extraordinary class *correspondence* to the needs of magnates and gentry alike by the feat of its stability. No other political order in modern British history can match its record—half a century of tranquil party monopoly, followed by another half century of party alternation within the same framework, virtually unmodified throughout.

Walpole's person and career must be seen within this context. The charge of 'opportunism' makes little sense. Entering Parliament at a time of Tory ascendancy, without immediate expectation of office or

90. In a footnote to 'Eighteenth-Century English Society', Thompson acknowledges the 'external strength' of the British State in this period, and comments that it was when its 'internal weakness' precipitated setbacks overseas that 'most of the issues of principle' were thrown up in mid-eighteenth century high politics: pp. 141-142. The remark is well-taken, but its object is not to be relegated to an aside.
91. Michael Mann, 'State and Society', 1130-1815: An Analysis of English State Finances', in *The Sources of Social Power*, London 1980 (forthcoming).

advancement, he started his political life a moderate Whig and remained one without major deviation thereafter—unlike many contemporaries, consistent in party and principle to his death. He acquired his experience and won his initial reputation as an administrator, not as a pilfering Paymaster-General, but as Secretary of War organizing the logistical background to Oudenarde and Zaragoza. His subsequent dominance within the ranks of the Whigs was due to the financial competence he displayed in the wake of the South Sea Bubble. His command of the Commons over two decades, from 1721 to 1741, was not the product of mere malversation and intimidation—bribes, threats and sinecures, as Tory critics claimed and Thompson by inference repeats. The 'packed assembly' was largely a myth. The bloc of government-controlled votes in Parliament never amounted to more than 150 MPs. Walpole's power rested on his ability to persuade and rally the consent of the independent back-benchers who always accounted for one-third to one-half of the House. 'Walpole quite clearly did not secure a majority in Parliament by corrupt means', writes the most recent and judicious authority on the subject.[92] He gained and kept it by the pursuit of policies favourable and acceptable to the propertied classes as a whole: low land taxes for the gentry, religious toleration for the merchants, stabilization of the constitutional settlement at home and of commercial hegemony abroad. Amidst all this, Walpole amassed a large private fortune by peculation and corruption. His spoils in office were undoubtedly larger than those of his predecessors, if only by reason of his longer tenure: there is little evidence that they were of qualitatively greater enormity. But there is no reason to fetishize this dimension of his career into a central criterion for assessing his work, any more than in the analogous cases of Talleyrand or Cavour, two other European statesmen notorious for their lack of monetary scruple. To do so is both unpolitical and unhistorical: as if the preoccupations of *Private Eye* were to be taken as a serious guide to research into the balance of social forces or the course of class struggle. Myopia of this sort has little to do with materialism: it merely reproduces the rhetorical reflex of contemporary journalism, reducing the War of the Spanish Succession to the private enrichment of the Duke of Marlborough.[93] Namier's cool observation that corruption in 18th century England can be seen as the index and instrument of a mollification

92. H.T. Dickinson, *Walpole and the Whig Supremacy*, London 1973, pp. 81-83, 150-155.
93. The burden, of course, of Swift's *Conduct of the Allies*.

of conflicts within the ruling class,[94] after the lethal proscriptions and executions of the previous century, takes us far closer to a genuine understanding of its functions than any number of obsessive pasquinades about thievery in high places, past or present. Walpole warrants neither the outrage of Thompson nor the encomia of Plumb.[95] His real hallmark is his remarkable representivity, in character and outlook, of the class which he steadily and effectively, but never outstandingly, led for twenty years. That class was generally pitiless and exploitative in its grasp of the world, as well as confident and creative in that age. Walpole shared most of its traits. He calls for no exceptional indignation. To describe him as England's 'least lovely Prime Minister' is a frivolous flourish. On what grounds should a socialist accept this gratuitous affidavit for such carriers of death as Castlereagh or Lloyd George?

The case of Swift can be dealt with more briefly, since Thompson says little of substance about him. A direct comparison with Walpole is a limited exercise, given the asymmetry in vocation and position between the two men. But certain points can be noted. Swift too, started his career as a moderate Whig, in 1705. But disappointed by what he deemed was a lack of proper perferment, he switched his allegiance to the Tory leaders in 1710, becoming their chief propagandist and winning fame for fulminations against Dutch, Austrian and German allies in the War of the Spanish Succession. Hoping for clerical promotion in England in exchange for his services, he was displaced to Ireland because of a vindictive assault on the Duchess of Somerset, one of the Queen's friends.[96] There he opted for the ultra-Tory faction of Bolingbroke in the crisis of 1713-14, demanding increased repression of dissent by the

94. For Namier, eighteenth-century corruption was 'a mark of English freedom and independence', since 'no one bribes where he can bully': *England in the Age of the American Revolution*, London 1930, pp.4-5. 'Bribery, to be really effective, has to be widespread and open; it has to be the custom of the land and cease to dishonour the recipients, so that its prizes may be attractive for the average self-respecting man. Such was political corruption in Great Britain about the middle of the eighteenth century.' *The Structure of Politics at the Accession of George III*, London 1929, p. 219.
95. 'The more I have come to know this great man, the stronger has my admiration grown': J.H. Plumb, *Sir Robert Walpole*, London 1956, vol. I, p. xi, who speaks of Walpole's 'richly varied and intensely human character', 'exquisite taste', 'finesse in human relations', 'empathy' and 'love of the visible world', not to mention his 'power of concentration' and 'steady, implacable dispatch of vast quantities of highly technical business'(ibid.). If these enthusiasms are disregarded, Plumb's biography can be taken as a portrait of Walpole that is often otherwise psychologically acute.
96. Whom he accused, without evidence or qualm, of murdering a former husband.

Established Church, permanent elimination of the Whigs from political life, systematic purges of parliament and army to secure them for Tory control. When the collapse of the projected Tory coup in London on the untimely death of the Queen frustrated these schemes, Swift in Dublin fell silent for some six years, in a country for which he frequently expressed loathing. In the 1720s, however, he took up the cause of Irish wrongs—monetary, economic, social—with great effect, in a renewed campaign against Whig rule whose major literary product is *Gulliver's Travels*. Soon afterwards, he was making overtures to Walpole (1726) and cultivating relations with the Hanoverian heir apparent—moves once again brought to nothing by venomous attacks on a friend of the Princess for an imaginary failure to secure the writer Gay, a fellow-postulant, a sufficiently lucrative sinecure at court. Preferment eluded him to the end of his days, despite further hopes of it in the 1730s.

This chequered career, in some ways not untypical of writers of the time, scarcely invites simple congratulation. The hand that Thompson would have us clasp was raised in anger and hatred against dissenters, commonwealthmen, foreigners, women, former personal friends and public foes alike. Its polemic was indifferent to truth.[97] Religious and political intolerance, ideological xenophobia and misogyny, distemper and unbalance Swift's work as a whole. The very quotation adduced as evidence of his qualities in *Whigs and Hunters* tells its own story: 'The Archbishop of Dublin attacked the Primate in the Castle for giving a good living to a certain animal called a Walsh Black, which the other excused, alleging he was preferred to it by Lord Townshend. It is a cant word for a deer stealer. This fellow was leader of a gang, and had the honour of hanging half a dozen of his fellows in quality of informer, which was his merit. If you cannot match me that in Italy, step to Muscovy, and from thence to the Hottentots.'[98] Here proper disdain for the informer mingles side by side with jealous concern for clerical

---

97. It is notable how often Irvin Ehrenpreis, a respectful and admiring biographer whose study is a monument of painstaking scholarship, has to register the operation of this trait: Swift's propensity for 'anonymous slanders', 'unsigned lies', 'multiple innuendoes', 'dishonest representations', 'lying allegations', 'invidious vituperation'. Ehrenpreis comments that Swift always avoided personal responsibility for his calumnies, unlike his one-time friend and ultimate opponent Steele, 'who was willing to put his real name to controversial publications and risk the consequences': *Swift, The Man, His Works, The Age*, vol. II, London 1967, pp. 444-445, 492-493, 530-532, 540-541, 705, 712.
98. WH, p. 221.

prebends ('a *good* living') and studied brutalism of language ('an animal') before issuing into the most banal chauvinism and racism (Muscovites and Hottentots). Thompson's praise of this passage as 'appropriate' and 'morally poised' is a strange lapse of attention. In general, intellectual or moral poise—a sense of balance or proportion—is the last quality Swift possessed. Even the writings for which he must be honoured, his denunciations of the misery of the Irish peasantry under the caul of English landlordism, among their other virtues lack this one. Bent on 'being used like a lord',[99] yet relegated to a modest exile, his sense of personal and social injustice fused explosively together in Ireland. But the savagery of Swift's satire, purporting to expose cruelty and inhumanity, compulsively partakes of it—the impulse to brutalize is the perpetual, chill shadow of the design to scandalize. The pathology of this violence has its sources elsewhere than in the condition of the Irish, and finds its outlets pervasively in his writing. Foiled ambition and thwarted feeling— Swift's radical blockage in public and private life—are the emotional fires that light the fury of his prose. The lack of disinterested pity or warmth of solidarity is manifest if we compare him with a contemporary like Fielding—from whom Thompson, with far more aptness, takes his epigraph to *Whigs and Hunters*. Leavis's judgement, in all its gravity, remains authoritative: 'A great writer—yes; that account still imposes itself as fitting, though his greatness is no matter of moral grandeur or human centrality; our sense of it is merely a sense of a great force. And this force, as we feel it, is conditioned by frustration and constriction; the channels of life have been blocked and perverted. That we should so often be invited to regard him as a moralist and an idealist would seem to be mainly a witness to the power of vanity, and the part that vanity can play in literary appreciation; *saeva indignatio* is an indulgence that solicits us all, and the use of literature by readers and critics for the projection of nobly suffering selves is familiar. No doubt, too, it is pleasant to believe that unusual capacity for egotistic animus means unusual distinction of intellect; but, as we have seen, there is no reason to lay stress on intellect in Swift... He was, in various ways, curiously unaware—the reverse of clairvoyant. He is distinguished by the intensity

---

99. 'All my endeavours, from a boy, to distinguish myself, were only for want of a great title and fortune, that I might be used like a Lord by those who have an opinion of my parts—whether right or wrong, it is no great matter': *The Correspondence of Jonathan Swift*, ed. F. Elrington Ball, London 1913, vol. IV, p. 78 (Letter to Pope).

of his feelings, not by insight into them, and he certainly does not impress us as a mind in possession of its experience.'[100]

The fineness of this assessment of Swift as a writer leaves little more to be said. There is an equivalent political lesson, however. The extraction of moral values from individual lives, for transmission down through history, is a much more complex and delicate affair than *The Poverty of Theory* suggests—as the very examples it gives have proved on closer inspection. Tory reversions, even in purer personifications than those of Swift, meant the triumph of bigotry, hierarchy, authority, legitimacy in early 18th century England.[101] The Whig consolidation cut off the experience of a regime controlled by the camarilla of 1714. *Some Free Thoughts on the Present State of Affairs*, written by Swift in that year, provides us, however, with a gaunt scenario of what its programme might have been.[102] Posterity has no reason to regret that England was governed by Walpole in the spirit of Defoe rather than ruled by Bolingbroke at the promptings of Swift.

More general reflections impose themselves in conclusion. Thompson is right to insist that Marx and Engels left no Ethics, and that the resultant gap was never made good in the Marxism which ensued after their deaths—to the danger of historical materialism as a theory and of the

100. *The Common Pursuit*, London 1976, pp. 86-87.

101. Swift's own *Project for the Advancement of Religion and the Reformation of Manners* (1708) is described by his biographer as 'a nightmare expansion of the Test Act'. So far as freedom of the press was concerned, 'the rage Swift exuded against journalists who had attacked either himself or the government in print' was such that in 1711 he 'begged the Secretary of State to make a lesson of them; but as it happened, neither the policy of the administration nor the practice of the courts of law supplied the opportunities Swift wanted; and those who were arrested could only be threatened and released.' *Swift, The Man, His Works, The Age*, vol. II, pp. 292, 517. In fact, of course, Bolingbroke did pass a Stamp Act in 1712, and it was ironically Walpole who had to set up a clandestine press in his own home, because no printer dared handle one of his pamphlets in the climate of Tory intimidation.

102. 'The Church of England should be preserved entire in all Her Rights, Powers and Privileges', 'All Schisms, Sects and Heresies discountenanced and kept under due subjection', 'Her open Enemies not trusted with the smallest degree of Civil or Military Power', 'an End of that Faction' be encompassed which had been prone 'to disturb and insult the Administration'—a 'wicked Confederacy' that 'cannot be too soon or too much disabled'—by taking steps to exclude any possibility of 'an ill Majority in a House of Commons', and to 'regulate the Army, and chiefly the Officers of those Troops which in their Turns have the care of Her Majesties Person': *Some Free Thoughts upon the Present State of Affairs*, in Herbert Davis and Irvin Ehrenpreis, eds., *Political Tracts 1713-1719*, Oxford 1953, pp. 88-89.

socialist movement as a practice. The sole significant exception is Trotsky, whose *Their Morals and Ours* remains a defensive and occasional case. Both Lukács and Sartre, it is interesting to note, planned to write major works on ethics, but in each case abandoned or postponed the project, finding ontology and aesthetics more tractable. Brecht wrestled persistently but unavailingly to stage a Marxist morality in his theatre. The *difficulty* of developing a materialist ethics, at once integrally historical and radically non-utilitarian, has proved daunting. It is this difficulty that Thompson underrates. Overlooking the good reasons why Marx and Engels rejected the 'ethical socialism' of the Utopians before them, and Luxemburg or Lenin resisted the 'ethical socialism' of Bernstein or Hardie after them, the argument of *The Poverty of Theory* tends towards an extrapolation of moral values from the historical past that involves a dual simplification. The primary continuity between past and present, which is necessarily *causal*, is displaced from focus—risking a rhetorical rather than strategic use of history. For historical materialism, as for socialist politics, what the past bequeaths the present is first and foremost a set of *lines of force* for *transformation*, not a gallery of model lives for imitation. These lines of force in turn incarnate certain values that are an active part of the process of social transformation itself—something Thompson has shown perhaps more eloquently than any other historian. Marxists have no cause to abstain from judgement of these values, as they were embodied in the past. But such judgement is only possible in full historical context, which is not the same thing as the *contemporary* context of the time. The danger of selecting individuals as emblems of opposing codes, to be adopted or repudiated by descendant generations, is that it so easily shortcircuits the complexity of this task. The archetypal cases chosen by Thompson are an illustration. Walpole is reduced to a mask of corruption—waiving the substance of his economic and political superintendancy, and its effective relation to the needs of the English ruling class. Swift is reduced to a voice crying havoc—ignoring the sources of his rage, the pattern of his loyalties, the consequences of his politics.

Picked out for display in *The Poverty of Theory*, these characterizations are to be read, so to speak, in the margins of *Whigs and Hunters*, the merits of whose main narrative is unaffected by them. Behind them, however, there is the temptation to countersign the categories of the

Tory opposition to the Whig ascendancy.[103] For were not the attacks of Swift or Gay grounded in direct experience? Were these not 'the most gifted writers of the time'—and so witnesses with a sympathetic affinity to one of the most gifted writers of our time? The latent appeal to 'Tory humanism' as a valid yardstick for assessing Walpole's government is a more serious weakness of *Whigs and Hunters*, on occasion leading, as we have seen, to an uncritical reproduction of contemporary polemic instead of the formulation of historical concepts based on modern knowledge— whose resources include, not only data unknown to any of the actors of the time, but also the record of the subsequent epoch—in other words of the *direction* of the time. Thompson reserves the term 'progress' for movements in the present alone, refusing it to processes in the past. More rationally, the opposite might be argued: the retrospective outcome of past conflicts is relatively settled and ascertainable, whereas the issues of the present are by their nature always fundamentally uncertain, subject to the indeterminacy of a future whose shape remains to be seen. A Marxist evaluation of the past is inseparable from an explanation of it: and an explanation must necessarily encompass its consequences, in all their ambiguity and contradiction. The present is never a fit judge of itself. Marx's conception of historical progress, which included the two terrible ordeals of the establishment of agrarian capitalism and of industrial capitalism in England—the very moments of *Whigs and Hunters* and *The Making of the English Working Class*, respectively—is a hard one. But even—especially—amidst the torments of the socialist movement in the 20th century, we have no cause to revise it.

---

103. An example: Thompson finds of the Bishop of Rochester, Francis Atterbury—one of Swift's associates—that 'his critique of Walpole was sober enough', on the grounds that he claimed that Walpole had obtained his parliamentary majorities 'at the expense of the morals of a people, who were remarkable for their honour and probity, and who had some share of it left till they came under his administration' (WH, p. 215). Such were his words after defeat and exile. When he was an active politician, as a Tory falcon in 1710, here was his opinion of the same subject: 'The voice of the people is the cry of hell, leading to idolatry, rebellion, murder, and all the wickedness the devil can suggest . . . nothing but fire from heaven can stop the cry, nothing but sulphurous flames can quell the voice of the people' (*The Voice of the People, No Voice of God*): see H.T. Dickinson, *Liberty and Property. Political Ideology in Eighteenth Century England*, London 1977, p. 45.

4
Stalinism

Having demolished, to his own satisfaction, the intellectual structure of Althusserian theory, Thompson ends *The Poverty of Theory* by attempting at once a social account and a political assessment of it. The two are dissociated in presentation, however, and discrepant in argument. Let us look at each in turn. The first argues that within the history of the socialist movement three great epochs can be discerned since the death of Marx, to which have corresponded pervasive outlooks and vocabularies formed by the dominant social experience of the time. From the 1890s to the mid 1930s, the growth of the European labour movement (before the First World War) and the development of the USSR (after the War) gave rise to the illusions of 'evolutionism'. 'Marxism was hence infiltrated by the vocabulary (and even premises) of economic and technical 'progress''.[1] This era was succeeded, between 1936 and 1946, by a period of decisive popular struggles against fascism culminating in the victory of the Allied forces in the Second World War, which produced a culture of 'voluntarism'. 'The vocabulary of Marxism became infiltrated from a new direction: that of authentic liberalism (the choices of the autonomous individual) and perhaps also of Romanticism (the rebellion of spirit against the rules of fact). Poetry, rather than natural science or sociology, was welcomed as a cousin.'[2] After the War, there were a few

1. PT, p. 263.
2. PT, p. 264.

outcrops of this voluntarism down to its 'late poetic flaring' in Cuba at the end of the 50s. But essentially from 1948 onwards, with the onset of the Cold War between East and West, a third epoch took shape in which history 'seemed to congeal in an instant into two monstrous antagonistic structures, each of which allowed only the smallest latitude of movement within its operative realm'.[3] The result was the spread of 'structuralism', which in 'its most pervasive accents . . . has been a *bourgeois* vocabulary, an apologia for the *status quo*'.[4] Althusserianism is a consummate manifestation of this process—the infiltration of a contraband 'sociological conservatism' into the thought-world of the Left, during 'three decades of Cold War stasis'. Today, 'the vocabulary of structuralism has pushed all else aside'.[5]

What can be said of this periodization? First and foremost, that it reveals a lack of historical sense disconcerting in a historian of Thompson's stature, yet one which seems a recurrent pattern in his comments on the 20th century. For how can the revolutionary Marxisms of Lenin, Trotsky or Luxemburg be described as exemplars of 'evolutionism'—the very vice of the Second International they most detested? Theoretical expressions of the October Revolution in Russia and the November Revolution in Germany, they were followed by even more intransigent rejections of the heritage of pre-war Social Democracy, born out of the Hungarian Commune and the Italian factory councils. Gramsci's *Revolution against 'Capital'* welcomed the triumph of the Bolsheviks as a defiance of the laws of Marx's political economy, while Lukács's *Changing Function of Historical Materialism* looked forward to the supersession of the primacy of the economic in history altogether.[6] Voluntarism, if the term has any meaning, is the very definition of these texts. Nor was their stance a mere reflection of the great crisis of 1918-21, confined to the immediate aftermath of the Russian Revolution and the end of the War. Thompson ignores the dramatic experience of the Third Period of the Comintern, which dominated the late 20s and early 30s, whose combat of 'class against class' and 'storm in the streets' marked a paroxysm of voluntarist politics whose like has never been seen since. By

3. PT, p. 265.
4. PT, pp. 265.
5. PT, pp. 265, 266.
6. See respectively Antonio Gramsci, *Selections from the Political Writings 1910-1920*, London 1977, pp. 34-37; Georg Lukács, *History and Class Consciousness*, London 171, pp. 223-256.

comparison, the rhetoric of the Popular Fronts after 1935 was emollient and their practice gradualist, deferring the morrow of socialism till after the day of democracy—unsuccessfully in France and Spain. In fact, if we survey the period 1936-1946 as a whole, what theories of 'political will and initiative' did it produce to compare with those of 1917-1936? Only one, which Thompson does not mention: the developing work of Mao in China, which goes back to 1928 in unaltered register. Finally, what justification is there for the claim that history 'underwent a sickening jerk of deceleration' after 1946? The Chinese Revolution was actually *ac*celerating in this conjuncture: the victory of the socialist movement in the most populous nation on earth—a decisive hinge of world history—occurred three years later, after the onset of alleged international stasis. The 50s saw the first successful breach in capitalism in the Western hemisphere, with the advent of the Cuban Revolution. The 60s were, among other things, the decade of Guevarism in Latin America—surely one of the least 'structuralist' currents in the history of socialism—and the upsurge of major working-class struggles in Western Europe, with the largest mass strike in history erupting in France: an event scarcely registered by Thompson in *The Poverty of Theory*, save as an impediment to more important business on the Left in England. Above all, the 70s have seen the triumph of the greatest feat of sustained revolutionary 'will' in the 20th century, with the defeat of US imperialism in Vietnam. Yet the Vietnamese Revolution does not rate a mention in Thompson's account of the past two decades. One can only conclude that it is omitted because it does not conform to his idea of what a socialist revolution should look like in the contemporary world (being relatively closely linked to one of the 'monstrous structures' whose function is held to be the imposition of a global stasis ruling out such movements in the first place). Angola or Nicaragua are the evidence of its continuing impact on the real balance of social-international forces. Even in England, the events of 1973-74 were a more imposing demonstration of the power of collective proletarian will than any episode in the comparatively tame domestic process from 1936 to 1946—from Baldwin to Attlee.

Of course, the three decades since the Second World War have seen major disasters and reverses for the cause of socialism as well: some of these are cited by Thompson (Hungary, Czechoslovakia, Chile) and the list could be extended (Indonesia, Bolivia, Portugal). There has been no homogeneous pattern or unilinear trend in any of the periods Thompson constructs. All of them have combined upsurges, plateaux, subsidences defeats, truces, victories, stalemates, distributed on a vast geographical scale that has itself guaranteed mutable contrast and complexity in every decade. What Thompson's account gives us is the selective report of his own subjective experience, overwhelmingly dominated by the struggles of the Popular Front and Resistance in Europe, with little memory of the earlier history of the Third International, and deep disappointment at the later failure of the Communist oppositions or unaffiliated Left to break the pattern of European politics after the death of Stalin. Disengagement from many of the major international developments of the past two decades seems to have followed. Hence the projection of structuralism as the ideology of a time imaginarily becalmed, that has in fact been one of gathering turbulence. So far as the object of the construction is concerned, the founding text of Althusser's work—'Contradiction and Over-Determination', published in 1962—is a theory of the matrices of social revolution. Ten years later, its author summed up his own view of the ensuing decade: 'A good deal of water has flowed under the bridge of history since 1960. The Workers' Movement has lived through many important events: the heroic and victorious resistance of the Vietnamese people against the most powerful imperialism in the world; the Proletarian Cultural Revolution in China (1966-1969); the greatest workers' strike in world history (ten million workers on strike for a month) in May 1968 in France—a strike which was "preceded" and "accompanied" by a deep ideological revolt among French students and petty-bourgeois intellectuals; the occupation of Czechoslovakia by the armies of the other countries of the Warsaw Pact; the war in Ireland, etc.'[7] The generalities of Thompson's account, in other words, tell us more of the astigmatism of the seer than of the particular properties of the seen. An explanation of Althusser's thought in terms of planetary doldrums is without worth.

Thompson, however, advances a second characterization of Althusser that is more extended and drastic. Diverging from the first, it occupies most of the latter part of *The Poverty of Theory* and provides the main conclusion of the essay. It is a political verdict. According to Thompson, Althusser has produced the completed theorization of the practice of Stalin. 'Althusserianism *is* Stalinism reduced to the paradigm of theory.

7. *Essays in Self-Criticism*, pp. 35-36.

It is Stalinism at last, theorized as ideology'.[8] Soviet doctrines during the life of the dictator lacked such a systematization. 'It is only in our own time that Stalinism has been given its true, rigorous and totally coherent theoretical expression. This is the Althusserian orrery.'[9] As such, it is a 'straightforward ideological police operation'.[10] Its aim is to repress the 'socialist humanism' and 'libertarian communism' which exploded in 1956 and represented 'a total critique' of Stalinism, and of which Thompson himself was a leading spokesman, 'itemizing the errors of Stalinist theory, one by one'.[11] Its political tenets are a circle of lies and delusions. For Althusser: 'the PCF is embodied proletarian ideology, Stalinism in decomposition is "socialist humanism", the murder of a revolution's cadres is the dictatorship of the proletariat, the substantial gains over decades of the Western working classes are an index of their more intense exploitation'.[12] For Thompson, on the other hand, no wave in the working-class movement can be conceived that is 'further to the right than Stalinism', or from the perspective of socialist liberty, none that is 'further to the "right" than the anti-historicism and anti-humanism of Althusser'.[13] Since Althusser claims, with a sort of justice, to have something to do with Marxism, which the experience of Stalinism had shown in any case the need to revise, it is necessary to have nothing more to do with Marxism as such, and to renounce the illusion that there ever was a 'common Marxist tradition'. On the contrary, 'there are *two* traditions' which are 'irreconcilable antagonists' today.[14] 'Between theology and reason there can be no room left for negotiation'. Dismissing the 'cant' of 'no enemies to the Left', Thompson ends by calling for 'unrelenting intellectual war' against Althusser and all 'such Marxisms'.[15]

The crescendo of violence that marks these final pages of *The Poverty of Theory*, an escalation of tone with few precedents on the British Left, can be set aside for the moment. Let us look rather at the substance of Thompson's charges against Althusser. The first question to ask is: what

8. PT, p. 374.
9. PT, p. 333.
10. PT, p. 375.
11. PT, p. 332.
12. PT, p. 375.
13. PT, pp. 326-327.
14. PT, pp. 380-381.
15. PT, p. 381.

evidence does he present for his claim that Althusser is the supreme officiant of Stalinism, surpassing the dictator himself in system and implacability of doctrine? The answer is surprising, for a professional historian. Thompson makes no effort to situate Althusser's thought in the French social or intellectual context of the past twenty years—which is simply ignored. He spends no time over Althusser's relationship, either to the French Communist Party itself, or to the international Communist movement, over that period. He devotes not a line to Althusser's actual pronouncements on political issues, in his numerous writings. Instead, we are given a set of rudimentary equations between putative features of Stalinist and Althusserian thought, at the most generic levels of abstraction: mechanism, dogmatism, anti-humanism, elitism, irrationalism. Even these are unsupported by any gesture at textual demonstration: the sole quotations from Stalin to be found in the whole essay are two formulations manifestly at variance with the views of Althusser, and in fact produced for comparison not with him but with the Parsonian sociologist Smelser.[16] Yet any historian, Marxist or non-Marxist, should know that the political character of a body of thought can only be established by a responsible study of its *texts* and *context*. Since there is scarcely a hint of Althusser's actual political record in *The Poverty of Theory*, it is necessary to recall some simple dates and facts.

Louis Althusser started to publish his first major essays 'On the Young Marx' (March-April 1961) and 'Contradiction and Over-Determination' (December 1962) in the early 60s. What was the conjuncture at the time in the international Communist movement? The unrest and revolt of 1956, which so indelibly colours Thompson's memories of the period, had been contained. In Russia, Khruschev was unchallenged master of the CPSU. In Eastern Europe, Kadar—despite initial repression and contrary to expectation—was starting to emerge as a relatively popular politician in Hungary, while Gomulka was becoming an increasingly unpopular one in Poland. In Western Europe, the major Communist Parties had survived the crisis of 1956 with relatively marginal losses— more significant in Italy than in France, but in both cases largely confined to intellectuals; the small party in England, by contrast, had suffered heavily with the exodus of a third of its members, mostly from the working class. But five or six years later no established leadership had

16. PT, pp. 270-271.

been shaken in Europe;[17] membership had increased again nearly everywhere; loyalty to the CPSU was still formally universal and unconditional. There was no need for an 'ideological police operation' against socialist humanism, because the political and ideological impetus behind it was spent. Its most serious and consequent representatives, the group in England around Thompson himself, were for the most part dropping out of active politics—scarcely under police pressures, but because of the familiar difficulties of building an independent Left outside the traditional structures of the Labour Party.

Meanwhile, a wholly new international situation had developed. In 1960, the dispute between Russia and China exploded, dividing the 'socialist camp' and dominating the ferment within the world communist movement for the next period. The founding moment of Althusser's work was *this* entirely different conflict. The Sino-Soviet dispute, which receives not so much as a mention in *The Poverty of Theory*, is the real political background to the writing of *For Marx* and *Reading Capital*. In these years, the fronts and issues of the 50s underwent a series of sudden shifts and subsidences, in an altered historical landscape. Typically, the rebels of 1956 had appealed to the humanism of the young Marx against the administrative and intellectual repression of Stalinism; they had defended the cause of national independence and local tradition against Russian monolithism; they had rejected manipulative and putschist practices in the labour movement, for a consensual popular politics. By the early 1960s, these themes had become standard slogans of the official Communist leaderships themselves. In Western Europe, the values of humanism were extolled from the balconies of the French Politbureau by its major ideologue, Garaudy, while in the USSR Khruschev's new party programme for the CPSU proclaimed 'Everything for Man'. National roads to socialism were everywhere exalted, not least by the CPGB. More and more, too, pacific and even parliamentary perspectives for superseding capitalism were defended, with the semi-imprimatur of a Soviet foreign policy now fully committed to the pursuit of 'peaceful coexistence' with the USA. It was against this whole constellation, in fact, that the Chinese Party unmasked its batteries in the spring of 1960, with the famous broadside of articles *Long Live Leninism*. The title was significant.

17. With the exception of Denmark, where Axel Larsen had uniquely led the majority of the CP into the creation of an independent socialist organization, the SF, much larger than the residual Party in 1956.

The debates of the post-'56 period in Europe had largely revolved round the antithesis Stalin/Young Marx. Lenin scarcely ever figured, as can be seen by consulting a journal like *The New Reasoner*, where his name is conspicuous by its absence.

Althusser's intervention in 1961-1962 was aimed at the Russian line internationally, and nationally at much of the official culture of the PCF, from a position sympathetic to the Chinese. It is no accident that he marked his intellectual debut within the party by one essay criticizing Soviet and East European philosophers—Lapine, Bakouradze, Pazhitnov, Schaff, Jahn[18]—for their reception of ideological themes fashionable in the West ('On the Young Marx'), followed by another reconstructing Lenin's theory of revolution ('Contradiction and Over-Determination'). His references to the USSR soon afterwards, far from being the accolades that Thompson, deaf to irony, takes them for, were sardonic criticisms ('Marxism and Humanism'). 'Terror, repression and dogmatism' had 'not yet been completely superseded', and the official blandishments of 'socialist humanism'[19] and repudiation of the 'cult of personality' were an ideological placebo—a substitute for genuine political measures to eliminate them in the USSR.[20] All this is there for anyone to see in the texts themselves, complete with their allusions to Mao. It had very little to do with Stalin. It is true that it was hostile to the philosophical aftermath of the late 50s. But was it altogether wrong to be so? A number of issues need to be distinguished here. It is indisputable that there was a widespread trend at the time to dissolve the achievements of Marx into the philosophical anthropology of his youth, which, however brilliant, was no substitute for his mature writings, and was frequently counterposed to them. Indeed Thompson himself on occasion complained of this tendency.[21] Against this stream, Althusser's

18. See *For Marx*, esp. pp. 55-70.

19. *For Marx*, p. 237.

20. Thompson cites Althusser as claiming that: 'In the USSR men are indeed now treated without any class distinctions, that is, as *persons*' (PT, p. 315). In fact, the passage quoted starts with the phrase '*The Soviets say*, in our country classes have disappeared . . .' etc (*For Marx*, p. 222, my italics). Similarly, he quotes Althusser as speaking of 'the world opening up before the Soviets' as one of 'infinite vistas of progress, of science, of culture, of bread and freedom, of free development—a world that can do without shadows or tragedies' (PT, pp. 315, 317). Again, the effect is achieved by the simple device of omitting the clause with which the sentence begins. '*The communism to which the Soviet Union is committed* is a world without economic exploitation . . .' etc (*For Marx*, p. 238). Official Russian professions are converted, by a stroke of the pen, into Althusserian assertions.

21. See 'Commitment in Politics', *Universities and Left Review*, No 6, Spring 1959, p. 51.

reinstatement of serious study of *Capital* and of *Pre-Capitalist Economic Formations* as the core of historical materialism was a major and lasting intellectual accomplishment—to which a Marxist of such different background and outlook as Cohen has recently paid tribute.[22]

A second question is political: was Althusser correct to sense the danger of a rightist outcome to the celebration of socialist humanism by the early 60s? The answer here must be more nuanced, but it will certainly not deny all justice to his charge. The revival of the ideas of the Young Marx was, among other things, also the work of many writers and commentators in the West who had no commitment to socialism: academics like Tucker or Avineri, priests like Bigo or Calvez were among the major interpreters of the new Marx. The influence of religion was never far away in this period, even among many intellectuals who were still socialist. The case of Garaudy (comparable in pastoral background to John Lewis) is well known, within the ranks of the orthodox Communist movement itself. Outside it, Fromm—anthologizer of *Socialist Humanism* in 1963—was dabbling in an unguent syncretism of faith and psychoanalysis.[23] Closer to Thompson's own circle, MacIntyre was fresh from providing books on Marxism for the Student Christian Movement, imbued with Anglican devotion.[24] Was there no evidence of rightism in these currents? We have merely to take the two philosophers Thompson himself cites most frequently and warmly in *The Poverty of Theory*. MacIntyre ended up in the pages of *Encounter* and *Survey*, while Kolakowski became the Koestler of the 70s, denouncing Marxism for its hubristic usurpation of religion ('deification of mankind') to the plaudits of *The Daily Telegraph*. Among the major political figures associated

22. *Karl Marx's Theory of History—A Defence*, p. x.
23. 'A new religion will develop within the next few hundred years, a religion which corresponds to the development of the human race. It will come into existence with the appearance of a new great teacher'—*The Sane Society*, London 1956, p. 351.
24. 'The task is to create a form of community which will exemplify the pattern of the gospel and which will renew continually its repentance for its conformity to the pattern of human sin... The true Christian community will be one of poverty and prayer'—'Its prayer will be classical prayer of Christendom. Paradoxically it is the contemporary study of Marxism which perhaps brings out most clearly what the classical methods of meditation have to say to us about the "dark night of the soul". It is a "dark night", an *ascesis* of poverty and questioning which must renew our politics. A community committed alike to politics and to prayer would serve in the renewal of the whole Church.' *Marxism: An Interpretation*, London 1953. In a remarkable demonstration of ideological continuity, the book was reissued by its author, with modest adjustments for latter-day loss of faith, as *Marxism and Christianity*, in 1969.

with the rebellions of 1956, Hervé became a Gaullist Deputy in France, Giolitti a Social-Democratic Minister in Italy. The risk of a collapse to the right was no figment of the imagination: it was to become a pitiful reality in some cases. In some, but not all. Where Althusser's judgement was wrong was in suggesting a generic political deduction from the theoretical premises of socialist humanism. For there were also principled and courageous opponents of Stalinism in 1956, who remained true to the causes of that year. Thompson himself is an outstanding example, with his fellow-editor Saville. There was no simple ideological fatality inscribed in the framework of socialist humanism: if its limits and weaknesses permitted a particular type of evolution to the right, they did not dictate one.

Ironically, Althusser's own options of the early 60s were to be put to a similar test, with a not dissimilar result. For over a decade his orientation—however delphically expressed at a time when the PCF was the most anti-Chinese party in the West—remained fixed towards China. The advent of the Cultural Revolution in 1966 greatly reinforced this inclination: the PRC now appeared to offer not merely a theoretical critique of the Soviet Union, but a practical model of an alternative and superior experience of socialist construction—governed by the 'mass line', the struggle against 'economism', the 'right to rebel' against bureaucratic privilege and constriction. The appeal of the unprecedented social process in China in these years was widespread in the West, attracting the interest and sympathy of many outside the ranks of the Communist movement itself.[25] Althusser's conviction of the political significance of the Chinese example in general and of the Cultural Revolution in particular can be seen very clearly from his declaration as late as June 1972 that: 'The only *historically existing* (left) "critique" of the fundamentals of the "Stalinian deviation" to be found—and which, moreover, is *contemporary* with this very deviation, and thus for the most part precedes the Twentieth Party Congress—is a concrete critique, one which exists in the facts, in the struggle, in the line, in the practices, their principles and their forms, of the Chinese Revolution. A silent critique,

25. In England, they included Raymond Williams (see Terry Eagleton and Brian Wicker, eds., *From Culture to Revolution*, London 1968, p. 298); *New Left Review*, up to the unveiling of the new Chinese foreign policy at the turn of the decade; possibly in some measure Edward Thompson himself, who mysteriously exempts China from his otherwise universal 'structural stasis' of world politics at the end of the decade—see PT, p. 265.

which speaks through its actions, the result of the political and ideological struggles of the Revolution, from the Long March to the Cultural Revolution and its results.'[26] A few months earlier, Nixon was being toasted in Peking, while US bombs rained on Vietnam. Within another few years, the Cultural Revolution was officially buried by the CCP as a disastrous decade of vendetta, regression and anarchy—its only durable legacy a foreign policy of ferocious reaction, far to the right even of Stalin's most cynical overtures to imperialism. If Althusser is to be taxed for his political record, he must be criticized for his ingenuous misjudgement of Mao's regime in China, rather than suppositious hankerings for Stalin's in Russia. The Chinese Revolution, in some respects historically more advanced than the Russian Revolution (scale of popular support, ordinal position in time), in others more backward (limits of working-class participation, absence of bourgeois culture), avoided the disasters of forced collectivization or mass purges, but never at any stage knew an operative experience of proletarian democracy. In a *chasse-croisé* of illusions, while the rebels of 1956 were to find the humanism of the Young Marx to which they pinned their colours soon absorbed as the official piety of the Western Communist leaderships they had once fought, the Leninism that Althusser had sought to recall was trampled under foot by the bureaucratic manipulation of the masses and diplomatic collusion with imperialism of the Chinese Party onto which he had naively projected it. In the West, the harvest of Maoism in turn yielded an abundant crop of transfuges to the right. Glucksmann and Foucault, formerly hailed by Althusser, vie today in Cold War zeal with Kolakowski, once saluted by Thompson. It is difficult to think of any adherent of socialist humanism who has sunk to quite such depths as literati like Sollers, recent champions of materialist anti-humanism.

Yet the inadequacies and mistakes of the oppositional stance inspired by China in 1960-1962 did not necessarily lead to an eventual break with Marxism, any more than those of the opposition inspired by Hungary or Poland in 1956-1957. For all his indulgence towards the Cultural Revolution, the balance of Althusser's political record was to be a perfectly defensible one. The publication of *For Marx* and *Reading Capital* in 1965, which made him an intellectual force in France, was an unwelcome shock to the PCF leadership, greeted with icy silence. Two

26. *Essays in Self-Criticism*, p. 92.

years later Althusser was counselling and reasoning fraternally with Debray over Cuban strategy on the eve of the Bolivian campaign.[27] When a crisis of national dimensions erupted in France, he intervened *against* the official positions of his party, with a generous and eloquent defence of the role of the students in the events of May 1968—which among other things reminded the PCF of the distrust it had earned by its conduct during the Algerian War.[28] At the same time, he was encouraging and aiding an oppositional critique from the left of the PCI's electoral practices in Italy—to the anger and discomfort of the party leadership there.[29] In 1972, he published his *Reply to John Lewis*—containing a trivial and tactical discussion of Stalinism, as if it were a mere philosophical deviation, demagogically playing to the rank-and-file reflexes of the PCF membership (equation of 'violent bourgeois anti-Communism' with 'Trotskyist anti-Stalinism'), which Thompson rightly condemns. But it is notable that even this text ends with a clear statement in support of the national mass movement represented by the Prague Spring in Czechoslovakia, and an endorsement of its demand for 'Socialism with a Human Face'.[30] In 1976, Althusser defended the cause of the Polish workers in the Baltic ports, and declared his solidarity with the Workers' Defense Committee in Poland. Prefacing a study of Lysenko in the same year, he stressed that in the USSR 'the repressive system of the Stalin period, including the camps, remains in existence, as do the basic principles of that period regarding social, political and cultural life', and remarked that the CPSU leadership 'have even gone back on the few poor glimpses of elucidation with which Khruschev awakened hope'.[31] In 1977 he was attempting to strike a difficult balance between the positive and negative elements in the PCF's orientation after its abandonment of the 'dictatorship of the proletariat': welcoming its commitment to popular liberties in the transition to socialism, and its alliance with the PS, but also warning against its underestimate of the dangers of imperialist intervention against a left government in France, its failure to create organs of popular

27. His long letter of March 1 1967, criticizing *Revolution in the Revolution?*, was published by Debray in *La Critique des Armes*, Paris 1974, pp. 262-269.
28. 'A propos de l'article de Michel Verret sur "Mai Etudiant"', *La Pensée*, June 1969, pp. 3-14.
29. M-A. Macciocchi, *Letters from Inside the Italian Communist Party to Louis Althusser*, London 1973; official reactions can be found pp. 323-335.
30. *Essays in Self-Criticism*, p. 77.
31. Preface to Dominique Lecourt, *Proletarian Science?*, London 1977, pp. 11-12.

unity from below, its lack of the elements of even bourgeois democracy within its own ranks.

In sum, there is not the slightest justification for Thompson's presentation of Althusser as a—*the*—consummate Stalinist. His political record was not a perfect one. For a long time he paid a high price in silences for his party card. But despite his subjective misconceptions about China, and the objective restrictions of the membership of the PCF, the net weight of his political intervention over fifteen years was on the side of a more democratic communism and a more militant internationalism. If they remained far from the practice of an open revolutionary Marxism, in their own idiom they bear comparison with the record of his critic over the same span of time. Describing his own withdrawal from active politics after 1968, Thompson writes: 'It was a time for reason to sulk in its tent'.[32] This description, which might be taken as self-serving, in fact does a disservice to its author. Not only has Achilles never won many admirers, but Thompson exaggerates the degree of his disengagement. For all his distaste now for the student radicalism of the late 60s, he edited one of the best volumes to emerge from the campus turmoil of the time, *Warwick University Limited*.[33] In 1970-1972 he wrote two superb articles on the power-workers' and the miners' strikes, as class confrontations in England.[34] An elegy to Allende in 1973 will be remembered.[35] British membership of the EEC was vehemently opposed in 1975.[36] On the other hand, it is true that on many major issues of the decade—from the May events in France to the victory of the Vietnamese Revolution, the upheavals in China to the occupation of Czechoslovakia, the fall of Nixon to the overthrow of Heath—Thompson seems to have said little: certainly less than he would have done at the turn of the 60s. Without public explanation, at some time in these years he joined the Labour Party.

So matters stood in February 1978, as the writing of *The Poverty of*

32. PT, p. ii.
33. London 1970. The book was an exposure of academic and industrial surveillance. The fine conclusion, 'Highly Confidential: A Personal Comment by the Editor', pp. 146-164, is one of the original starting-points of Thompson's preoccupation with civil liberties at the end of the 70s.
34. 'Sir, Writing by Candlelight', *New Society*, December 24, 1970; 'A Special Case', *New Society*, February 24, 1972.
35. 'Homage to Salvador Allende', Spokesman Broadsheet, Nottingham, September 30, 1973.
36. *Sunday Times*, April 27, 1975.

Theory came to a close with its impassioned attack on Althusser as the arch-Stalinist incarnate. Scarcely before the ink had dried on it, Althusser's manifesto *Ce qui ne peut plus durer dans le Parti Communiste* was appearing in France. Seldom can a polemical charge have collapsed quite so speedily and completely.[37] The whole edifice of Thompson's characterization lay scattered before the irrefutable evidence of Althusser's actual convictions. Althusser's savage indictment of the bureaucratic regime and sectarian politics of the PCF made the notion of him as the personification of Stalinism patently ridiculous. Rather than alter or retract it, however, Thompson appended a postscript to his text, throwing up two lines of defence of it. On the one hand, he attempts to minimize the scope and force of Althusser's critique of the French Party apparatus. Now it is true that Althusser fails to call for the right to form organized tendencies within the PCF, and appears to be unaware that this was normal practice within the Bolshevik Party throughout most of Lenin's life-time. But then, neither was this a major demand of Thompson when he was fighting a struggle within the CPGB.[38] In general, if we compare *Ce qui ne peut plus durer* with *The Reasoner*, Althusser's assault on the command structure and internal organization of the party is far more scathing and systematic. In fact, it is probably safe to say that Althusser's manifesto of April 1978 is the most violent oppositional charter ever published within a party in the post-war history of Western Communism. Thompson complains of its timing—that it appeared twenty years after the rebellions of 1956, and on the occasion of the defeat of the Left in the March legislative elections. But both are quite intelligible in terms of Althusser's long-term choice to remain within the Communist movement. This option involved paying the price of silence on a range of fundamental issues in order to maintain activity in the major party of the French working class. A similar decision—based on practical judgement of relative advantages and disadvantages—was made in the late 50s by many other intellectuals respected by Thompson: Eric Hobsbawm in England or Paolo Spriano in Italy, for example. The latitude of political expression permitted within the CPGB or PCI, of course, widened over the years much more than in the PCF. But it was

37. Althusser's articles were published in *Le Monde*, 24-27 April 1978.
38. Ken Alexander was the major critic of democratic centralism, as interpreted by the party leadership: see his articles on the subject in *The Reasoner*, No 1, July 1956, and *World News*, September 7, 1956.

precisely the rigidity of bureaucratic control and censorship within the French party which explains the chronology of Althusser's assault on it. Prior to the debacle of spring 1978, to defy the leadership of the PCF publicly across the whole range of its immediate practice and policies was to incur certain expulsion. Althusser chose the moment of his initiative politically and deliberately—the hour when the party apparatus was deeply shaken and discredited among Communist militants and electors alike, and was no longer able to apply its traditional sanctions. In other words, he waited for a serious internal crisis before striking: a perfectly rational calculation, conventional in military thinking. Even so, the opposition for which he stood remained rather isolated in the party, as the sequel proved—making clear what his situation would have been a few years earlier, when the balance of forces was far less favourable. In the event, the PCF leadership was able to contain the threat of a generalized revolt from below, and to restabilize its authority over its membership. Yet despite this defeat, Althusser's manifesto has achieved a signal gain. Freedom of expression has been secured within the French Party—its extent henceforward measurable by the pitch of his philippic. Today, there is probably more genuine liberty of discussion in the PCF than in the drugged consensus of the PCI.

Thompson seems to sense the weakness of his final attempt to cling to the description of Althusser as an inveterate Stalinist. For half-way through his Postscript, he suddenly changes tack. Declaring that 'what concerned' him in *The Poverty of Theory* 'was not the particular situation of Althusser in France', he concedes that 'the signs, and the complexities, of that situation I may not always have correctly read'.[39] This tacit admission of error receives no further exploration, however. Instead, Thompson announces that his real concern all along was not Althusser's work itself, 'but the influence of transposed Althusserian thought outside of France', above all in England, and of the 'import agencies' responsible for this. He goes on: '*New Left Review* (and New Left Books) hold a particular responsibility for this, since over the past fifteen years they have issued, to the accompaniment of ecstatic "presentations" and theoretical heavy breathing, every product, however banal, of the Althusserian *fabrik*; and from France or about France, they have *issued nothing else* [his italics]. So that, whatever esoteric reservations the

39. PT, pp. 404-405.

Review's editors may hold as to Althusser, the imposition has been passed upon an innocent public that the French proletariat = the PCF, a Party supposedly composed of a heroic, uncomplicated, militant "base", adjoined to which are rigorous and lucid Marxist theorists, imbricated in the concrete life of the Party.'[40] Probably written in a hurry, perhaps off balance, it would be unfair to judge the Postscript on the same scales as *The Poverty of Theory* itself. But it must be said that this paragraph is a travesty of the truth, unworthy of its author. Has NLR published nothing but 'ecstatic presentations' of Althusser's work? Long before Thompson addressed himself to the task, the review had published a systematic series of critiques of Althusser: of his philosophy (Geras, no. 71; Glucksmann, no. 72); of his theory of history (Vilar, no. 80); of his politics (Gerratana, no. 101/102). I have defended Althusser against the wildness of Thompson's charges here: but among other colleagues and contributors, I too criticized both his speculative constructions and his political illusions (*Considerations on Western Marxism*; NLR 100). Has NLB 'issued nothing else' from France apart from the products of the 'Althusserian *fabrik*'? Does the work of the historians Lucien Febvre (*The Coming of the Book*) or Pierre Vilar (*A History of Gold and Money*), Georges Lefebvre (*The Great Fear*) or Albert Soboul (*The French Revolution*) really fall under this description? Dead or alive, they would have been surprised to learn of it. What, for that matter, of the philosophers Jean-Paul Sartre (*Critique of Dialectical Reason*) or Lucien Goldmann (*Immanuel Kant*), the very humanist adversaries whom Althusser expressly constructed his theories against? The economist Arghiri Emmanuel (*Unequal Exchange*) or the sociologist Lucien Malson (*Wolf Children*)? Thompson's claim is a simple absurdity. His final accusation is no less so. When did NLR 'impose upon an innocent public' the proposition that 'the French proletariat = the PCF, a Party supposedly composed of a heroic, uncomplicated, militant "base", adjoined to which are rigorous and lucid Marxists theorists, imbricated in the concrete life of the Party'? The 'fairy-story' here is entirely Thompson's. If he had scrupled to look at the review, instead of hastily inventing this fiction, he would have found articles like Jean-Marie Vincent's 'The PCF and its History' or Ernest Mandel's 'The Lessons of May 1968', not to speak of the latter's *From Stalinism to Eurocommunism*,[41] whose surgical

40. PT, p. 405.
41. NLR 50; London 1978.

sharpness and clarity speak for themselves. Swivelling round at the last minute from 'the situation of Althusser in France' to the 'import' of his ideas in England, as the ostensible target of his polemic, Thompson adds nothing to his case. A historian, not to speak of a socialist, should be more sensible of accuracy and equity.

There remains another question, however. In itself, Thompson's picture of Althusser as a Stalinist may be absurd. But construable within it, is there not the much more persuasive claim that Althusser's anti-Stalinism was less principled and passionate than that of Thompson? Here the answer must ungrudgingly and certainly be yes. The moral and political intensity of Thompson's rejection of the heritage of Stalin, after he had left the British Party in 1956, is far greater than anything Althusser was to display over the next decades. In part, the difference was inscribed the divergence of starting-points. Any critique of the CPSU inspired by the Chinese polemics of 1960 onwards, rather than by the Twentieth Congress or the Hungarian Revolt of 1956, contained an inbuilt restraint against all-out assault on the dictator and his regime. The famous article *On the Question of Stalin*, in which the CCP gave its verdict on his historical role, was published in the *Renminribao* in September 1963, just as Althusser's 'On the Materialist Dialectic' was appearing in France. Among the costs of credulity in Maoism as an alternative to Khruschevism in the 60s was this one. Thompson, to his honour, never shared it. In *The Poverty of Theory*, however, he makes claims well beyond this merited contrast. For central to the whole latter part of his essay is the thesis that Thompson, with the aid of socialist humanism, was possessed of a complete insight into Stalinism in 1956—a 'total critique' of its 'practice and theory'.[42] Today, this remains the 'unfinished agenda' of history, temporarily 'pushed aside' by the callow usurpation of subsequent Marxisms, but ultimately unanswerable as a 'moral critique' which was at the same time 'a very specific and practical political critique'.[43] Again and again, Thompson returns to the idea that *1956* was the year of the historical epiphany in which Stalinism for the first time received its ethical quietus, its complete intellectual exposure, its final political death-sentence for socialists. Then and only then did 'the two traditions' within Marxism, theology versus reason,

42. PT, p. 324.
43. PT, pp. 375, 369.

irremediably divide, and *since* then all developments can be judged by whether they have lived up to or fallen short of that moment of apocalyptic revelation.

Can this account be accepted? The answer to it is surely twofold. *Before* the charmed year of the Twentieth Party Congress, there was a very long tradition of Marxist analysis and discussion of Stalinism, by revolutionary socialists. Its major current, of course, was founded by Trotsky. The critique of the USSR that he constructed from the mid-20s onwards was charged with a burning moral and political indignation some three decades before the lights of 1956. But it was also an enterprise of materialist *social theory*, an attempt at a *historical explanation*, of Stalinism. The fundamental hypotheses of *The Revolution Betrayed* (1936) remain unsurpassed to this day as a framework for investigation of Soviet society. Trotsky's work was in turn developed and amplified by Isaac Deutscher, in his biography of Stalin (1952), and many other writings, above all his trilogy on Trotsky himself. If these were the peaks of historico-political study of Stalinism on the Left, there also rose an extensive range of memoirs and exposés indicting the realities of the dictatorial regime in Russia: Souvarine's *Staline*, Gide's *Retour de l'URSS*, Serge's *Memoirs of a Revolutionary*, to name only a few. Thompson today rebukes Althusser for the tardiness of his critique of Stalinism, characteristically asking: '*Where was Althusser in 1956?*'.[44] Then for a brief sentence, he admits that the logic of the question is an uncomfortable one for him too. Where was Thompson in 1952 (Doctor's Plot) or 1951 (Slansky Trial), for example? But he brushes this train of thought aside, by emphasizing an essential difference: 'In 1956 it was at length officially revealed that Stalinism had, for decades, been swatting men down like flies'. Is the *official* announcement of Stalin's crimes then to mark the frontier between venial and mortal responsibility? The suggestion would seem to be that it was understandable to dismiss Trotsky and ignore Serge, but inexcusable not to heed Khruschev or Mikoyan. Thompson can hardly take this seriously himself. What excuse was there for credence in the infamous Rajk Trial, for which after 1956 he once told his readers in a brisk, bad phrase he did not intend to be 'crippled by remorse'?[45]

---

44. PT, p. 324.
45. 'Socialism and the Intellectuals', *Universities and Left Review*, No 1, Spring 1957, p. 36. The effect of the phrase is dismissal of due responsibility by rhetorical inflation of it.

An abundant literature already existed on the show-trials in the USSR, which anyone truly concerned with the subject could scarcely have avoided. Instead, he apparently contented himself with Andrew Rothstein.[46]

Of course, it is also possible that in reality Thompson never wholly believed in the Moscow Trials, suspected the existence of the labour camps, was aware of Stalin's role in the Spanish, Greek or Chinese Revolutions, but kept silent because he thought it more useful and responsible to work in the most devoted working-class party available in Britain at the time, hoping for better days to come. There would have been some Communists among the rebels of 1956, virtually certainly, who thought like this after the War. In many cases, a mixture of motives is probable. But neither assumption—innocence of knowledge or estimate of relative advantage—gives much ground for railing at later revolts. The fact is that the year 1956 confers no special historical privilege or exemption on Thompson. To assess its contribution to a socialist critique of Stalinism, it is necessary to look at the actual composition and output of the Communist oppositions of the time. In Eastern Europe, where the social and national explosions lent them a mass character, many courageous articles and some fine poems were written in the brief period of ebullition from the spring to the autumn—not to speak of the heroism of those who fought in the streets when the test of arms came. But little intellectual work of lasting substance survived the crisis. The major thinker to rally to the causes of that year was Lukács, who never theorized them: philosophically antithetical to Althusser, in his political relationship to the Hungarian Party he remained very similar to the latter in his attitude to the French Party. The limits of the Marxist literature on Stalinism inspired by 1956 in Eastern Europe can be seen by looking forward to the landmarks that came afterwards. Nothing emerged comparable in stature to the major work of Medvedev in the 60s or Bahro in the 70s.

In Western Europe, the oppositions had more space and time to develop a radical and systematic analysis of the nature and origins of

---

46. See *William Morris—Romantic to Revolutionary*, London 1955, where on the strength of an article by Rothstein, 'Culture in the Soviet Factory', he told his readers: 'Twenty years ago even among Socialists and Communists, many must have regarded Morris's picture of "A Factory as it Might Be" as an unpractical poet's dream: today visitors return from the Soviet Union with stories of the poet's dream already fulfilled.' p. 760.

Stalinism as a historical phenomenon. Thompson invites his younger readers to inquire: 'Did you identify the sources of Stalinism? Did you construct a better Theory?'[47] This, of course, is the second question that needs to be asked. We have seen that Thompson ignores the entire tradition of Marxist theoretical engagement with the Soviet Union before 1956. What then have he or his associates produced in the twenty or so years since? The answer is a curiously contradictory one. In England, *The New Reasoner* maintained from 1957 to 1959 a record of socialist documentation on Eastern Europe and the USSR without equal on the Left in any country. No issue was complete without articles on or translations from the Communist world. Among these were the essays by Thompson himself to which he refers—eloquent Western equivalents of the Eastern manifestoes of the time—and poems and stories by Dery, Yashin, Hikmet, Wazyk, Ilyes, Woroszylski, Brecht and others. But with the cessation of *The New Reasoner* in late 1959, this interest dwindled away. There is scant reflection of it in the *New Left Review* of 1960-1961. In France, the achievement was smaller. There the typical product of those years was Edgar Morin's autobiographical memoir of his time in the PCF, *Autocritique*. In Italy, a few ephemeral pamphlets appeared. By the early 60s, the momentum of '56 appears to have run out. For all the passionate polemics and self-questioning of the hour, it might be said that overall it is the dearth of sustained study of Stalinism that is remarkable, rather than any pattern of cumulative research. Did the levy of '56 produce a single substantial book, or even analytic essay, on the USSR in the later Khruschev years? Did it investigate the roots of the Sino-Soviet conflict? Did it have much to say about China, before or after the Cultural Revolution? Did it follow the evolution of Russian or Eastern European societies in the epoch of Brezhnev? One writer in *The Reasoner* and *The New Reasoner* made a distinguished contribution in this area— R.W. Davies,[48] who went on to collaborate with E.H. Carr in *The Foundation of a Planned Economy*. But he seems to have been a figure somewhat apart from his peers of the time. In general, real knowledge of Stalinism was advanced in these years by professional scholars like Carr,

---

47. PT, p. 374.
48. See 'Some Notes on the 1937-38 Purges', *The Reasoner*, no. 3, November 1956, and 'The Russian Economy', *The New Reasoner*, no. 10, Autumn 1959. The former article is strangely similar to the explanation it sketches of the Yezhovschina to that advanced by Althusser's pupil Grahame Lock, in his Introduction to *Essays in Self-Criticism*. The solitary book review on the USSR in the early *New Left Review* (no. 5) was also by Davies.

Nove or Rigby, or by Trotskyists like Mandel or Maitan. The mainstream of '56 proved in the end surprisingly thin, and left rather little trace.[49] In part, this was due to the lack of specialized skills and interests in Russia, Eastern Europe and China among the intellectuals who left the Communist movement in that year. Their attention was more naturally turned towards their own societies. But even here, it is striking how little progress was made in a materialist understanding of the persistence of the loyalty commanded by the bureaucratic structures and traditions of the major Communist parties among vanguard workers and large masses of members and electors in the West, without benefit of political coercion or ideological monopoly: a problem largely unbroached by Marxists to this day. Deeper reasons were at work in the subsequent direction of the rebels of 1956 than a mere withdrawal from the disappointments of destalinization in the East.

It is difficult not to wonder whether the results of the socialist humanism of the time were not so analytically meagre because of a premise continually visible in *The Poverty of Theory*: the belief that the real work was already done—the *moral* critique of Stalinism which rendered painstaking sociological or historical inquiry into the dynamics of Eastern societies supernumerary, or secondary. The prolonged silence on the Soviet Union or China which followed the effervescence of 1956-1959 was perhaps in this sense the logical outcome of what might genuinely be called a substitution of moralism for historical materialism. Instead of a tracking of the complex causal processes leading from the death of Stalin to the equilibrium of Brezhnev, we have a passing on of the torch of ethical protest across the decades, from 1956 to some time in the future when the 'unfinished agenda' of socialist humanism will be taken up again. The relationship between past and present set out in Thompson's canon of historiography finds a faithful reflection in his definition of politics here. An uncritical cult of 1956 is the practical consequence of a conception of history as a chrestomathy of moral examples. Ultimately it leads to an abandonment of the responsibilities of continuous intellectual analysis and explanation. *The Poverty of Theory* itself furnishes the disturbing proof of this. The treatment of Althusser as a Stalinist is, as we have seen, a trifling caricature of

49. Elsewhere, Thompson himself virtually concedes this. In his letter to Kolakowski, he speaks of 'the few constructive and enduring consequences' of the intellectual turbulence of 1956: PT, p. 93.

Althusser. But it also trifles in a different way with the nature of Stalinism. For the Stalinist regime in Russia was a colossal politico-institutional complex, born in a backward country dominated by extreme scarcity and surrounded by armed enemies, consolidated amidst the profoundest social convulsions and bonded by the material interests of a privileged bureaucratic stratum created by the Revolution itself. The cataclysm of the forced collectivization, the terror of the purges, the hecatombs of the Second World War, together decimating the Soviet population, were specific to this Stalinism. Its hallmark was loss of life—through sanguinary repression or insensate blunder—on an enormous scale.

With the death of the autocrat who gave his name to the system, Stalinism in its classical sense soon came to an end in Russia. There remained a rigid party dictatorship, dedicated at once to the industrialization of a planned economy, the defence of state property against the pressure of imperialism, and the protection of its privileges from the masses of workers and peasants—still a negation of socialist democracy, but no longer an apparatus of generalized terror. Stalinism in this secondary sense has proved to possess a much wider historical basis. So far this century, it has constituted the format of all regimes to emerge from successful socialist revolutions, with the partial exception of Cuba. For all their otherwise significant differences, China, Yugoslavia and Vietnam essentially represent variations of this model. In one case only, the terror of imperialism produced an experience more terrible than that of the tyranny of Stalin: the Cambodian dictatorship, put to an end by a more clement neighbour. Other, lesser deformities of Russian Stalinism have on occasion been exceeded: the cult of personality in North Korea, for example, has eclipsed any precedent. But by and large the socialist revolutions since October have benefited from the change in the world balance of forces it set in motion: the costs of social transformation, in political brutality and irrationality, have been proportionately less. Stalinism has been at once replicated and mitigated outside Russia, wherever the construction of socialism has been attempted in poor and backward social formations locked in struggle with colonial domination or imperial aggression. The arc of its spread in the underdeveloped world forms one of the major historical patterns of the 20th century.

How on earth, then, could Althusserianism, the recondite product of a tiny fraction of the intelligentsia in a highly developed capitalist country, emerge to give a complete *post hoc* theorization of this phenomenon? In either sense of the term Stalinism, the very idea defies the imagination. Thompson even intends it in the first, as Stalin's bloody magistrature itself. What conceivable material basis or historical logic connects two such utterly dissimilar and disproportionate forces? At no point does Thompson attempt to supply an explanation. Instead, perhaps sensing the impossibility of doing so, he propels himself into a *fuite en avant* of widening generalization—conjuring up one moment the threat of a 'new ruling class' in the West, the next future despotic rulers in the Third World, seizing upon Althusserianism as a heaven-sent ideology. Dark hints of the Khmers Rouges mingle with warnings of nihilism in the Polytechnics.[50] The sheer fantasy of this composite picture of Althusser—posthumous ghost-writer of Stalin, unseen counsellor of Pol Pot, spawner of a myriad budding Nechaievs—is astonishing. Elsewhere, still casting about for some explanation of his work, Thompson more bathetically presents it as a product of the congenital elitism of Western academics and other intellectuals, spoilt by free education and comfortable jobs today, but otherwise a mere descendant of the traditions of Bentham, Coleridge or Webb.[51] The cataract of contradictory accounts towards the end of *The Poverty of Theory* can be taken only as a testimony of an underlying lack of interest in their nominal object itself. The stertorous assertions that Althusserianism is the perfected codification of the practices of bureaucratic terror in the USSR actually involve—contrary to their intentions—a trivialization of Stalin's dictatorship. They are no advertisement for the materialist wisdom of 1956.

At the same time, Thompson's political judgements of Stalinism in its broader contemporary sense have also gone seriously astray in *The Poverty of Theory*. 'From my own position', he tells us, 'I cannot conceive of any wave in the working-class movement being further to the "right" than Stalinism.'[52] With this dire sentence, he slips back to what is in fact a classical Cold War position. For Stalinist movements, in the sense in which he is here using the term—Communist parties modelled on the authoritarian traditions of the later CPSU—are not mere survivals of a reactionary past: on the contrary, some have proved capable of still continuing to play a revolutionary world-historical role, right through the

50. PT, pp. 379, 380, 397.
51. PT, p. 377.
52. PT, p. 326.

60s and 70s. What else was the Vietnamese Revolution—the greatest epic of anti-imperialist struggle in the 20th century? The filiation from Stalingrad to Saigon is plain for anyone to see. The contradiction between liberation and regimentation, emancipation and duress, has been far less drastic in Vietnam than in the USSR. But the overall shape of the historical process is kindred. If Thompson could really conceive of no wave to the right of Stalinism in the workers' movement, the logic of his position would have been concurrence with Shirley Williams and Lee Kuan Yew in their violent denunciations of the NLF within the ranks of the Second International. In fact, although the Vietnamese Revolution receives little emphasis from him today, he did stand for solidarity with it. Vulgar anti-communism is expressly disavowed elsewhere in *The Poverty of Theory*. But this does not inhibit Thompson from a volley of ferocious onslaughts against the PCF, that come ill from an uncomplaining member of the British Labour Party—an organization whose particular record on Vietnam (not to speak of Rhodesia, Malaya, Greece) was beneath contempt, and whose general character even its admirers might hesitate to describe as actually to the 'left' of the PCF. It is not, of course, that the choice of a socialist to work within the Labour Party in Britain is necessarily wrong or incomprehensible: a similar type of case can be made for it as for the option taken by Althusser to work within the Communist Party in France. In either case, a disintoxicated calculation of relative utility is no doubt involved. But precisely for this reason, it is unseemly for Thompson to pillory Althusser for membership of a Communist party, in a text which fails to take any distance from the Social Democratic party to which he now belongs. The drift of the declaration that there are 'no enemies to the right' of Stalinism within the labour movement is acceptance of social democracy as the lesser evil. It is impossible to believe that Thompson really holds this view. Everything in his political temper speaks against it. It is much more probable that the pronouncement is a flight of the pen, let out in the heat of the moment. Rather than the sign of a new and deep-seated accommodation to Cold War categories, it is simply evidence of the limitations and dangers of 'theory understood as polemic'.

The political and theoretical deficiencies of Althusser's work have not been eluded here. They are eminently subject to fair socialist criticism. But Thompson's style of polemic in *The Poverty of Theory* makes no attempt at such fairness. There is, in fact, an occasional suggestion in

Thompson's writing that a historian may be dispensed from his ordinary obligations to truth when dealing with contemporaries—that something less than the exacting standards required of the past will do in the present, where personal involvement in its conflicts precludes objectivity anyway. In an attractive interview given in the United States, he remarks: 'When it comes to the 20th century I am almost sure that younger historians must do the work because of my too great involvement in some episodes. I don't think I can write about these as a historian. I can write political theory, but I can't write as a historian about 1945. Because I am too much in there myself. There is a necessary distance to make possible an objective analysis.'[53] The argument is a curious contradiction of the epistemological claims for experience that are so central to *The Poverty of Theory*—as can be seen from a parallel comment on the history of Communism in the British labour movement: 'Those of us who have lived the experience will never be able to hold it at the distance requisite for analysis'.[54] But the consequence Thompson seems to draw from it is not a need for greater care, but a licence for greater looseness, of judgement. For he goes on: 'The historian may tend to be a bit too generous because a historian has to attend and listen to very disparate groups of people and try and understand their value-system and their consciousness. Obviously in a very committed situation you can't always afford that kind of generosity'.[55] In fact generosity is less appropriate a term for the proper practice of the historian than justice. It is all too clear that in what he took to be the 'very committed situation' in which he was writing *The Poverty of Theory*, Thompson felt subjectively unable to afford the one: the objective result was to sacrifice the other. The same interview contains its own correction. It continues: 'But if you afford it [generosity] too little then you are impelled into the kind of sectarian position in which you are repeatedly making errors of judgement in your relations with other people. We have seen a lot of that recently. Historical consciousness ought to assist one to understand the possibilities of transformation and the possibilities within people.' It is just that consciousness which was needed in *The Poverty of Theory*, and is so wanting.

Thompson's conviction that Althusser *must* be a hardened Stalinist is plainly based in large part on the unrelenting determinism of his work: a

53. 'An Interview with E.P. Thompson', *Radical History Review*, III, 4, Fall 1976, p. 17.
54. PT, p. 75.
55. 'An Interview with E.P. Thompson', p. 17.

philosophical denial of the role of human agency in history is read as a theorization of the practical repression of living men and women. Althusserian anti-humanism is thus equated with an inhuman Stalinism, in which the 'supports' of Balibar's relations of production are virtually assimilated to the victims of Beria's execution squads. An analytic structuralism, in other words, becomes another name for moral nihilism. But if Thompson had allowed a normal historical consciousness to inform his attention to Althusser, he would perhaps have recalled that in the history of philosophy there is no intrinsic relation between a causal determinism and a callous amoralism. If anything, the contrary is true. The most radical and implacable determinist of all, Baruch Spinoza, was known in his own life-time as the noblest and gentlest of men, and was canonized by his successors as the 'saint of philosophers'. The categories of Althusser's thought are derived directly, as I have tried to show else-where, from Spinoza's monism. There is no reason to suppose, from his theoretical tenets, that his ethical outlook would be especially different. There exist few glimpses of Althusser in print. But it is worth citing the memory that Régis Debray—politically and intellectually a very different Marxist—had of him, from his cell in a Bolivian prison: 'He tactfully gave us the chance of working with him, in such a way that we did not realize it was he who was actually doing the work, that he was working for us. We knew he was a communist, and under his influence, though without telling him, we became so too. But with him it was a whole-hearted conviction, as could be seen not only from his written works, but from the affection and generosity with which he guided our steps in that direction. For what his students saw as his personal qualities were in fact those of every activist.' [56]

Althusser's own person and writing are one thing. The influence of his ideas—the phenomenon of 'Althusserianism'—is another. Is Thompson more pertinent in his verdict on the latter? There can be no doubt that in England a species of spin-off from Althusser's work occurred in the 70s which does answer to some of Thompson's severest strictures. The writings of Hirst, Hindess and their associates notoriously effected a *reductio ad absurdum* of some of Althusser's ideas—before successively rejecting Althusser himself as too empiricist, then their own earlier notions as too rationalist, and finally Marx as too revolutionary. But this

56. *Prison Writings*, London 1973, p. 198.

weightless iconoclasm, however understandably a provocation to Thompson, has never been part of the mainstream of Althusserian work—which it has expressly renounced, along with Marxism. The real question lies elsewhere. Is it the case, as Thompson claims, that the overall record of Althusserianism has been a 'blight on the mind', as a 'wholly reactionary ideology', whose reified categories 'it will never be possible' to apply or test in the writing of history?[57] The answer is that, so far from this being true, Althusserianism has proved remarkably *productive—generating an impressively wide range of works dealing with the real world, both past and present*. Guy Bois's *Crisis of Feudalism* is a landmark of mediaeval scholarship, combining meticulous empirical research with rigorous conceptual exposition of the dynamics of Norman feudalism. Michel Aglietta's *Theory of Capitalist Regulation* is a pioneering political economy of the development of US capitalism. Nicos Poulantzas's *Fascism and Dictatorship* is a detailed comparative investigation of German and Italian fascism. Pierre-Philippe Rey's *Colonialism, Neo-Colonialism and the Transition to Capitalism* is a major anthropological study of the impact of French colonialism in the Congo. Robert Linhart's *Lenin, the Peasants and Taylor* re-examines the formative conditions of the Bolshevik breakthrough towards socialism in the Soviet Union. Roger Establet and Christian Baudelot's *Capitalist School in France* provides a thorough social-statistical survey of the French educational system. Erik Olin Wright's *Class Structure and Income Determination* is a comprehensive empirical study of the bases of economic inequality in the United States. Göran Therborn's *Science, Class and Society* is a critical history of classical European sociology, his *What Does the Ruling Class Do When it Rules?* a unique conspectus of the contrasting organizational structures of feudal, capitalist and socialist states.[58]

These books are only a sample of the very large literature closely or distantly inspired by Althusser's work that has emerged in the last decade. They are confined to substantive studies of topics of importance

57. PT, pp. 352, 375, 287.
58. Guy Bois, *Crise du féodalisme*, Paris 1977; Michel Aglietta, *Régulation et crises du capitalisme*, Paris 1976; Nicos Poulantzas, *Fascisme et dictature*, Paris 1970; Pierre-Philippe Rey, *Colonialisme, néo-colonialisme et transition au capitalisme*, Paris 1971; Robert Linhart, *Lénine, les paysans, Taylor*, Paris 1976; Christian Baudelot and Roger Establet, *L'Ecole capitaliste en France*, Paris 1971; Erik Olin Wright, *Class Structure and Income Determination*, New York 1979; Göran Therborn, *Science, Class and Society*, London 1976; *What Does the Ruling Class Do When it Rules?*, London 1978.

by any reckoning—excluding predominantly epistemological or purely theoretical writings. Even within these limits, the list above is far from exhaustive. Nor is it immune from faults—ranging from undue Maoist coloration in some cases to insufficiently critical use of sources in others. But it does incontestably indicate the vitality of Althusserianism as an intellectual force capable of stimulating and informing concrete inquiry among economists, political scientists, historians, sociologists and anthropologists alike. It would be difficult to deny that the overall balance-sheet of Althusser's impact has in this sense been positive for the real development of historical materialism. Indeed, if we ask ourselves what comparable gamut of works Thompsonism, to risk the term, has given rise to, the answer is evidently more modest. Where, the reader of *The Poverty of Theory* might be tempted to inquire, are the Thompsonian explorations of the trajectory of advanced industrial capitalism, the mechanisms of the crisis of feudalism, the role of primitive accumulation in colonialism, the relationship between classes in the building of socialism, the patterns of educational opportunity or of income distribution in bourgeois democracies, the intellectual history of the social sciences, or the nature of fascism? The temptation should be resisted, because no comparison between Althusser and Thompson along these lines would be a strict one. It is not just that Thompson's own historical work carries a weight and authority in its own field far beyond that of any single Althusserian study to date. It is also that a historian teaches by example, in a discipline where a long period of maturation is normal among new practitioners, while a philosopher can instruct by system, generalizing concepts and theses relatively rapidly across a number of disciplines. Finally, of course, Thompson should not be isolated as an individual from the brilliant group of English Marxist historians of his own generation, even if the accents and interests of his work are certainly distinctive within it. A comparison of the achievement of this Marxist historiography as a whole with the legacy of Althusser would look very different. But it would be one between equals, within a common socialist culture that had grown beyond mutual anathemas. Younger Marxists in Britain today are, in fact, already seeking a critical balance or synthesis between these two diverse traditions.[59]

59. See the impressive volume produced by the Centre for Contemporary Cultural Studies at Birmingham: John Clarke, Chas Critcher and Richard Johnson, eds., *Working-Class Culture*, esp. 'Culture and the Historians', pp. 41-71, and 'Three Problematics: Elements of a Theory of Working-Class Culture', pp. 201-232, by Richard Johnson.

It is against the very thought of any such commerce or exchange that Thompson would interpose his most vehement veto. *The Poverty of Theory* ends with the declaration of a general jehad against Althusserianism—a call to a new War of Religion on the Left. The recklessness of this summons, for the well-being of what Morris called socialist fellowship, scarcely needs emphasis. Its very vastness and vagueness give it away: 'I declare unrelenting intellectual war against such Marxisms'.[60] Which? Apparently, 'Theoretical practice (and allied Marxisms)'.[61] To which Thompson has himself written the best reply, rebuking Kolakowski for precisely the procedure he now employs: the same 'undiscriminating commination against a section of the Left', 'made in so imprecise a form', with its singular counterpart to 'that small phrase, dropped in so quietly, as to "all those other social utopias" '.[62] But it is not just their indiscriminacy which is wrong with Thompson's concluding menaces. It is the assumption contained in the epigraph from Marx blazoned at the head of *The Poverty of Theory* as a whole: 'To leave error unrefuted is to encourage intellectual immorality'. A favourite motto of Thompson, its authority should be rejected. For an intellectual error is *not* a moral crime, and to confuse the two is a licence for the fanatic and the pharisee. The tone of long stretches of Thompson's attack on Althusser bears witness to the dismal consequences of this maxim. 'Monstrous', 'vaporous', 'nonsense', 'rubbish', 'bourgeois ride', 'police operation'— the dictionary is ransacked for variations of abuse. The harmfulness of this style of polemic to the possibilities of rational or comradely communication on the Left can be in no doubt. The long and disastrous tradition that lies behind it is sufficient reminder of that. To call Althusser a police agent of Stalinism today, in the branch of ideology, is certainly milder than to call Slansky an intelligence agent of capitalism yesterday, but the habits of language involved are not entirely unrelated. It is understandable that Thompson should have been exasperated by the generic *hauteur* of Althusser's treatment of socialist humanism or of professional historiography, by his lack of any inclination for the ordinary duties and decencies of critical dialogue on the Left. But in reacting against these faults, he has overtrumped them with his own.

Behind the violence of his assault on Althusser, in fact, there can be

60. PT, p. 380.
61. PT, p. 380.
62. PT, pp. 127-128.

traced a deeper and more general disaffection from the present. For Althusserianism is just 'one more astonishing aberrant spectacle added to the phantasmagoria of our time. It is a bad time for the rational mind to live: for a rational mind in the Marxist tradition it is a time that cannot be endured.'[63] The wider historical judgement involved here is a strange one for a Marxist: has any passage in the past decades compared in darkness with the late 30s, the time of triumphant Nazism and the Great Purges, which yet still form part of a poetic epoch for Thompson? But even locally, confining ourselves to the intellectual landscape of the Left alone, is it really the case that the shadows have been thickening so sombrely, to well-nigh nightmare pitch, in these last years? Thompson has given us the testimony of his sensations in this time. The honesty of his report is not to be questioned, but its rationality can be. We may assess the degree of its validity, perhaps, by comparing his reactions to the change in the cultural climate of the Left in England since the 60s to those of the fellow socialist whose ideas he most often acknowledges in *The Poverty of Theory* as close to his own. Raymond Williams has described the broadening of Marxist culture in Britain, of which the introduction of Althusser's work has been one element, rather differently: 'It was in this new situation that I felt the excitement of contact with more new Marxist work: the later work of Lukács, the later work of Sartre, the developing work of Goldmann and of Althusser, the variable and developing syntheses of Marxism and some forms of structuralism. At the same time, within this significant new activity, there was further access to older work, notably that of the Frankfurt School (in its most significant period in the 20s and 30s) and especially the work of Walter Benjamin; the extraordinarily original work of Antonio Gramsci; and, as a decisive element of a new sense of the tradition, newly translated work of Marx and especially of the *Grundrisse*. As all this came in, during the 60s and early 70s, I often reflected, and in Cambridge had direct cause to reflect, on the contrast between the situation of the socialist student of literature in 1940 and 1970. More generally I had reason to reflect on the contrast for any student of literature, in a situation in which an argument that had drifted into deadlock, or into local and partial positions, in the late 30s and 40s, was being vigorously and significantly reopened . . . My own long and often internal and solitary debate with

63. PT, p. 216.

what I had known as Marxism now took its place in a serious and extending international inquiry. I had opportunities to extend my discussions in Italy, in Scandinavia, in France, in North America, and in Germany, and with visitors from Hungary, Yugoslavia and the Soviet Union. This book is a result of that period of discussion, in an international context in which I have the sense, for the first time in my life, of belonging to a sphere and dimension of *work* in which I could feel at home.'[64] Even allowing for the different situations in literary and historical studies, the quality of response is antithetical. The 'unendurable time for a rational mind in the Marxist tradition' here becomes 'the first' in which such a mind 'could feel at home'. Experience, touchstone of the Thompsonian world, reveals its waywardness.

64. *Marxism and Literature*, pp. 4-5.

5

Internationalism

The tour of *The Poverty of Theory* is now completed. It has traversed a wide range of theoretical and political problems confronting contemporary socialism—from the status and logic of history as a discipline, to the course and limits of Marx's intellectual achievement, from the part of human choice and initiative in the generation of social structures, to the basis and nature of Stalinism as a type of political regime and organizational movement. Throughout, the focus of debate has been Thompson's polemic with Althusser over all of these issues. Each of them has been considered here, at some length, in that light. There remains, however, a final duty to be acquitted. It can scarcely escape any reader of *The Poverty of Theory* as a whole—the book rather than the essay—that one of its recurrent themes, whether as aside, undertone or outright pronunciamento, is Thompson's quarrel with the present *New Left Review*, a journal of which he was a founder. The Preface starts out with a brusque blow at Tom Nairn. 'The Peculiarities of the English' is, as is well known, a sharp attack on the essays on British society and history written by Nairn and myself in the early 60s—now spiced with further gibes meticulously preserved for release nearly fifteen years later. The 'Open Letter to Leszek Kolakowski' devotes much of its introduction to a more general characterization and condemnation of the editorial practice of NLR. The collection then ends as it began, with an 'Afternote' which, as we have seen, turns its fire away from Althusser to *New Left*

Review and New Left Books. It would be wrong to evade the insistence of this pattern. The risks of a perpetual feud are too clear: they should be exorcised. I will therefore try in conclusion to bring the relations between Edward Thompson and *New Left Review* since the early 60s into some more fraternal order—at the same time inviting correction or amendment of it in the same spirit.

The fullest account of the differences that Thompson perceives to lie between himself and us is to be found in his 'Letter' to Kolakowski. There he lists five main areas of discord. The first is what he calls the 'exclusion' of earlier editors and contributors from the discourse of the journal—'not only has the review turned away from its founders, but it has passed over their thought without examination'.[1] Is this charge really valid? Stated as it is, it is not difficult to refute. NLR was the first journal anywhere to publish an extended assessment of *The Making of the English Working Class*. The essay by Tom Nairn on it may have displeased Thompson, but the admiration and seriousness of its approach to his book can scarcely be doubted. Ralph Miliband's study of *The State in Capitalist Society* was appraised by Nicos Poulantzas, to whom he rejoined in the pages of the Review, in a debate widely noticed at home and abroad. Peter Worsley's *Third World* and Eric Hobsbawm's *Age of Revolution* were reviewed at length by Victor Kiernan, and Hobsbawm's *Labouring Men* by Gareth Stedman Jones. Raymond Williams's work was the subject of a major debate between Terry Eagleton and Anthony Barnett. Miliband, Hobsbawm, Williams, Kiernan, Hilton have in turn all contributed with some regularity to NLR. It is true, on the other hand, that not every founder or contributor to *The New Reasoner* or *Universities and Left Review* was published or discussed in NLR as it developed from the early 60s onwards. If Thompson had spoken of selection rather than exclusion he would have been more justified. Some part of the blame for this certainly lies with the Review, for reasons I will discuss. But part of the responsibility for it was simply the diverse destiny of many of the original individuals involved, not all of whom even remained on the Left. It is surely not without some significance that *The Socialist Register* itself, edited by Ralph Miliband and John Saville, which Thompson describes as 'the last survivor in the direct line of continuity from the old New Left', he also notes, has 'not involved all the tendencies which co-existed

1. PT, p. 105.

fruitfully in the older movement'.[2] Wider reasons were at work in the disintegration of the old New Left than mere impiety on the part of the new editors of NLR.

Thompson's second criticism is that the review has 'severely limited' the 'interest in and dialogue with' Communist dissent that 'marked the tradition of *The New Reasoner*'.[3] In fact, as we have seen, that interest had declined sharply in the early *New Left Review* itself, of 1960-1961. The record of the new editorial committee was not significantly different for some time; if its interest in the Communist world was greater, its coverage was very irregular and uncertain. Thompson could not fail to register the falling away from the proud standards of *The New Reasoner* in either case. However, by the time he was writing his criticisms of the review in 1973, his claim was no longer valid—not to speak of its republication today. For NLR has over the past decade included texts by leading Marxist dissidents from virtually every major Communist country in Europe: Roy and Zhores Medvedev from Russia, Rudolf Bahro from East Germany, Jiri Pelikan from Czechoslovakia, Miklos Haraszti from Hungary, Zaga Golubovic from Yugoslavia, Edward Baluka and his fellow shipyard-workers from Poland—in some cases for the first time anywhere in the English-speaking world. Successive articles by Tamara Deutscher have monitored the course of the new Soviet oppositions during the 70s. Even anti-socialist dissidents like Solzhenitsyn have been carefully assessed, by a range of authors.

Thompson's third complaint is that NLR has effected a 'narrowing of intellectual referents' and exerted 'an insistent pressure to reassert Marxism as doctrine'.[4] This is a vaguer charge, to which it is not easy to know how to reply. But so far as intellectual references are concerned, it could plausibly be argued that the Review has if anything widened them beyond the stock of its immediate inheritance. Among major thinkers with no connection to historical materialism discussed more amply or for the first time in NLR since 1962 have been such obvious figures as Freud, Weber, Darwin, Hegel, Rousseau, Lévi-Strauss. While rather than insisting on Marxism as a single 'doctrine', it has emphasized the plurality and diversity of schools of thought within 20th century Marxism, and has purposively published criticisms of all of them—as can

2. PT, p. 102.
3. PT, p. 105.
4. PT, p. 105.

readily be seen in the volume of its essays collected as *Western Marxism—A Critical Reader*.

Fourthly, Thompson contends that NLR has practised 'an obligatory rejection of the empirical mode of investigation' and given 'structural organization of concepts' a 'Hegelian priority' over 'substantive analysis'.[5] This description corresponds very little to the actual contents of the Review. One of the hallmarks of NLR, on the contrary, has been the attention to empirical data of its major political essays. The standard Review article of the past two decades has typically deployed a broader gamut of statistical and factual information, nearly always set in historical context, than was customary in either *The New Reasoner* or the early *New Left Review*. A random glance at any selection of its issues will confirm this, whether the subject be West Germany, Turkey, Japan, Argentina, Ceylon or India, the British economy or the American class structure, the pattern of industrialization in the underdeveloped capitalist countries or the origins of bourgeois democracy in the advanced capitalist countries. The need for empirical controls has been both advocated and applied in the editorial practice of the Review.

Fifthly, and finally, Thompson doubts whether we have 'ever absorbed or worked through the full historical experience of Stalinism'.[6] The premise here is the now familiar assumption that an experience as such delivers its own lessons together with it. To which it is again necessary to reply that different lessons can be drawn from the same historical experience—a point ironically made by the very invocation Thompson uses in the text. 'You and I would certainly doubt it', he told Kolakowski, as if the lessons were at least plain and common to two veterans of '56—an illusion that Kolakowski's reply quickly dispelled,[7] not to speak of the well-worn political 'moral' he subsequently went on to draw from the experience in question. At all events, so far as the 'mutant tradition' of NLR is concerned, it need only be said that it was to publish more material on the historical origins and development of Stalinism in the USSR than either the initial *New Left Review* or *The New Reasoner* before it. The prolonged debate between Ernest Mandel, Nicolas Krassó and Monty Johnstone in the mid 60s had no prior equivalent in either length or

5. PT, p. 105.
6. PT, p. 105.
7. 'My Correct Views on Everything', in *The Socialist Register 1974*, pp. 1-20, described as 'a tragic document' by the editors of the *Register*.

depth in the earlier journals. Subsequent texts by Medvedev, Carr, Halliday, Mészáros, Miliband, Nove, and repeatedly by Mandel again, have continued close exploration of the meaning and legacy of Stalinism in Russia and of related forms of bureaucratic rule in China.

In other words, Thompson's strictures on NLR largely mistake their object. The record of the Review over the years has certainly contained its share of errors, omissions and illusions. But its performance on the scores with which Thompson taxes it can be defended without ire or strain. No great chasm seems to exist between his position and ours on any of the substantive questions he raises. Does this mean, then, that there are no grounds for the dispute that indubitably broke out between us over a decade ago, and still apparently remains unrepaired? No. But to understand it, we must look beyond the rather tenuous bill of particulars presented in 1973. The real basis for the genuine grievance felt by Thompson against the present NLR surely lies in the circumstances of the change in personnel and control of the Review itself, in 1962-1963. It is this to which the first and most substantial, even if overstated, of his criticisms alludes. Thompson reproaches myself and the others on the new editorial committee of the Review on two essential counts here—for administratively 'dismissing'[8] the founders of the Review from the board, while failing to articulate our theoretical differences with them, and thereafter with disregarding Thompson and his colleagues in the development of a new style of NLR. What happened seems to me more complex. It is untrue that the old board was 'dismissed' by myself or by the new, as any participant of the time can testify. No such action was ever possible: as Thompson in effect concedes a few lines later, when he speaks of the old New Left 'electing for its own administrative dissolution'[9]—which is an accurate description. The notion of an editorial coup is a legend. This does not dispose of the peculiarity of the transition, nevertheless. Thompson is right to maintain that a parting of practical direction occurred without any adequate intellectual accounting of it by us. It was the evidence of that 'fracture' which, of course, motivated the silent disengagement from NLR by him and others in 1962. Thereafter there was no policy to exclude the work of the old board from the journal: but it is also true that the new editorial committee did not make a systematic effort to solicit and integrate it either. A major turnover of

8. PT, p. 102.
9. PT, p. 102.

contributors *de facto* occurred with the new format of the Review. By the mid 60s Thompson was surely not alone in his distance from it.

What was our share of responsibility in this? To calibrate it accurately, it is necessary to recall the circumstances that brought *New Left Review* into existence in the first place. The journal was created from a fusion of *The New Reasoner* and *Universities and Left Review* in 1960; its first editor was Stuart Hall, from the ULR side of the merger, working under a large board drawn from within and without the two previous journals. Benefiting from the dual prestige and loyalty commanded by its predecessors, the new Review was conceived as the organ of a broad socialist movement, informally organized in New Left Clubs across the country, and centrally focused around the Campaign for Nuclear Disarmament, which was then registering rapid advances within the Labour Party. Yet despite these fair prospects, within two years NLR was in acute crisis. CND was abruptly checked inside the Labour Party; the Clubs declined; the board of the Review was divided and uncertain of direction; the sales of the journal were falling. In effect, the political basis on which the journal had been launched was giving way, and no new one was readily discernible. The resignation of the editor, under conflicting pressures from the board, created a vacuum in late 1961. After a series of provisional arrangements, which produced one remarkable issue of the Review, it was filled—for lack of any other alternative—by the original nucleus of the present editorial committee of NLR: in the first instance, myself, Tom Nairn and Robin Blackburn.

Two points may be stressed about this strange outcome. The material and intellectual resources at the disposal of the old board were incomparably greater, in every respect, than those of the small group which started to edit the Review in 1962. Yet no one stepped forward from it to take up the responsibility of rescuing and reconstructing the journal. We found ourselves trying to do so, in default of any other candidates for the task. There was no usurpation in the process of succession: in the strict, neutral sense of the term, there was an abdication. The further peculiarity of the change-over lay in the character of the new incumbents— novices with no political or editorial experience, not even mainstream younger recruits from the New Left movement, in their early twenties: one was still an undergraduate. The loss of quality and response in the halting periodical that struggled to survive in 1962-1963, compared with the maturity of *The New Reasoner* or the vitality of *Universities and Left*

Review, was painfully evident to all at the time. It was compounded by the exaggerated sense of generational distance typical of that age, accentuated by the particular climate of the decade. We freely spoke of the 'Old Guard' among ourselves ... at a time when Thompson was just over 35. It is a normal process for youth to seclude itself to some extent in its own mental world for a period, turning away from its elders in search of its own identity and direction. This we certainly did. What was unnatural was for this process to occur in a political journal recently created by others who were themselves in their prime. The sense of exclusion of which Thompson speaks has its origin in this peculiar dislocation. If we had possessed greater maturity, there would have been more equal and fluent collaboration; if they had been veterans, there would have been easier acceptance of our need to find our own feet. In between either, the two sides drifted apart. Since we were editing the Review, Thompson can with justice fix major responsibility on us. But granting this, it may still be wondered whether any editorial group or policy was capable of reviving and reuniting the New Left of 1962. For if Stuart Hall, far closer in authority and outlook to the majority, was unable to secure the harmonious and fruitful interaction of the old board of the Review, was it ever likely we would succeed? The question can at least be posed. An answer may perhaps best be left to the judgement of others besides Thompson or myself who were involved in the events of the time. It is worth noting, at any rate, the view of Ralph Miliband, who regards the very decision to fuse *The New Reasoner*, of which he was one of the editors, with *Universities and Left Review* as ill-starred, leading inevitably to the later difficulties of *New Left Review* as a combined project.[10] The possibility of recreating the model of *The New Reasoner*, however, was open in 1962, when the future of NLR was in the balance: it was not taken. Other commitments probably by now had priority. Who can criticize them, when among other things they gave us *The Making of the English Working Class*, which was published the next year?

It took approximately two years for the new editorial group to develop stable bearings. When it did so, by 1964, the Left was confronted by a quite new situation in England. For the first time, the national crisis of British capitalism was unmistakable: the long Conservative regime of the 50s was visibly sinking, as the failure of CND and the eclipse of the New

---

10. 'John Saville: A Presentation', in David Martin and David Rubinstein (eds), *Ideology and the Labour Movement. Essays Presented to John Saville*, London 1979, pp. 25-27.

Left were succeeded by the revival of the fortunes of the Labour Party. The programme NLR set itself was to try to comprehend this conjuncture, for which little in the heritage of the old journal had prepared us. The result was the series of essays written by Tom Nairn and myself in 1964-65, on the British ruling order, the English working class, the Labour Party, and the Left of the previous decade. The novelty of these texts, by comparison with anything published in the earlier NLR or its predecessor journals, was simply that they sought to provide a systematic *historical* explanation of the configuration of class forces in English society and the nature of the present crisis of British capitalism. It may seem surprising that members of the old New Left board, studded with eminent historians, had never addressed themselves to this task. But it is so. Perhaps the very rigours of professional practice inhibited hybrid excursions between past and present. At all events, without either these advantages or apprehensions, we attempted to sketch out some cumulative Marxist account of our own history and society. It was this venture which brought down the vials of Thompson's wrath publicly on our heads. In 'The Peculiarities of the English', published in *The Socialist Register* in 1965, he attacked our essays aggressively and unrelentingly.

What had they done to provoke this denunciation? We had committed no uncomradely hostilities against Thompson—on the contrary, as I have pointed out, we had saluted his work with the greatest respect. We were seeking to introduce a more historical perspective on contemporary British politics—an enterprise that should in principle have commended itself to the founders of NLR. We emphasized the schematic and provisional nature of our theses, as the start rather than the end of a wider discussion. All this seems now, and seemed at the time, blameless enough. But we also unwisely declared our belief that the tradition of Marxism had hitherto been relatively weak in Britain, while ourselves resorting to categories derived from Marxist traditions in Italy and France. It was this injurious judgement that was surely the immediate ground for Thompson's explosive reaction. For it could indeed be read as a tacit dismissal of the work of the older New Left, or rather of that part of it (not necessarily majoritarian) which was attached to Marxism. In point of fact, the question itself was a moot one. To understand our attitude at the time, it is necessary to recall that the major flowering of English Marxist historiography post-dated our entry into NLR in 1962. In the next two years, *The Age of Revolution* and *The Making of the English*

Working Class were published, but we were very conscious that the 'mature works of Marxist historians' were 'only now beginning to emerge and consolidate each other'.[11] *From Reformation to Industrial Revolution, Industry and Empire, The World Turned Upside Down, The Lords of Humankind, Bondmen Made Free, Whigs and Hunters, The Age of Capital*—all lay in the future. We should perhaps have been able to discount against them all the same. In any event, we were certainly overlooking the achievement of Maurice Dobb, and above all neglecting the giant figure of Morris in the previous century. So there was real cause for Thompson's reflex of indignation. On the other hand, it was also true—as we subsequently pointed out—that *The Reasoner*, under the joint pen of Edward Thompson and John Saville themselves, had a few years earlier pronounced the very same verdict on British Marxism of which we were culpable: 'weak and shallow', in their words.[12] There was thus room for argument here, according to emphasis and context. I now think our emphasis was misplaced. But this did not in itself warrant a wholesale philippic against our analyses in the Review. 'The Peculiarities of the English' is in many ways a marvellous essay in its own right, as an exercise of historical imagination—as I can see today even more clearly than at the time. But it would not have suffered or been substantially altered one whit if it had shed its rebarbative armoury of invective against ourselves. It could have been written as a rejoinder in good temper and comradely respect, with every concrete thesis and pertinent criticism or rebuke intact. Instead, it adopted a tone from the outset that Thompson had never displayed even to enemies on the Right: where muffled by the scruples of his editors in 1965, now restored to its pristine pitch in *The Poverty of Theory* today.

This was a mistake, and an unnecessary one. It led inexorably to retaliation in kind. My own reply, 'Socialism and Pseudo-Empiricism',[13] was written with a useless violence that I regret. The extent to which it was a departure from the norms of socialist discourse which we set ourselves can be seen from the fact that to this day it remains an entirely

11. 'Origins of the Present Crisis', NLR 23, January-February 1964, p. 27.
12. *The Reasoner*, no. 1, July 1956, p. 5. John Saville reiterated much the same view in the first issue of *The New Reasoner*. 'Marxism has struck few sparks in the political and intellectual life of Britain since 1945': *The New Reasoner*, no. 1, Summer 1957, p. 78. Perhaps the original judgement was more that of Saville than of Thompson—a possibility I overlooked at the time.
13. NLR 35, January-February 1966.

isolated episode in the annals of NLR, which has never published anything like it again. But in mitigation, it must be said that we felt we were
fighting for our survival against an attempt to annihilate us by weight of
superior authority and systematic travesty. Anything short of a reply at
full tilt seemed inadequate to fend off this threat, as the Review was just
beginning to acquire a new shape and stability. Even so, although my
vocabulary exceeded Thompson's in harshness, it was also at the same
time more handsome: at no point did I deny the real merits of 'The
Peculiarities of the English', or fail to praise those cameos and arguments
which still today most command my admiration within it. The article
ended, in fact, by welcoming the historical debate that had thus been
initiated. Nevertheless, it contained one section that was bound to
aggravate the dispute fatally. Going beyond self-defence, I moved to
counter-attack Thompson's own political and editorial writing in *The
New Reasoner* and *New Left Review*. The purpose of doing so, as I
stressed at the time, was not to arraign Thompson for his past but to
explain why we had felt it necessary to make a break with the style of
commentary on British politics which his leading articles and 'letters to
readers' from 1958 to 1961 had—we thought—exemplified, and to
attempt instead a different type of socialist analysis. The substance of the
argument I made can be left to the arbitration of contemporary readers.
But there can be no doubt that the formulation of it was very wounding.
The blade of polemic, once unsheathed, all too often ends in carnage. For
that I must express my apology. The most constructive amends I can
make here will be to try to correct two charges that I levelled at
Thompson then, and which I regard as by and large misinterpretations
today. These concern, respectively, the allegations of 'nationalism' and
'moralism' that I pressed against Thompson in 1965. In each a genuine
divergence was at stake, as I think can be shown, but was misrepresented
by these terms. A reconstruction of the real differences may, it can be
hoped, help to resolve some of the unreal division that has separated the
two cohorts of the New Left since the mid-60s.

In his Preface to *The Poverty of Theory*, Thompson takes Tom Nairn to
task for the error of describing his politics as a 'populist socialism', and of
attributing to him a 'cultural nationalism'.[14] He presents Nairn's account

14. PT, p. iii.

as a hostile one, whereas in fact any reader who consults the passage in question will see that it is the opposite: written in praise of a 'progressive and generous cultural movement', imbued with a 'romanticism not infallibly Tory in its results', capable of a 'political contribution' that 'Marxism by itself could never furnish', that constitutes a 'critical hope' for England.[15] Beyond his misunderstanding of Nairn's purpose, however, Thompson proceeds to the firm declaration: 'I feel it necessary to make a plain repudiation. At no time have I ever held up a banner of "populist socialism". If there has been a banner, it has been that of socialist internationalism.'[16] On the first count little need be said here. It was I who launched the label of 'populism' in 1965. Prejudicial in the context in which I used the term, it is not inevitably so. In mellower mood, in fact, Thompson has on occasion invoked it himself. To see why, there is no better discussion than the balanced and sympathetic assessment of its changing meanings on the British Left by Raymond Williams, from whose conclusions I hazard the guess that neither Thompson, Tom Nairn nor I would now dissent in any significant respect.[17] The more important statement is the ensuing affirmative. Here it is necessary to be categorical. Thompson is absolutely entitled to claim, with the utmost force, the standard of socialist internationalism as his own. The record of solidarity that he cites—Yugoslavia, Bulgaria, Korea, Egypt, Cyprus, Algeria, Cuba, Vietnam, Chile—speaks for itself. Any suggestion of suspicion on this plane would be false and absurd.

There is, however, more than one valid type of internationalism. It is worth looking more closely at the particular complexion of Thompson's own form. The best starting-point for doing so is undoubtedly the collection of letters written by his brother, Frank Thompson, killed in the Bulgarian Resistance in 1944, which he jointly edited after the Second World War.[18] This memoir provides a moving insight into the biographical depth of his internationalist commitment. For his brother's correspondence, from the successive stations to which he was posted—Libya, Egypt, Syria, Persia, Sicily, Bulgaria—not only reveals an astonishing maturity, gaiety and courage. It also breathes in every line an

15. *The Break-Up of Britain*, London 1977, p. 304.
16. PT, p. iii.
17. 'Notes on British Marxism since the War', NLR 100, pp. 86-88.
18. T.J. Thompson and E.P. Thompson, eds., *There is a Spirit in Europe—A Memoir of Frank Thompson*, London 1947.

incomparable spirit of Communist internationalism. By the time of his execution by Bulgarian fascists at the age of 24, Frank Thompson studied or spoke some nine European languages—Russian, French, German, Italian, Serbo-Croat, Greek, Bulgarian, Czech and Polish. 'Frank lived and wrote as a European',[19] commented his brother after his death, and there can have been few soldiers in the Second World War, in any country, of whom this seems so impressively true. Edward Thompson followed his brother into the Communist Party, at seventeen, and into the war, at nineteen. We can be sure that this personal and political succession must have been decisive in his own life. The ideals expressed in Frank Thompson's letters were his immediate fraternal legacy. Fighting in the Italian campaign, and volunteer construction in Yugoslavia and Bulgaria after the war, sealed them in practice. The best description of the significance of this period for him is his own. It was 'an extraordinary formative moment in which it was possible to be deeply committed even to the point of life itself in support of a particular political struggle which was at the same time a popular struggle; that is, one didn't feel a sense of being isolated in any way from the peoples of Europe or the peoples of Britain.'[20]

The Second World War, 'a very delicate moment in human civilization',[21] thus provides in his own account the key to many of Thompson's later political attitudes. To understand its impact fully, it is necessary to explore exactly the meaning of that unity of a 'particular political struggle' with a 'popular struggle' which he reports. What do these two terms denote? We may take it that the first is the cause of Communism, the second of anti-fascism. Thompson is right to emphasize the *popular* nexus created by the fusion of the two in the countries where the Resistance was strongest (France, Italy, Norway, Slovakia, Yugoslavia, Albania, Bulgaria, Greece—not to speak of China, the Philippines or Vietnam in Asia). But there is another way of defining the same linkage that is historically more precise. From 1941 onwards, the Second World War permitted a unique fusion of *international* and *national* causes on the Left. The real meaning and power of the Resistance movements lay in this juncture. Unconditional devotion to the international goals of communism could be combined with intransigent leadership of the fight for

19. *There is a Spirit in Europe*, p. 20.
20. 'An Interview with E.P. Thompson', p. 10.
21. Ibid., p. 10.

national liberation from German occupation. Out of the unity of the two were born socialist revolutions in Yugoslavia and Albania, China and Vietnam, together with several quasi-revolutions elsewhere, notably in Czechoslovakia and Bulgaria. Nationalism and internationalism marched together across most of Europe and much of Asia in the military conflagration of the time. The harmony between them was not universal, of course. By definition, Germany was excluded from it. There the 'particular political struggle' could never become at the same time a 'popular struggle', because the people were mobilized in a national cause pitted against that of all others. The Third Reich was the one continental country which produced no significant mass Resistance and led to no growth—rather a catastrophic decline—in the Communist movement. Britain was also something of a special case. In the passage cited above, Thompson assimilates it to the rest of Europe. But in the memoir to his brother of 1947, he wrote more accurately: 'Few of us in Britain have understood the tragedy through which Europe has passed or the strength of the renaissance into which she is now entering. England is divided from Europe, not only by the channel, but by the experiences in which we have not shared'.[22] Not merely did Britain escape Nazi invasion: it was also the only European power to keep its huge colonial empire virtually intact throughout the war. The national struggle with Germany consequently preserved far more traditional overtones, remaining at a lower ideal-political threshold than elsewhere, in a conflict still linked in collective memory and association with earlier contests for imperial dominion against continental enemies, Habsburg, Bourbon or Napoleonic. The patriotism of paramountcy under threat was necessarily rather different from the nationalism of defeat and occupation. Nevertheless, the general coordinates held for the local communists here too. Internationalism and nationalism were non-contradictory in the common war effort.

For a short time the union between them lasted after the War, at least on the surface of events. At home, the election of a Labour government in 1945 created the atmosphere of a 'brief episode of optimistic socialist populism'.[23] Abroad, Thompson's work with a railway brigade in Bosnia (1947) expressed the communist dimension of the euphoric aftermath of victory—international solidarity directly in the service of national

22. *There is a Spirit in Europe*, p. 20.
23. *Warwick University Limited*, p. 162.

independence.[24] The moral-practical cast of this socialist internationalism has been a permanent characteristic of Thompson's outlook ever since, and perhaps of many others of his generation. By late 1947, however, the wartime idyll was over. With the onset of the Cold War, the Cominform was established by Stalin and Zhdanov to reassert a uniform subordination of the European Communist Parties, East or West, to the CPSU. A few months later it was appropriately in Yugoslavia that the principles of national liberation clashed irreconcilably with this ostensibly international process of *Gleichschaltung*. We do not know how Thompson reacted to the denunciation of Tito as a fascist by the Cominform:[25] but the strain for many party members in the West must have been very great. Yet the sharp 'left' turn of '48-'50 in the international communist movement did not lead to any full-scale return to earlier Comintern norms. The nominal autonomy of each party remained the same: the mandatory discipline of the Third International was replaced by mere 'sharing of information' in the Cominform. With the outbreak of the Korean War, the official line of the world communist movement swung massively back to exaltation of 'national' demands, as the CPSU strove to divide the Western bloc by fostering anti-American sentiments and struggles within it. At the 19th Party Congress in 1952, a year before his death, Stalin announced that the working-class movement must now everywhere 'pick up the national and democratic banner which the bourgeoisie had abandoned in the mire'. The hands of the European Communist Parties have remained, in one sense, compulsively clutching it to this day. In England, the early 50s were thus marked by an official simulacrum of the lost unities of the war. *The British Road to*

24. Accounts of the experience were collected under the title *The Railway—An Adventure in Construction* edited by Thompson, and published by the British-Yugoslav Association, London 1948. Among other contributors were Martin Eve, Peter Worsley and Francis Klingender. Thompson was Commandant of the British Brigade, and wrote the longest report. In this very early text, his characteristic emphases are already clear and strong. Describing the selfless spirit of volunteer work on the Samac-Sarajevo line, he wrote: 'It would be impossible to understand any of this story without accepting this change of values': p. 3. Further impressions of Yugoslavia and Bulgaria can be found in his article, 'Comments on a Peoples's Culture', *Our Time*, October 1947, which speaks of 'human nature itself being changed by human agency.'

25. A reaction that would be of especial interest since *The Railway*, with its epigraph from Tito and bi-national imprimatur, must have appeared only a few short months before the Cominform denunciation of the Yugoslav government in June 1948 as a 'terrorist regime'. Significantly, there was already no Russian contingent among the foreign brigades in Bosnia during the summer of 1947.

Socialism—sealed with Stalin's approval—was issued in 1951, stressing the particularity of English conditions and the positive role of Parliament. The CPGB, like its brother parties elsewhere, fought hard and well against the Korean War—a struggle in which Thompson was active. Conferences on *The American Threat to British Culture* were organized, less happily, in which Thompson also participated.[26] Nationalism and internationalism were welded together once more within the organizational system of Stalinism.

Yet below the surface, something had changed. By the mid 50s it was impossible for the more intelligent and independent minds in the British Party to harbour exactly the same views of the USSR as had been current during the War. Latent doubt and suspicion, in many cases perhaps not fully conscious, now often existed where complete confidence had prevailed before. It was precisely in reaction against 'Russian' methods and East European 'models' that Communists like these started to accentuate English resources and traditions. A genuine ambiguity was inscribed in this project from the start. For on the one hand their intention was effectively anti-Stalinist—an attempt to recover and assert democratic communist values and directions. On the other hand, a positive orientation towards the national past was assiduously promoted by the Stalinist officialdom of the party itself. In this one respect, there was a paradoxical 'fit' between the overt ideological interests of functionaries and freethinkers alike. Thompson's first major intellectual work germinated within it. Vigorously intervening against a blatant attempt by a US academic to confiscate William Morris for reaction, in an article for the party publication *Arena* in 1951, he was invited by the editor to write a longer piece on Morris, at a time when the latter (Jack Lindsay) was himself publishing articles claiming Coleridge as our national dialectician.[27] From the commission grew the great book that was published in 1955, recovering the figure of Morris as a revolutionary socialist radically incompatible with the orthodox ethos of Stalinism.

Thus when the break with the Communist Party came in 1956, the political and theoretical ground for it had already been to a considerable extent prepared. Nothing is more striking in Thompson's development

26. *Arena*, vol. II, no. 8, June-July 1951.
27. See E.P. Thompson, 'The Murder of William Morris', *Arena*, II, no. 7, April-May 1951; Jack Lindsay, 'Samuel Taylor Coleridge', *Arena*, II, nos. 6-7, February-March/April-May 1951; 'An Interview with E.P. Thompson', pp. 12, 14.

than the coherence and continuity of his thought, across his Communist and non-Communist phases—one he rightly points to with pride in the Postscript to *William Morris* twenty years later. The occasion for his rupture with the CPGB was the Soviet intervention in Hungary. Outside the Party, Thompson sought to fight a joint struggle with the Communist oppositions of that year throughout Europe. National causes—above all those of Poland and Hungary—could now be seen as genuinely at one with an international movement. *The New Reasoner* was the expression of that hope. Thompson's parting salute as a Communist to the readers of the Journal in 1959 signalled the end of this immediate perspective. The New Left, however, as it took shape at the same time, reconjugated something of the same political pattern in another arena. For the major focus of its activity was the Campaign for Nuclear Disarmament—a mass movement which simultaneously insisted on Britain's capacity to 'lead the world', as it was often put at the time, by setting a moral example of renunciation of atomic weapons to all other countries, and at the same time emphasized the universalist goals of international peace and solidarity with colonial peoples. The genealogy of CND as a type of political campaign was a peculiarly English one, very different from that of the postwar reconstruction brigades. But its internationalism too—at once generous and ingenuous—was strongly pragmatic and moral in cast. So long as it kept its momentum, CND recalled in the later 50s certain elements of the popular mobilization of the 40s. The relative congruity of the critical moments of Thompson's political formation is in these respects remarkable. Throughout, as we have seen, there was attraction rather than tension between its national and international poles. Practical political solidarity with the struggles of the oppressed abroad—classes or peoples, went together with intellectual and theoretical concentration on native traditions of dream and resistance at home.

It is important to remember the latter aspect as well. Thompson's *culture* up to the early 60s remained profoundly English. The absence of reference to the Marxism that emerged after the First World War on the continent is not surprising, since Lukács and Gramsci, let alone the Frankfurt School or later arrivals, were generally unknown in Britain at the time. More significant is the lack of interest in the classical tradition of revolutionary Marxism in the 20th century. Thompson's world before or after 1956 scarcely registers the existence of Lenin. Trotsky impinges not at all. In relaxed mood, Thompson frankly acknowledges this circumscription himself: 'This, if I am honest, is my self, my sensibility. Take Marx and Vico and a few European novelists away, and my most intimate pantheon would be a provincial tea-party: a gathering of the English and the Anglo-Irish. Talk of free-will and determinism, and I think first of Milton. Talk of man's inhumanity, I think of Swift. Talk of morality and revolution, and my mind is off with Wordsworth's Solitary. Talk of the problems of self-activity and creative labour in socialist society, and I am in an instant back with William Morris'.[28] It would not be just to call this declaration 'cultural nationalism', but it may readily be seen that in irascible mood—unfortunately not infrequent since the mid 60s—the same sensibility can become aggressively nationalist: *in culture*. The tones of the colloquium of '51, of some of the polemic with us in '65, of pronouncements on the EEC in 75, of parts of the anathema against Althusser, do stray towards such cultural nationalism—albeit momentarily and perhaps, as Thompson would see it, under foreign 'provocation'. The reaction is no more than skin-deep, usually in response to particular irritants. But it tells us something important—not demeaning—about the *type* of socialist internationalism Thompson has so long and so valiantly defended.

The conditions that formed the present *New Left Review* were very different from this history. They were colder. Untouched by the afterglow of the War, we never knew the popular élan of the 40s. It was the reactionary consolidation of the 50s that dominated our consciousness. That 'base period', as Raymond Williams has called it,[29] was marked throughout the West by Cold War mobilization at every institutional and ideological level. In Britain, its major idiom was glutinously chauvinist—reverent worship of Westminster, ubiquitous cult of constitutional moderation and common sense, ritualized exaltation of tradition and precedent. The 'left' variant of the political culture of the time descended from the maudlin social patriotism of Orwell: the 'right' variant from the anthems to the wisdom of gradualist 'experience' of thinkers like Oakeshott. The bulk of the working class was passive and integrated into the national 'consensus'—one of the great ideological themes of the decade. The UK appeared a stable bastion of the Free

28. PT, p. 109.
29. *Politics and Letters*, London 1979, p. 135.

World. The major threats to British capitalism came, not at home, but abroad: from the colonial revolts in successive theatres of the post-war empire—Kenya, Cyprus, Egypt, Guyana, Aden. In other words, the constellation of national and international forces operative on the British Left (as well as, most notably, the French) was completely transformed. Internationalism now required frontal rejection of national mystifications, at the most immediate political level. No socialist demonstrated more consistent solidarity with movements of colonial liberation in these years than Thompson. But as we have seen, the rise of the Campaign for Nuclear Disarmament at the same time fostered the hope of a renewed reconciliation of British national initiative with the universal cause of world peace, within a resurgent popular movement in England. We viewed the prospects of CND somewhat more sceptically. I have explained why elsewhere.[30] The campaign was a predominantly middle-class phenomenon, mass in numbers but not proletarian in weight. The ambiguity of the term 'popular' concealed the crucial sociological difference—one of the reasons for our distrust of populism. It was also unable to generate any historical or materialist understanding of the international conflict—the Cold War—against which its moral protest was directed. For to do so would have involved a complex assessment of the contradictions between imperialist and communist blocs, and within each of them, which was beyond the liberal categories it inherited from the tradition of radical humanitarian campaigns stretching back to the 19th century in England. Its failure at the turn of the 60s was inscribed in these limits of its horizon. The collapse of CND, which brought down with it the hopes of the New Left as a political movement, was rapidly followed by the crystallization of the prolonged crisis of British capitalism which we have been living ever since.

These coordinates determined the emergence of a type of internationalism in the NLR after 1963 quite distinct from that of its predecessors. Its relationship to English nationalism, of whatever stripe, was one of hostility rather than harmony. A fierce hatred of the reigning cultural conformism in Britain, decked out in every patriotic colour, inspired it from the start. We felt no inclination to delve into the native past for a more progressive or alternative tradition to counterpose to the official celebrations of English cultural empiricism and political

---

30. 'The Left in the Fifties', NLR 29, January-February 1965, pp. 10-13.

constitutionalism. For us, the central historical fact which such enter-prises always seemed designed to burke or minimize was the failure of British society to generate any mass socialist movement or significant revolutionary party in the 20th century—alone among major nations in Europe. This view was accompanied, however, by an undue simplifica-tion of assumptions about the general relationship of contemporary socialist culture to the past, and a characteristic underestimate of certain strengths and resources within English radical traditions. On the other hand, each generation has its own task to fulfil. Our dissatisfaction with what Thompson himself at one point calls 'a hostile national culture both smug and resistant to intellectuality and failing in self-confidence'[31] drove us outwards, to try and appropriate a wider cultural universe. The internationalism that resulted was a *theoretical* one. It was founded on the conviction that just as historical materialism was born in the mid-19th century from the confluence of at least three different national systems of thought—German philosophy, French politics and English economics—so it could only be expected to develop freely and fruitfully in the mid-20th century from an equal, or rather even greater, breaking of national barriers. In a word: we did not believe in Marxism in one country.

NLR set out from the mid-sixties onwards to introduce the major intel-lectual systems of continental socialism in the post-classical epoch into the culture of the British Left. Successive translations and presentations were made of the work of Lukács, Korsch, Gramsci, Adorno, Della Volpe, Colletti, Goldmann, Sartre, Althusser, Timpanaro and other thinkers—most of whom were effectively unknown in England at the time. We also, of course, sought to popularize the writings of Marx himself by creating a Pelican Library that was to include the first transla-tion of the *Grundrisse* and complete version of *Capital*. At the same time, this labour was not merely one of passive exposition and intermediation. The review also criticized, calmly and systematically, every one of the theoretical schools within 'Western Marxism', taking it for granted that it was the duty of an independent socialist journal to do so. Finally, and most fundamentally, NLR tried to utilize the acquisitions of a widened historical materialism to analyse its own society. Here the decisive influence was Gramsci, whose concepts were deployed by the Review in its explorations of English history and politics a decade before they

31. PT, p. 109.

became a vogue elsewhere. Thus internationalization of discourse did not lead to abstraction from national realities. On the contrary, it served—among other ends—to bring these more sharply and specifically into focus. For the framework of the resultant analyses of England was itself comparative and international. The crisis of the British bourgeois order was interpreted through the prism of unequal development within the capitalist world as a whole. The internationalism of inquiry at which NLR aimed in these years thus had two dimensions: it was cultural, in the sense of drawing on the theoretical resources of a wide range of Marxist work abroad, and it was political as a principle of causal explanation of the domestic society. Rather than national independence, global interdependence was the tacit starting-point for assessing the contemporary conjuncture in Britain. Hence not only the strongly (if not always accurately) comparative cast of the review's work on England itself, but also the serial studies of other societies—advanced capitalist, underdeveloped or communist—which formed one of the staple categories of NLR coverage at the same time. This combination was new on the British Left, and represented a gain.

Against it there was a loss. The popular register that comes from participation in a real mass movement was missing. There was no denial of the necessities of a moral-practical internationalism as well, but in the absence of any genuine socialist swell carrying them within British society, their impetus inevitably ebbed for a time. Although the surrounding argument is over-stated, Thompson is right to stress in *The Poverty of Theory* the critical lack of any real popular context for Marxist theoretical work in this period: 'the kind of experience of mass political activity, in which intellectuals have played a minority and a subordinate (sometimes overly subordinate) part alongside comrades with practical positions of leadership within their own communities and places of work—this kind of experience has largely passed [younger Marxists] by.'[32] On the other hand, that historical situation—so different from the 'experience of anti-fascist struggle, War and Resistance' of Thompson's own generation—demanded another sort of political stamina. This can be seen rather clearly if Thompson's attitude towards the international communist movement in these years is compared with our own. As we have seen, Thompson invested the most ardent hopes in the Communist

32. PT, p. 376.

oppositions that emerged after the 20th Party Congress of the CPSU. These held out for him the prospect of a return to the best values of the Resistance period, now fortified by a lucidly democratic anti-Stalinism. When the challenge of '56-'58 faded, however, and the major Communist parties across the world were 'normalized', his interest correspondingly waned. By 1960-1961, it is striking that the early *New Left Review* virtually ignored Communism as a world phenomenon altogether: in twelve issues under the old board, one article and one book-review comprised the total of its attention to one third of the world, and one half (at least) of the international labour movement. Thereafter, developments within the Communist bloc attracted Thompson's interest so little that, as we have noted above, he appears to have virtually forgotten the existence of the Sino-Soviet dispute when he came to write about Althusser's politics of the mid-60s. Disappointment seems to have led to disengagement, as if once the current of popular initiative as he knew or envisaged it ceased to flow, his own energies too were switched off.

Our position was in this respect a different one. Unlike Thompson, we had had few illusions in Stalinism. We took our earliest knowledge of the USSR from Isaac Deutscher, rather than Andrew Rothstein.[33] We viewed the East European turmoil of '56 with sympathy, but without finality. The Cuban Revolution of '59 appeared to us more important and hopeful for the future. Thereafter the Sino-Soviet conflict, the first stirrings of Italian polycentrism, the Cultural Revolution in China, the Cuban expeditions in Latin America and in Africa, the Czechoslovak Spring, the fall of Gomulka in Poland, the advent of Eurocommunism, the record of Brezhnevism in the USSR, all seemed worthy of the closest attention and analysis. Nor was this continuing concern with the complex futures of the Communist movements across the world a merely intellectual one. Members of NLR were active in the Cuban and Czech Solidarity Committees from their inception, in the organization of the International Tribunal on Vietnam. Above all, the Review took its part in the Vietnam Solidarity Campaign—the most important single political mobilization

---

33. It is worth recalling the official Communist treatment of Deutscher in the early 50s. For Rothstein, his biography of Stalin was 'outrageous' and 'grotesque', 'the latest version of the Trotskyite Encyclopaedia', a vicious compendium 'called upon to play its part in the propaganda for a third world war' (*sic*). See 'Stalin: A Novel Biography', *The Modern Quarterly*, vol. 5, no. 2, p. 122.

of the British Left in the 60s, which at its height commanded mass demonstrations equal to those of CND in numbers, and surpassing them in militancy. VSC inherited much, in methods and inspirers, from CND; but it also represented a break with the traditions of both CND and the Peace Movement of Thompson's Communist period. For it called, not for peace but for victory, not for neutralism but for socialism in Vietnam. Opposed as adventurist by the British Communist Party, belaboured by the police at the behest of the British Labour Party, whose government was a firm ally of American imperialism, it was the VSC which rallied a major popular force in the streets and whose themes answered to the realities of the war in Indochina. In *The Poverty of Theory*, the tone of Thompson's references to the movement of solidarity with the Vietnamese Revolution is faintly deprecating, as if it could be defined by its penumbral dishevelment or bravado. In fact, the international resistance to the American aggression in Vietnam was the most successful anti-imperialist campaign in the history of capitalism. Above all, in the United States itself it was a crucial determinant of the collapse of the American war effort: even its blindest forms contributed to the downfall of the Nixon regime, in their inducement of the siege paranoia of Watergate. There has been no more remarkable and effective achievement of socialist internationalism in our century than the struggle waged by the US Left, seconded by its counterparts in the 'allied' countries, in aid of Vietnamese Communism. *New Left Review* provided what arguably remains to this day the best synthesis of the historical meaning of this signal moment in Göran Therborn's text, written during the Tet Offensive, 'From Petrograd to Saigon'.[34]

Solidarity with the Vietnamese Revolution was a cause that pitted internationalism frontally against nationalism in the USA itself. It is no accident that in America the most consistent, as in England and France the most pioneering, impulse within the broader movement against the War in Vietnam came from sections of the Fourth International. For the tradition founded by Trotsky—whose originating act was rejection of 'socialism in one country'—has always incarnated the most intransigent refusal to compromise with national sentiments within the ranks of the labour movement in the developed world. Quite logically, that tradition became in time a central and unevadable pole of political reference within

34. NLR 48, March-April 1968, pp. 3-11.

NLR. Here we touch one of the most submerged yet substantial real differences of all between Thompson and ourselves. For in some ways nothing is more striking in his outlook since the revolt of 1956 than its blankness before the main alternative heritage of revolutionary Marxism since the October Revolution. For him, it is as if the history of the Communist movement had started in 1936. There is virtually no mention in his writings of any major event or debate within the Third International before that date. The few careless allusions to Trotskyism that can be found are uniformly trivial and pejorative, generally conforming to a common trope of this generation of intellectuals—the off-hand suggestion that Trotskyism is really no more than another version of Stalinism.[35] What this recurrent claim really represents is a refusal to turn back beyond the immediate biographical cycle of illusion and disillusion with the official Communism of the 30s and 40s, an involuntary rejection of any other history. A recent friendly critic of Thompson has made the essential point very well: the early New Left 'refused to come to grips with the Communist tradition in its original Leninist form and with the Left Opposition tradition that arose from it. It largely ignored the whole historical experience from 1914 to 1956. Significantly, it hardly discussed the Communist International.'[36] We have already noted the absence of Lenin from Thompson's reconstruction of Marxism after '56.

---

35. Typical in this respect is the original article on 'Socialist Humanism' in the first number of *The New Reasoner*, where he feared the danger 'if the fall of the Soviet bureaucracy is long delayed, of the Trotskyist ideology taking root, and if victorious, leading to similar distortions and confusions'. For 'Trotskyism is also a self-consistent ideology, being at root an "anti-Stalinism" (just as there were once anti-Popes)', with 'the same false conceptual framework and attitudes—the same economic behaviourism, cult of the elite, moral nihilism.' The intellectual weight of these assessments is suggested by the comment that follows. Complaining that for Trotskyism ' "workers' councils" and "soviets" must be imposed as the only orthodoxy,' he went on: 'But Britain teems with Soviets. We have a General Soviet of the TUC and trades soviets in every town: peace soviets and national soviets of women, elective parish, urban district and borough soviets'. *The New Reasoner*, no. 1, pp. 139, 140. His latest asides strike the same note. Some 'Marxists of a Trotskyist derivation' may eventually 'rescue themselves' from their own ideas—a redemption much needed, since 'Trotskyism reinforced the Stalinist intellectual system, by rehearsing the same legends and setting up identical blocks': PT, pp. 122-123, 325. The attempt to equate the legacies of Stalin and Trotsky is an old one. Trotsky dealt with it himself, in words of some contemporary relevance. Having rejected Stalinism, he noted, many people 'cannot help seeking indemnification in postulates of abstract morality for the disillusionment and abasement of ideals they have experienced'—'They have a ready answer: "Trotskyism is no better than Stalinism" '. *Their Morals and Ours*, New York 1942, p. 19.
36. Duncan Hallas, 'How Can We Move On?', *The Socialist Register 1976*, p. 7.

His repression of Trotsky is at first sight more surprising. For not only did Trotsky provide the first and most durable Marxist theory of Stalinism—the prime object of Thompson's concern after leaving the British Party. But he was also the first great Marxist *historian*. In fact, for a long time *The History of the Russian Revolution* remained unique in the literature of historical materialism. No other classical Marxist had so profound a sense of the changing tempers and creative capacities of the masses of working men and women, pushing at the foundations of an archaic social order 'from below'—while at the same time preeminently able to chart the complex shifts and clashes of organized political forces 'from above'. Yet this supreme example of a properly socialist historical imagination finds not the smallest echo in Thompson's work—typically not even in *The Poverty of Theory* itself, throughout its extended pursuit of the relations between history and politics. What are the reasons for so large a repression? They must surely be sought in the timing of Thompson's formation as a Communist. We have seen the overwhelming importance of the Second World War in his political memory and sensibility. It was precisely the ordinary terms of this conflict that Trotsky, at the end of his life, rejected—denouncing the outbreak of hostilities in 1939 as an inter-imperialist struggle comparable to 1914. This judgement was in my view a major political error[37]—for the working class had every reason to defend bourgeois democracy against fascism at an international as well as at a national level. The mistake was shared, of course, by the Comintern itself. The invasion of the USSR in 1941 transformed the character of the War. Stalinists and Trotskyists alike rallied to the defence of the Soviet workers' state—but with a difference: the former according unconditional primacy to the anti-fascist struggle in its own right within the camp of the capitalist Allies and occupied countries, typically under the leadership of bourgeois governments in place or in exile, the latter refusing any compromise with 'democratic imperialism'. After the War, the Fourth International never ceased to criticize the Communist Resistance movements for their policies of national union. It is in that historical divide, in which political right and wrong were inextricably mixed on either side, that Thompson's lack of any

---

37. See *Considerations on Western Marxism*, pp. 119-120. For a complex and balanced analysis of the Second World War by a Trotskyist who was active in the Resistance, see Ernest Mandel's recent discussion in *Revolutionary Marxism Today*, London 1979, pp. 162-170; for all its interest, however, it does not affect my judgement of Trotsky's position in 1939.

comprehension or acknowledgment of the Trotskyist tradition virtually certainly lies.

For our part, an encounter with the work of Trotsky was an inevitable process in the attempt to recover a coherent revolutionary Marxism after the political reflux of the early 60s. In our case, the formative influence of Isaac Deutscher was obviously of primary importance; the initial issue of the recast NLR in 1963 led with an essay by him on the divisions within International Communism, and the last text he published before his death in 1967, on the Middle East War, was an interview with NLR.[38] From the mid-60s onwards Ernest Mandel—the leading living spokesman of the Fourth International—was the most frequent external contributor to the Review, in which he debated the record of Trotsky with a member of the editorial committee itself, a former pupil of Lukács and participant in the Budapest Workers' Council, as well as with a loyal member of the British Communist Party—the first time such an exchange occurred anywhere in the world. Thereafter NLR never lost sight of the centrality of Trotsky's heritage, even while its own editors varied widely among themselves in their particular assessments of it, and none was ever uncritical of it. My own reservations I have set out elsewhere.[39] This engagement with the thought of Trotsky was, of course, by no means confined to *New Left Review*. In different ways, and with diverse interpretations, it has been a very general phenomenon among the younger generation of socialist militants in Britain in the past decade—far more so than the Althusserianism which preoccupies Thompson.

For our purposes here, the importance of this heritage lay in the standard and model of internationalism it embodied. Throughout his life, Trotsky was an unremitting adversary of every form of social patriotism or great-power chauvinism: no revolutionary ever preached or practised so long and so consistently proletarian internationalism, in his own politics. At the same time, no other socialist has had the same degree of insight into the culture and society of other nations besides his own as Trotsky displayed in his writings on Germany, France and England, as well as Russia. Finally, Trotsky was the first Marxist to found a historical account of the nature, and a political strategy for the future, of his own nation on a theory of its integration into the international imperialist

38. See NLR 23, January-February 1964, and 44, July-August 1967.
39. *Considerations on Western Marxism*, pp. 118-121.

order.[40] Political, cultural and theoretical, the dimensions of this internationalism overtop any before or since. It was not immune from failings or mistakes, some of them major ones. But its moral and intellectual grandeur has only grown with the passage of time, and the unfolding of other strands in the labour movement. So far, it is this tradition alone that has proved capable of an adult view of socialism on a *world* scale, as anyone who reads Mandel's recent *Revolutionary Marxism Today* may see for themselves. A natural and critical contact with it should have been a common element in the politics of the older and younger levies of the New Left. In fact, it was to prove a further dividing-line.

Yet that division is an increasingly unnecessary one. For the contrast between the two patterns of internationalism to be found in Thompson's work and our own was never an absolute one, and has become less so as the conjuncture has changed. Today, the actual positions associated with either are much more relative and mutable, on contemporary issues. Thompson and the local section of the Fourth International, for example, were united in stoutly opposing British entry into the European Economic Community: Tom Nairn and Raymond Williams, a socialist with a very similar political and generational background to that of Thompson, joined in advocating it. Within NLR, Nairn was to defend the emancipatory potential of popular national movements in Scotland and Wales—his plea for them from the left resting on bases much closer to the association between internationalism and nationalism of Thompson's formative years than to the polarization of the two characteristic of NLR's earlier writing on England. Meanwhile, such elementary duties of socialists across frontiers as the campaign for the release of Rudolf Bahro have brought us all together—Communists, Trotskyists, New Leftists, Labourists. There will never be, and there ought never to be, one single format of socialist internationalism. Here as elsewhere, variety of tenor and emphasis is not a drawback but an asset for the growth of a vital political culture of the Left. Thompson's identity and our own are unlikely ever to be confused, in their characteristic ways of trying to make sense of the mosaic of nations in which classes exist and the struggle for socialism develops. But need they still be counterposed?

40. See e.g. *Results and Prospects*, New York 1978, p. 108.

6

Utopias

The second misconstruction for which I was responsible in 1965 was the suggestion that Thompson's most distinctive political concerns could be reduced to the category of 'moralism'. I continue to think that much of the rhetoric of '58-'61 which I taxed with the term is among the weakest part of Thompson's writing—its increasingly desperate note a reflection of unnegotiated strains and difficulties in the New Left of the time. But in criticizing it, with whatever justice, I committed the serious mistake of failing to see the real force and originality of Thompson's engagement with the issues of communist morality proper in his major work. The proving-ground here was *William Morris*. My recollection is that, strangely, this book never acquired the same centrality or currency within the New Left—at least its youngest recruits—as Williams's *Culture and Society* or *The Long Revolution*, or even Hoggart's *Uses of Literacy*. Looking back, this seems incomprehensible. Probably, however, the accidents of dating and of idiom had something to do with their different fortunes. *William Morris* was published in 1955, two years before the existence of either *The New Reasoner* or *Universities and Left Review*, and was written in a more militant and Communist vocabulary than was to be usual in the New Left—whereas Williams's and Hoggart's work coincided exactly with its emergence and corresponded more closely to its language. At all events, whatever their respective receptions in 1958-1960, there is no doubt that the cadet group which remodelled

NLR in 1964-1965 entirely failed to register the significance of Thompson's first major book. This can be seen most obviously in its denial of any important Marxist past in England—a wilful way of over-looking Morris, whose genius Thompson had declared to be 'peculiarly English';[1] but most essentially in its insensitivity to the major claim for Morris's greatness entered by Thompson—his 'moral realism': not only the 'practical moral example of his life' and the 'profound moral insight of his political and artistic writings', but 'the appeal to the moral consciousness as a vital agency of social change'.[2] This claim is convincingly substantiated by Thompson's study. Today its qualities have probably achieved duly wide acknowledgment for the first time, with the reissue of the book in its revised edition. The *Postscript* with which it now ends, surveying the literature on Morris in the intervening twenty years, must be accounted one of Thompson's most important political and theoretical statements in its own right. It reintroduces Morris directly into the quick of contemporary socialist debate by laying special stress on the nature and stature of his utopianism. In reparation for past neglect, let me make some observations on the Morris newly present—we may hope now definitively—in this revised edition.

Thompson's argument in his *Postscript* can be resumed as follows. The original version of his book was concerned at once to show the extraordinary originality of Morris's moral and political imagination and to reclaim him for revolutionary Marxism. In doing so, it tacitly suggested that there was no significant contradiction or even tension between these two aims. Today, however, this presumption of innocent unity can no longer be sustained. Morris had developed a profound critique of capitalism out of his own Romantic background, before his discovery of Marx's thought, and that critique continued to inform his socialist writing after he had learnt from Marxism—yielding a moral vision of communism that was to be critically lacking in the orthodox Marxist tradition, to its detriment. Thus 'it is more important to understand him as a (transformed) Romantic than as a (conforming) Marxist'.[3] Indeed 'his importance within the Marxist tradition may be seen, today, less in the fact of his adhesion to it than in the Marxist "absences" or failures to meet that adhesion half-way. Morris's

1. WM, p. 728.
2. WM, pp. 717, 721.
3. WM, p. 786.

"conversion" to Marxism offered a juncture which Marxism failed to reciprocate'.[4] To establish these points, Thompson turns to the work of two French scholars—Paul Meier, a Communist, and Miguel Abensour, a libertarian. While conceding that Meier's massive study *William Morris—the Marxist Dreamer* is 'weighty' and (up to a point) 'helpful', he reproaches it with assimilating Morris 'curtly' within 'a myth of Marxist orthodoxy', and thereby producing an end-result that is 'not only repressive' but also 'distancing and boring'.[5] Abensour's account, by contrast, can be unequivocally welcomed. It proposes a new reading of *News From Nowhere* which rehabilitates its utopianism as a break from the tradition of diagrammatic model-building of future societies towards a freer heuristic reverie distinguished by 'its *open*, speculative quality, and its *detachment* of the imagination from the demands of conceptual precision'.[6] This enterprise enabled Morris to enter 'Utopia's proper and new-found space: *the education of desire*'—the kindling of aspiration towards a better life through an 'uninterrupted interrogation' of present values that is also a 'criticism of all that we understand by "politics"'.[7] Commending these formulations of Abensour, Thompson proceeds: 'What may be involved, in "the case of Morris", is the whole problem of the subordination of the imaginative utopian faculties within the later Marxist tradition: its lack of a moral self-consciousness or even a vocabulary of desire, its inability to project any images of the future, or even its tendency to fall back in lieu of these upon the Utilitarian's earthly paradise—the maximization of economic growth'.[8] Morris's utopian communism, independently derived from the Romantic tradition, had a generosity and confidence of vision missing from the mainstream of historical materialism, then or later—whose very definition as a science has restricted its human range. For the goal of communism itself is 'unobtainable without the prior education of desire or "need". And science cannot tell us what to desire or how to desire. Morris saw it as a task of Socialists (his own first task) to help people find out their wants, to encourage them to want more, to challenge them to want differently, and to envisage a society of the future in which people, freed at last of

4. WM, p. 786.
5. WM, pp. 780, 802.
6. WM, p. 790.
7. WM, p. 791.
8. WM, p. 792.

necessity, might choose between different wants.'[9] Thompson then moves to the decisive conclusion of his essay: 'It should now be clear that there is a sense in which Morris, as a Utopian and a moralist, can never be assimilated to Marxism, not because of any contradiction of purposes, but because one may not assimilate desire to knowledge, and because the attempt to do so is to confuse two different operative principles of culture. So that I've phrased the problem wrongly, and Marxism requires less a re-ordering of its parts than a sense of humility before those parts of culture which it can never order.'[10] The closing injunction of the passage adjures Marxism to 'close down one counter in its universal pharmacy, and cease dispensing potions of analysis to cure the maladies of desire'.[11]

The seduction of this rich and meditative postscript is a powerful one. Its clauses, however, need to be discriminated from one another, for a proper assessment of its argument. The central claim that Morris's utopianism represents a feat of moral imagination without equivalent in the work of Marx, ignored without reason by Engels, and abandoned without sequel or echo in much later Marxism, is surely right. Morris's thought remained in this sense an isolated peak within socialist literature for at least half a century after his death. Today, too, Thompson is entirely justified in summoning historical materialism again to take full and self-critical measure of Morris's greatness. However, his ulterior theorization of the reasons why Marxism as a whole long failed to take up the legacy of Morris cannot be so easily accepted. The former, he maintains, pertains—or at least pretends—to 'knowledge', the latter to 'desire'. These are 'two different operative principles of culture' which may not be assimilated to each other. Spelling out the distinction, he writes: 'The motions of desire may be legible in the text of necessity, and may then become subject to rational explanation and criticism. But such criticism can scarcely touch these motions at their source.'[12] What is wrong with this account? Essentially that it substitutes an *ontological* for a *historical* explanation of the record of relations between Morris and Marxism.

9. WM, p. 806.
10. WM, p. 807.
11. WM, p. 807.
12. WM, p. 807.

This can be seen very clearly if we stop to examine for a moment the key term in it. The pivot of Thompson's reinterpretation in the *Postscript* is the notion of 'desire'. It is left quite undefined in the text. But the authority for its use is signalled without ambiguity: Abensour. What does the latter intend by it? All we are given is as follows. For Abensour, the role of utopian thought is 'to teach desire to desire, to desire better, to desire more, and above all to desire in a different way'.[13] What way? What does it mean to 'teach desire to desire'? The cloudy tautology should be adequate warning. What has insinuated itself in Thompson's blameless text here is a fashionable philosophy of Parisian irrationalism. The catchword of Desire has, in fact, been one of the slogans of the subjectivist *Schwärmerei* that followed disillusionment with the social revolt of 1968—celebrated in such writings as Jean-Paul Dollé's *Désir et Révolution* and Deleuze and Guattari's *Anti-Oedipe*, the expression of a dejected post-lapsarian anarchism. Intellectually, the category operates as a licence for the exercise of any fantasy freed from the responsibility of cognitive controls. A passage from Abensour cited by Thompson exalts 'the desire to make a breakthrough, to risk an adventure, or an experience, in the fullest sense of the word, which allows one to glimpse, to see or even to think what a theoretical text could never, by its very nature, allow us to think, enclosed as it is within the limits of a clear and observable meaning'[14]—a candid invitation to obscurantism. Politically, the notion of desire here can lead with the greatest facility to hoary superstition and reaction. Thus Abensour himself has recently ushered forward a volume in which his co-thinkers Clastres and Lefort propound the view that the origin of the State in primitive societies lies in the masochistic 'desire' to be dominated of the oppressed classes

13. WM, p. 791.
14. WM, p. 791.
15. See Abensour's edition of Etienne de La Boétie's *Discours sur la servitude volontaire*, Paris 1976, with its 'Présentation—les leçons de la servitude et leur destin' by Miguel Abensour and Marcel Gauchet, and its two successive afterwords by Pierre Clastres and Claude Lefort. For Clastres, 'societies with a State' are founded on 'the desire for submission'—'there is no feasible desire for power without the correlative desire for submission' (p. 239 ff). In Lefort's companion meditations, 'the desire of servitude' divined by La Boétie springs from 'the charm of the Name of One' in a secret yearning for uniformity as 'social narcissism', realized through 'the desire of each, whatever their hierarchical position, to identify with the tyrant by becoming master of another'—'such is the chain of identification that the lowest of slaves still wishes himself a god' (pp. 273-274, 301).

themselves.[15] Such elucubrations are light-years away from Thompson. But their possibility is inscribed in the metaphysical vacancy of the term itself—which can legitimate the desire for death and destruction, just as much as the desire for life and liberty, as its origins in Nietzsche make plain. Neither Marxism nor socialism have anything to gain from traffic with it, unless it is given what in this irrationalism it is so expressly constructed to refuse—a clear and observable meaning.

Thompson does not furnish one in his *Postscript*. Unaware of the background of his borrowing, he doubtless saw no pressing reason to do so, and need not be unduly faulted for it. However, it cannot be denied that he also takes over the *opposition* between desire and knowledge typical of this vogue and seeks to construe the reception of Morris through it. In doing so, he concedes that 'the motions of desire may be legible in the text of necessity, and may then become subject to rational explanation and criticism'—yet immediately goes on: 'But such criticism can scarcely touch these motions at their source'. It is not entirely clear what this phrase means, but taken literally it is certainly untenable: are we to say that the sources of cruelty, for example, are beyond criticism? A contradictory and more satisfactory address to the same question can be found in earlier remarks, where he writes: 'The "education of desire" is not beyond the criticism of sense and of feeling, although the procedures of criticism must be closer to those of creative literature than those of political theory. There are disciplined and undisciplined ways of "dreaming", but the discipline is of the imagination and not of science. It remains to be shown that Morris's utopian thought survives this criticism, as well as the criticism of ninety rather sombre years. I have not changed my view that it does.'[16] The best way of responding to this is to take up the challenge and see whether rational explanation cannot touch some of the sources of Morris's utopianism, and rational criticism indicate some of its limits, in ways not already available in Thompson's magisterial study.

The first point to be made is that although the new *Postscript* lays such central emphasis on the *utopian* vision of Morris, neither it nor the book itself really asks what were the historical conditions of this particular utopianism—what made it possible? Yet when an achievement is as rare as Morris's in this respect proved to be, it is surely of especial interest to

16. WM, p. 793.

inquire into the circumstances that enabled it. Why was it so unlike any of the numerous utopias before it? Why was it followed by so few utopias of any sort after it? Part of the answer to the first question, of course, lies in the juncture of Romanticism and Marxism in Morris's thought, which Thompson's study in general traces so admirably. But this intellectual fusion occurred in the development of a thinker with a material life-situation of an unusual sort. Many socialist theorists of the 19th century came from well-off families—some of them ruined or reduced by subsequent vicissitudes (Saint-Simon, Fourier), others rising in prosperity in later life (Owen, Engels). None, however, enjoyed quite the position of Morris. Exact assessments of his father's fortune are lacking. But on MacKail's evidence, he may have been among the 250 richest men in England.[17] At the age of 21, his son inherited an income of about £20,000 a year in current values. Beyond this, of course, the Morris Firm was to become a highly successful enterprise in its own right: at his death Morris left a personal estate, setting aside real property, worth about one million pounds at today's prices.[18] It seems likely that this wealth was one material substratum of the sensuous ease and freedom of Morris's capacity to visualize the lineaments of a society of abundance beyond capitalism. Morris himself was moral realist enough to be aware of the possibility of this connection. In *The Society of the Future*, he wrote: 'I daresay that you will find some of my visions strange enough. One reason which will make some of you think them strange is a sad and shameful one. I have always belonged to the well-to-do classes and was born into luxury, so that necessarily I ask much more of the future than many of you do.'[19] Few major socialists have been more exempt from the deforming pressures of scarcity in their own lives and imaginations. The contrast with Marx is striking. In itself, of course, mere prosperity prompted nothing. It was its combination with Morris's other and incomparably greater fortune that was significant for the shape of Morris's utopianism. For Morris was also a practising artist of the highest gifts, for whom ordinary work was daily creation. Professionally, he was thus delivered from drudgery too. The contrast with Engels, also if more modestly well-off, is equally striking.

17. See *The Life of William Morris*, London 1899, vol. I, p. 14, in the light of W.D. Rubinstein, 'The Victorian Middle Classes: Wealth, Occupation and Geography,' *Economic History Review* XXX, November 1977.
18. Probate value of £55,000 in 1896, adjusted by *Economist* index.
19. 'The Society of the Future', in May Morris, ed., *William Morris, Artist, Writer, Socialist*, Oxford 1936, vol. II, p. 455.

Moreover, the major fields of Morris's practice were plastic arts, which are themselves distinctive within the forms of aesthetic composition for eluding the division between mental and manual labour. Yet at the same time, he was also a poet and a writer. Thus one might say that in his figurations of the future, Morris was able to draw on unique resources in his *present*, which brought him tangibly nearer to the conditions he imagined than any of his communist contemporaries: secure wealth, creative work, polymathic skills. These were some of the material roots of the moral range of his dreams, at once in their liberty and their limits. For if we look at the Utopia of *News from Nowhere* itself—his fullest representation of a communist society—these formative conditions are everywhere active principles of its design.

In his *Postscript* Thompson remarks, as we have seen, that Utopian thought 'is not beyond the criticism of sense and feeling, although the procedures must be closer to those of creative literature than those of political theory'.[20] This prescription, in many ways an attractive one, recalls a tendency in *The Poverty of Theory* to link 'values' with 'feelings' as against 'ideas'. Marx, it will be remembered, was there censured for an undue rationalism, insensitive to that 'half of culture' which 'may be described as affective and moral consciousness'.[21] Now if the general emphasis of Thompson's corrective can well be accepted, his formulations of it subtly err in the opposite direction. For values are not only sentiments, they are also beliefs. Moral awareness is not to be simply elided with affective sensation: it is always a matter of intellectual conviction as well. Without principles, passions have no ethical bearing. Values normally and necessarily rest on a delicate *equilibrium* of 'ideas' and 'feelings'. Any unilateral extrapolation of them from one sphere or the other risks deformation of their nature. The practical results can be seen in such emblematic contrasts as the famous quarrel between Russell and Lawrence: a brittle and over-cerebral rationalism at loggerheads with a thickened and truculent instinctualism. The relevance of these reflections to Thompson's treatment of Morris is this. The depreciation of 'political theory' as a valid guide to criticism of utopian thought, and laudatory description of the latter as a refusal of its 'knowledge', seem to permit too causal an attitude towards precise evaluation of *News from Nowhere*.

20. WM, p. 793.
21. PT, p. 363.

Thompson's treatment of Meier's work is symptomatic here. His argument that Meier on occasion exaggerates the degree of direct correspondence and derivation between themes in Morris and propositions in Marx or Engels is in itself perfectly fair. Meier does indeed tend to overstate the philological connection between the two bodies of thought. But this is only one, and far from the most important, feature of his long work. When Thompson proceeds to assert that Meier 'curtly assimilates Morris within a myth of Marxist orthodoxy', he goes seriously astray. For one thing, a study of some 600 pages can scarcely—whatever else it may be deemed—be called 'curt'. In point of fact, Meier's major enterprise, a meticulous and sensitive *critical* reading of *News from Nowhere*, is hardly registered by Thompson at all. Yet it compares impressively with his own remarks on *News from Nowhere*, a work which is allocated just six pages out of 800 in *William Morris—from Romantic to Revolutionary*, rather less space than that given to such verse romances as *The Defence of Guinevere*: treatment that might well be termed cursory. Nor is this a mere quantitative quibble. The few paragraphs Thompson devotes to *News from Nowhere* do not contain any real critical probing of it at all. They content themselves with suggesting that if 'one thing is lacking', namely 'an eager intellectual life' in its vision of the future, Morris himself 'knew life would not be exactly like this in any real society'.[22] By contrast, Meier examines with the greatest delicacy and detail every narrative episode and thematic element in *News from Nowhere*, in a remarkable feat of sustained intelligence and interpretation. The results, far from being 'boring and distancing' as Thompson would let his readers believe, are fascinating and illuminating. They do not amount to a crude annexation of Morris to Marxism, but rather to a persuasive sounding of the differences as well as the central congruities between the two. Pointing out that *News from Nowhere* is the first utopia to be written that possesses both a real geography—England, the Thames Valley—and a retrospective history—going back to the 'great change' of power in 1952-1954, Meier shows the care with which Morris constructed his image of the future along lines in keeping with the Marxist theory of the transition to a classless society in two stages—socialism ('from each according to their abilities') and communism ('to each according to their needs'). The material abundance of the world William Guest traverses is

22. WM, p. 697.

founded on the facilities of an advanced technology that has abolished all industrial drudgery, leaving only creative work to be performed. State, law and money have withered away, together with social divisions and national boundaries. The division between town and country has largely disappeared. Spontaneous self-regulation by a common morality has replaced every form of administrative coercion. A joyful emancipation and equality form the very texture of social relationships. So far, Morris's Utopia appears to approximate closely to the scenarios of Marx or Engels. But at the same time, a whole series of features distinguish it from views that could either factually or hypothetically be ascribed to the founders of historical materialism themselves. Meier scrupulously notes these, with an admirable tact and respect. In the aureate atmosphere of Morris's future, where 'all work done with pleasure and worthy of praise produces art',[23] there is a general revival of craft labour in every area of social life. Technology and energy exist, but are confined off-stage to repetitive or disagreeable tasks. Economically, the forces of production have ceased to advance. Culturally, science has become a marginal pursuit, yielding no new major discoveries or inventions. Education has been dismantled, leaving children to learn from life rather than schools or books. Knowledge of or interest in the past has widely dwindled. Literary forms have contracted: the novel is vanishing. Politics, too, have disappeared—small motes are enough to deal with sporadic local issues. Marriage is no longer a legal contract, but the position of women is semi-domestic: their roles, freely chosen, are predominantly housework and motherhood. Population, on the other hand, is incongruously stable. Travel, despite the absence of frontiers, appears minimal. The 22nd century is an 'epoch of repose'.

Now it would be possible to compare, point by point, the assumptions and attitudes implicit in this series of projections with pronouncements by Marx or Engels. This would not be a barren or uninteresting exercise. Certain conclusions would emerge of some salience. Raymond Williams has recently criticized Morris's utopianism for attaching 'the notion of social simplicity' to communism—arguing that in fact 'the break towards socialism can only be towards an unimaginably greater complexity'.[24] This fundamental observation—as 'theoretical' as one could wish—applies in good measure to Marx and Engels, and for that matter Lenin,

23. *Art and Labour*, London 1884, p. 116.
24. *Politics and Letters*, pp. 128-129.

too. The evaporation of politics in a classless society, for example, is a premise common to all four thinkers inherited from Saint-Simon—whose illusory axiom that the 'government of men' would one day be entirely replaced by the 'administration of things' was to have harmful consequences of a very material sort in Bolshevik practice after the October Revolution. But there is no doubt that the impulse towards simplification went much further in Morris than it would have done in Marx or Engels. *News from Nowhere* describes a society in which the division of labour has been surmounted by regression behind the range of potential occupations in capitalist society rather than beyond them, and even then only for one sex. In fact, the discrimination of women is less than it might seem at first sight, since men too are predominantly assigned manual roles in a world which celebrates an essentially similar physical dexterity in homes, on the roads or in the fields. Unseen, machinery and technology effortlessly support this universe. This combination, a collective transvaluation of Morris's personal life-situation, would have been unthinkable for Marx. Not merely because he would have been unlikely to pass over so lightly the problems of economic allocation even amidst abundance, but also because by vocation and conviction alike he would have accorded a far higher place to intellectual labour in any communist society of the future. Morris's vision is effectively an *inversion* of the present—manual labour, now the last species of social exertion, becomes the first, while mental, which today occupies first rank, will be tomorrow demoted to the last: hence the summary dispatch of science, education, fiction, history or other intellectual pursuits. For Marx, on the contrary, 'knowledge' was itself a fundamental and illimitable human 'desire'. Science, far from being sequestered in a few excentric rural retreats, would pervade all economic life, providing the normal framework of everyday production. Manual and mental labour would exchange and coalesce at progressively higher levels of integration, in rhythm with moving forces of production. Creative work would not necessarily be carefree pleasure. Marx had another, less sensuous paradigm than handicrafts in mind when he thought of unalienated labour. Rebuking Fourier for the notion that such work would be like 'play', which he scorned as the dream of 'a naive shopgirl', he wrote: 'Really free work, such as composing, is at the same time the most grimly serious, the most intense exertion'.[25] The image of the

25. *Grundrisse*, p. 611 (translation modified)

artist here is closer to that of Beethoven or Flaubert than—say—Blake or Chaucer, admired by Morris. Since Marx ventured little on the subject of women, it is difficult to know how he would have envisaged their position in communism, but it is possible that he would not have diverged very greatly from Morris's version of it. Engels, on the other hand, had much more decided views on the liberation of women, and would never have countenanced a redomesticated future for them, any more than Lenin. All these differences are well worth reflection. Not all of them are exclusive oppositions. There is no reason to think, for example, that the practice of art could ever be reduced to a single existential standard, across or even within its different forms—Morris's theory of its springs, deriving from Ruskin, is plainly too narrow: a much greater variety of aesthetic production, encompassing and surpassing both Morris's and Marx's ideals, seems a more credible horizon for an emancipated society.

But the really important conclusion to be drawn from *News from Nowhere* does not lie at the level of any of these individual comparisons, often inequitable as Morris committed himself so boldly where Marx or Engels were so reticent. It touches the contours of Morris's Utopia as a whole. For what his projection of the future generally involves is a consistent repression of the history of capitalism. Morris's rejection of the previous four hundred years of European civilization was, in fact, virtually absolute.[26] This is the common meaning of all the particular limitations of *News from Nowhere*. Culturally, he accepted little after the mediaeval period. The Renaissance, the Reformation and the Enlightenment he disliked equally: the art or science they produced signified little or nothing to him. The radicalism of this perspective sets him apart even within the Romantic tradition he shared, whose real revulsion was from the Industrial Revolution. The majority of the early Romantics were by no means uniformly hostile to the pre-industrial epochs of early modern history: it was they, indeed, who universalized Shakespeare and introduced the 19th century cult of the Renaissance. In some ways, the very intransigence of Morris's retrospection brought him closer to socialism—in particular his movement beyond a conventional mediaevalism to an ideal anchorage prior to the advent of feudal society itself, in the clan equality of Viking Iceland, an enthusiasm he shared with Engels. But in other ways, it set systematic limits to the type of communism he could

26. See Meier's comment, *William Morris—The Marxist Dreamer*, London 1978, p. 549.

imagine. Technology, science, schools, novels, history, travel, feminism were each of them products of an entire cycle of bourgeois civilization eradicated from his range of sympathy. Hence the kind of censorship under which they fall—a marginalization or suppression—in *News from Nowhere*.

We can now see why Thompson's suggestion that Morris's 'independent derivation of Communism out of the logic of the Romantic tradition'[27] yielded a moral-political Utopianism in some sense beyond the reach of Marxism, is wrong. For historical materialism at its strongest has always been defined by its *supersession* of the antithesis between Romanticism and Utilitarianism which *News from Nowhere*, for all its splendour, reiterates. The immediate prompting for its composition, as is well known, was the recent success of Bellamy's *Looking Backward*—a crassly neo-Benthamite utopia of mechanized industrial regimentation. Furiously rejecting this 'cockney paradise' as he called it, Morris produced a kind of craftsman's paradise. There can be no comparison between the political or literary quality of the two. But the tourniquet of their opposition is a very old one. Marx wrote in the *Grundrisse*: 'It is as ridiculous to yearn for a return to an original fullness as it is to believe that with this present emptiness history has come to a standstill. The bourgeois viewpoint has never advanced beyond this antithesis between itself and the romantic viewpoint and therefore the latter will accompany it as its legitimate antithesis up to its blessed end.'[28] This sense of the dialectical complementarity of Utilitarianism and Romanticism is what distinguishes classical Marxism from the many attempts by socialists at one time or another to construct an opposition to capitalism from either standpoint: denunciation of its irrationality or inhumanity alone. For each is capable of either progressive or reactionary 'derivations'—Mill or Zola can be set against Carlyle or Barrès, just as much as Shelley or Ruskin can be set against Ure or Spencer.[29] There is no one 'logic' of either tradition, each of which has proved capable of a rainbow of political metamorphoses. The duty of socialists today is not to pit one against the other yet again, but to set both intellectually in their changing historical settings and to prepare practically the conditions for the long-awaited blessing of their mutual end.

27. WM, p. 802.
28. *Grundrisse*, p. 162.
29. See the excellent discussion in Gareth Stedman Jones, 'The Marxism of the Early Lukács', in *Western Marxism—A Critical Reader*, pp. 23-24.

Marx was able to envisage such an eventual terminus because he had the majestic legacy of Hegel behind him. It was from within the categories and procedures of classical German philosophy that he could pose the possibility, not merely of a bond between, but of a synthesis beyond either of two chief cultural antagonists of his own day. This sense is lacking in the paired English thinkers to whom Thompson has above all turned for a native revolutionary inheritance—Blake and Morris: each of whom had an acute feel for dialectical opposition, but much less for surpassal or synthesis. On the other hand, the very Hegelian background that was formative of Marx was also one that precisely inhibited—even tabooed—long-term speculation about the future: *The Philosophy of History* closes irrevocably in the plenitude of the present. It is not surprising that Marx or Engels never sought to explore the shape of a communist society. Such efforts went against the grain of their whole outlook, fortified further in its aversion to utopias by the socialism they had encountered in their youth. The field they left open was entered, to his great honour and our great debt, by William Morris. None of the valid criticisms that can and must be made of *News from Nowhere* detract from the daring of his enterprise. The work of the founders of historical materialism has no equal to it, and in that sense Thompson is entirely right to insist on the *autonomy* of the value of Morris's Utopianism. Where he is wrong is in suggesting that this Utopianism is also beyond the jurisdiction of Marxist theory or materialist knowledge. In fact, as we have seen, the immense parenthesis at the centre of Morris's dream of the future, that folds away half a millenium of human development, is eminently subject to a properly Marxist criticism. Morris himself, in his modesty, would have been the last to claim immunity from it in his own time. 'Up at the League,' begins *News from Nowhere*, 'there had been a brisk conversational discussion as to what would happen on the Morrow of the Revolution'—'six persons present and consequently six sections of the party represented':[30] the journey into the imagination that follows is, from the outset, the conjecture of just one of them.

What was the subsequent fortune of Morris's Utopianism? Thompson

---

30. *News from Nowhere*, in A.L. Morton, ed., *Three Works by William Morris*, London 1977, p. 101. John Goode, in his otherwise illuminating essay on Morris, reads this passage too solemnly, I think, as an invocation of 'the destructive individualism which the story escapes from': 'William Morris and the Dream of Revolution', in John Lucas, ed., *Literature and Politics in the Nineteenth Century*, London 1971, p. 275. The tone is rather humorously self-ironic.

presents it as one of implacable neglect by 'a Marxism which could not reciprocate or live without disdain alongside Morris'. The actual history has been somewhat more complex than this, as can be seen from the fact that it was a sequence of Communists—Page Arnot in the 30s, Thompson in the 50s, Meier in the 70s—who have been primarily responsible for recovering Morris as a revolutionary thinker and reinstating his work in a common socialist culture. The lapse of centrality which these terms imply was a real one. But its explanation is to be found less in the moral deficiencies of Marxism than in the intellectual form and historical timing of Morris's work. *News from Nowhere* and its companion essays were written after the advent of Marx, and in the light of his theory, although they did not coincide with it; and before the expansion of the Second International or the victory of the Russian Revolution. The very insignificance of socialism as a political force in England, at a time when no mass labour movement existed to pose urgent day-to-day problems of mobilization, encouraged a tendency to futurism, of which Morris was the greatest but not the only exponent. The growth of organized working-class parties before the First World War everywhere saw a decline of this meditative tradition, as immediate tactical issues increasingly came to the fore. A decade later, the outbreak of the October Revolution transformed the whole landscape of socialist thought. From now on, the construction of a communist society was no longer a matter of speculative theory, but of experimental practice—or so it seemed, as the doctrines of Socialism in One Country, in contravention of classical Marxism, were proclaimed and generally accepted. The deep longing for another human order which had found expression in the utopias of the 19th century was now fastened to the—often scarcely less imaginary—society in the USSR. The new Soviet State was real enough, of course. But its reality was quite different from anything that could have furnished material for a genuine utopia in the West: the sombre process of primitive socialist accumulation, amidst barbarity and shortage, a ruthless labour discipline and countless casualties. The break-neck drive towards industrialization, which in the end saved Russia and Europe from Nazism, was presented as if it were a rapture of social harmony and felicity. Utilitarian in its means and goals, the official utopianism of the Five Year Plans was Romantic in its iconography and rhetoric, hailing from every loud-speaker the creative pleasure of the shock-worker in his labour. The spell of these images lasted long: down even to the first edition of *William Morris*.[31] So long as they did, Morris's utopianism was necessarily at a discount because of its eclipse of technology and science: a world where the forces of production were stationary was hard to relate to a society dominated by the objective of all-out economic growth.

In the West, the same difficulty was in a direct sense not so acute, although even there Morris's foreshortening of history was a major obstacle to the later reception of his work, as scientific and industrial problems multiplied. Perhaps more important, however, was the form of his work. For Thompson, the term 'system' is nearly always pejorative. In *The Poverty of Theory* it signifies intellectual closure, cramp, repression, unreason. The dangers to which Thompson points are indisputable, within Marxist or any other form of social or philosophical inquiry. But he is at the same time insufficiently aware of the strengths of systematic, as against scattered or piecemeal, modes of thought. They are twofold. Firstly, a genuine theoretical system demands a certain degree of overt connection and coherence between its constituent parts. It thereby not only works against lazy or inconsequent thinking: it also exposes its own premises and logic more clearly to criticism. Secondly, the order of such a system typically permits a greater degree of continuity with it after its origination, whether in the form of assimilation or development. Thought laid out as theory in this sense is at once easier to appropriate over time, and more immediately amenable to correction or modification in a cumulative tradition. It is the latter consideration that is important for the destiny of Morris's work. His thought was coherent enough in substance, by any standards. But its form was largely unsystematic—variously strewn through prose and verse romances, lectures and articles alike. Attractive yet *ad hoc*, this dispersal told against it afterwards. For the lessons of Morris to be learnt, either for emulation or amendment, they had first to be assembled. This they were not. Some of the major political texts themselves were not even readily available until the two supplementary volumes of his work were belatedly published by his daughter in 1936. A good part of the reason why Morris became so posthumously *isolated* a figure probably lies in this difficulty. For that isolation was never one from Marxists alone: it was from virtually all later currents of the socialist movement in Britain. Systems have their costs, as Thompson has argued: but lack of system too has its price,

31. Where 'Stalin's blue-print of the advance to Communism' is held to 'promise fulfilment' to the claims of Morris: *William Morris*, 1955, pp. 760-761.

and in this case it was paid in limited influence. In the absence of a consolidated canon of thought, Morris's communism was to be soon effaced in the homely alternative image, so readily available, of the English artist and designer. The posthumous fate of Blake, Shelley or even Wilde reveals something of the same pattern, perhaps a peculiarly national one. A purely aesthetic reconstruction took place, which for long separated Morris from successor generations on the Left.

Was Marxism in the West meanwhile unable to generate any utopian thought of its own? Not quite. The Frankfurt tradition contributed two idiosyncratic *chefs d'oeuvre* of utopian register, Adorno's *Minima Moralia* and Marcuse's *Eros and Civilization*. In a vastly different idiom, both have significant affinities with Morris's work. Each envisages a liberated society as one not of perpetual motion, but of tranquil rest. Each reveals a sceptical suspicion of modern science and technology, and a calculated rejection of the promethean motifs in Marx—a renunciation of any prospect of ceaseless economic growth. Each recalls the intimacy rather than the conflict of man with nature—a theme central to the whole Frankfurt School, whose first historical formulation by a socialist actually occurs in one of the least noticed and loveliest passages of *News from Nowhere*.[32] Each links ethics directly to aesthetics, as did Morris, as the principle of a world at last delivered from oppression and inequality. The two, of course, also diverge in important ways, between themselves and from the emphases of Morris. The lattice-work of aphorisms in *Minima Moralia* seeks to afford glimpses of a free future through minute observation of the imprisoned present: its morality is constructed as a set of impossible maxims for living within capitalism. The Orphic world of *Eros and Civilization*, on the other hand, is projected beyond any determinate contemporary horizon. Its regulative notions are drawn from Schiller's Enlightenment vision of art as sensuous play, and Freud's metapsychology of libidinal economy. Both works are more concerned with sexual life than was Morris, and both have a more intellectual conception of art. But the major difference is, of course, the aristocratic—at times esoteric—cast of the work of Adorno and Marcuse, and its distance from active politics. What has disappeared completely from the Frankfurt tradition is the *popular* texture of Morris's writing and the organic connection between his utopian imagination and his militant

32. *News from Nowhere*, p. 367.

conception of the *transition* between capitalism and communism. For Morris, utopian images of the future were indispensable for revolutionary struggle against *reformism* in the present: 'It is essential that the ideal of the new society should always be kept before the eyes of the working classes, lest the *continuity* of the demands of the people should be broken, or lest they should be misdirected.'[33]

This sense of the relationship between utopian and quotidian politics has been restored to us again today by Rudolf Bahro, whose *Alternative* is the finest Marxist attempt yet written to think the future. It is only necessary to indicate the ways in which it represents a departure from previous utopian traditions. First, unlike any predecessor, it is a product of the historical experience of the actual construction of a society beyond capitalism. Not coincidentally, the DDR is economically and socially the most advanced country in the Communist world: and at the same time the only one to share a common culture with a leading capitalist state. Secondly, it is the work of a man conversant from personal practice with the structures of a modern industrial economy, yet whose competences have cross-cut the compartments of its division of labour, in a career successively as agricultural organizer, cultural journalist and industrial consultant. Thirdly, and decisively, it represents a socialist figuration of the future beyond the antithesis between Romanticism and Utilitarianism—the first to give something like concrete shape, however preliminary, to Marx's hope. Unlike the romantic utopias of either Morris or Marcuse, Bahro's world is based on full acceptance of modern science and the necessary complexity of industrial society. The achievements of the epoch of capitalist civilization are integral to it, the Renaissance and Enlightenment proudly claimed as its heritage. Unlike the Utilitarian utopias of Bellamy or others, it refuses any neutral imperatives to machinery and declines economic growth as any longer a paramount objective. Education, far from disappearing, is radically raised and generalized to all. Within its compass, technical and mathematical studies balance with aesthetic, historical and philosophical formation. Labour is *re*divided at once by the universalization of higher education, the general obligation to participate in simple operative work, and the diminution of time devoted to production. In the space for life so liberated, *politics*—far from receding—acquires full centrality and dignity

33. *Socialism—Its Growth and Outcome*, London 1893, p. 278.

for the first time, as the 'general labour' of democratic direction of the affairs of society as a whole. Bahro's vision of the future is by no means beyond criticism. It greatly overestimates the level of economic development in Eastern Europe,[34] and abstracts from current struggles and demands within it, with the result that its institutional articulation (party system, commune structures) remains very weak. But of its intellectual significance, for socialists in the West as in the East, there can be no doubt. Marxism today has given birth to a major Utopia. The terms of Thompson's counterposition of the two manifestly no longer hold. Common socialist debate over the nature of a world beyond classes, in the doughty spirit of the first lines of *News from Nowhere*, can resume again.

---

34. It is for this reason, essentially, that Bahro's thought can be described without derogation as utopian. In general, the historical capacity to project a future qualitatively beyond the confines of the present has typically involved overshooting the limits of the realizable, in transforming the horizons of the conceivable—a condition in turn of other and later liberations. This is true of themes in Marx or Lenin as well. In that sense, all creative socialist thought is likely to possess a utopian dimension.

7
Strategies

We have considered Morris's thought so far through the lens of Thompson's view of it as essentially an exemplary form of utopianism. Focused in this way, *A Dream of John Ball* and *News from Nowhere* are suggestively described as 'richly imaginative moralities'.[1] There is, however, another Morris to whom we owe no less homage, who was concerned not only with moralities but *strategies*. Here we immediately encounter a paradox. Although Thompson's study contains the materials for a portrait of Morris as a revolutionary thinker of astonishing lucidity and originality in the field of socialist strategy, it is one that he inexplicably does not draw. Morris's different pronouncements on the crucial questions of the struggle for *power*, his successive scenarios for the *overthrow* of capitalism, are scrupulously cited, yet never organized or inter-related into a political assessment of his changing conceptions of the means to attack and destroy the bourgeois State. The whole strategic dimension of his thought is given virtually no weight in the final summing up of his achievement, and is ignored altogether in the revaluation of the *Postscript*. Yet it is very remarkable in its own right. For what we witness in Morris's political writings is the *first frontal engagement with reformism in the history of Marxism*.

The very notion of 'reformism', the belief in the possibility of attaining

1. WM, p. 717.

socialism by gradual and peaceful reforms within the framework of a
neutral parliamentary State, has no distinct existence in the work of
Marx. The phenomenon itself, as a major trend in the labour movement,
largely post-dates his death. Within the next two decades, however, it
started to acquire more visible shape and substance in Europe. But it was
not until the controversy over 'revisionism' exploded in the SPD in the
late 1890s that the modern concept of reformism really emerged in
socialist politics. It is perfectly evident that Engels still lacked any such
theoretical category in the final decade of his life, when confronted with
the growing moderation of German Social Democracy: the result can be
seen in the persistent ambiguity and indeterminacy of his own political
commentaries in these years, which for all his indomitable revolutionary
temper were later to be widely interpreted as recommendations of an
electoral evolution towards socialism. Thompson notes and reproves,
with justice, the failure of Engels to respond to Morris's moral
imagination. But what is scarcely less—perhaps even more—arresting is
his failure to register Morris's strategic insight. For Morris was intellectually much tougher and more clairvoyant in his assessments of the
choices before the nascent labour movement than Engels. The reason for
this undoubtedly lay in his greater familiarity with the citadel of future
reformist illusions—the bourgeois-democratic parliament. England,
with the oldest and most consecrated parliamentary system in Europe,
was to produce the deepest and most durable mass reformism in the next
century. Where Marx and Engels sought an occasional explanation of the
political passivity or moderation of the British working class in the
imperial economic position of England in the 19th century, Morris had a
much greater understanding of its potential political bases, that would
long outlive English international hegemony to produce the persistence
of Labourism in the 20th century. He looked at reformism full in the face,
where they merely glimpsed it out of the corner of their eyes. The range
of strategic options he considered was a product of this revolutionary
engagement. They went well beyond anything to be found in Marx or
Engels.

Morris's first public pronouncement as a leader of the Socialist League
in January 1885, two years after his own discovery of Marxism and two
weeks after the split in the SDF, declared unambiguously: 'The discontented must know what they are aiming at when they overthrow the old
order of things. My belief is that the old order can only be overthrown by

force; and for that reason, it is all the more necessary that the revolution should be, not an ignorant, but an intelligent revolution'—organized and led by trained proletarian cadres, 'who should act as the instructors of the masses and as their leaders during critical periods of the movement'.[2] This general statement of revolutionary intent was followed a year later by an exposition of the theoretical rationale for it. 'There are undoubtedly many who are genuine democrats', he wrote, 'who have it in their heads that it is both possible and desirable to capture the constitutional Parliament and turn it into a real popular assembly, which, with the people behind it, might lead us peaceably and constitutionally into the great Revolution.' The hope of such reformers was 'to get a body of representatives elected to Parliament, and by them to get measure after measure passed which will tend towards this goal; nor would some of them, perhaps most of them, be discontented if by this means we could glide into complete State Socialism'.[3] Morris's judgement of this comfortable perspective was uncompromising. 'Those who think that they can deal with our present system in this piece-meal way very much underrate the strength of the tremendous organization under which we live, and which appoints to each of us his place, and if we do not chance to fit it, grinds us down till we do. Nothing but a tremendous force can deal with this force: it will not suffer itself to be dismembered, nor to lose anything which really is its essence without putting forth all its force in resistance; rather than lose anything which it considers of importance, it will pull the roof of the world down upon its head.'[4] The argument here is a fundamental and novel one, which cannot be found in Marx himself: for the first time the *structural unity* of the capitalist order is clearly posed as the insurmountable obstacle to any sequence of partial reforms being capable of peacefully changing it into socialism—'it will not suffer itself to be dismembered'. The principle so firmly enunciated here was to have a long subsequent history, as a central tenet of revolutionary Marxism after Lenin. Morris, however, did not leave matters there. He went on, in one of the flashes of strategic imagination that were characteristic of his genius, to evoke the possibility of a reformist government in parliament actually attempting to implement a piecemeal programme for radical

2. 'A Talk with William Morris on Socialism', *Daily News* 8 January 1885, p. 5.
3. 'Whigs, Democrats and Socialists' (lecture given in 1886), in *Signs of Change*, London 1888, pp. 40, 43.
4. 'Whigs, Democrats and Socialists', p. 46.

social change. What would then happen? 'I grant these semi-Socialist Democrats that there is one hope for their tampering piece-meal with our Society; if by chance they excite people into seriously, however blindly, claiming one or other of these things in question, and could be successful in Parliament in driving it through, they would certainly draw on a great civil war, and such a war once let loose would not end but either with the full triumph of Socialism or its extinction for the present'.[5] Morris here effectively wrote the script of the Chilean tragedy nearly a century in advance: from the 'piecemeal tampering' of a well-intentioned government to the 'blind excitation' of the masses aroused by it, 'drawing on' the blows of a brutal military assault, accomplishing the 'extinction' of the cause of socialism 'for the present'.

In 1887 he once again directly characterized and denounced belief in what he called a 'system of cumulative reforms' to be 'carried out by means of Parliament and a bourgeois executive',[6] which he warned would prove to be peculiarly rampant in the national political culture of England. 'Socialist members [of Parliament] will be in the future looked on with complacency by the government classes as serving towards the end of propping the stability of robber society in the safest and least troublesome manner by beguiling them to take part in their own government. A great invention, and well worthy of the reputation of the Briton for practicality—and swindling! How much better than the coarse old-world iron repression of that blunderer Bismarck'.[7] Showing an early grasp of the mobile dynamics of capitalist domination in a representative State, he went on: 'The two courses [before the ruling class] are fraud and force, and doubtless in a commercial country like this the resources of fraud would be exhausted before the ruling class betook itself to open force.'[8] What should be the course of the oppressed classes? Once again, Morris's answer was an extraordinary presage of the revolutionary

5. 'Whigs, Democrats and Socialists', p. 46. Elsewhere, he referred sardonically to the prospect of 'tormenting the constitutional Parliament into cumulative reforms to bring us to the crisis of Revolution': see 'The Policy of Abstention,' p. 451.
6. 'The Policy of Abstention', in May Morris, ed., *William Morris, Artist, Writer, Socialist*, II, p. 437. As the title implies, the limitation of Morris's views at this time was his (never absolute) parliamentary abstentionism—a mistake politically separable from the analytic force of his insight into the mechanisms of capitalist domination in England. The relation between the two issues was not to be adequately resolved within the socialist movement until the advent of the Third International.
7. 'The Policy of Abstention', pp. 439-440.
8. 'The Policy of Abstention', p. 441.

experience of the next century, from 1905 onwards. In a few pregnant sentences, he advocated the creation of rival institutions of popular sovereignty, outside and against parliament, educating the masses in their own self-government, and issuing decrees enforced by powers of strike, cooperation and boycott, subverting and displacing those of 'the Westminster Committee'. 'Let us try, rather, to sustain a great body of workers outside Parliament, call it the labour parliament if you will, and when that is done be sure that its decrees will be obeyed and not those of the Westminster Committee'. This 'revolutionary body will find its duties divided into two parts, the maintenance of its people while things are advancing to the final struggle, and resistance to the constitutional authority': such a 'Labour Combination' would thereby 'educate its members in administration so that on the morrow of the revolution they would be able, from a thorough knowledge of the wants and capabilities of the workers, to carry on affairs with the least possible amount of blunders' and so 'offer no opportunity to the counter-revolution'.⁹ This seems to have been the first Marxist scenario for *dual power* since the Address to the Communist League of 1850, a text unknown to Morris and left without subsequent development in Marx himself—a notion entirely absent from Engels's writings at the time.

These ideas were given extended embodiment in the long chapter 'How the Change Came' in *News from Nowhere*. Morris left no doubt as to what he regarded as the principal and fundamental trait of the transition from capitalism to socialism. 'Tell me one thing, if you can,' asks his visitor from the 19th century, 'did the change, the "revolution" it used to be called, come peacefully?' His interlocutor replies: 'Peacefully? What peace was there amongst those poor confused wretches of the nineteenth century? It was war from beginning to end: bitter war, till hope and pleasure put an end to it.'—'Do you mean actual fighting with weapons? Or the strikes and lock-outs and starvation of which we have heard?'— 'Both, both'.¹⁰ The process of the English Revolution of 1952-1954,

9. 'The Policy of Abstention', pp. 446, 448, 452. So far as the potential of strikes was concerned, Morris showed a typical prescience in a lecture given a few years later. Addressing an audience in the North, he was reported as declaring: 'What was the hinge that labour depended upon at present? Coal mining. They therefore knew they could enforce their claims—that was to say, by a strike of the coal miners of the United Kingdom, backed by all the intelligence of labour. That was one of the possible instruments of rebellion which was perhaps not so far ahead of us (Applause)': *Leeds Mercury*, March 26 1890, 'The Class Struggle: An Address by Mr William Morris'.
10. *News from Nowhere*, pp. 287-288.

thereafter recounted in detail, comprises an escalating sequence of class struggles, finally erupting into civil war, of remarkable complexity and verisimilitude. Partial reforms of workers' conditions by a liberal government, under pressure from a rising labour movement, succeed only in undermining the rate of profit and disrupting capital accumulation without affecting the nature of the economic system. The result is a series of recessions, amidst increasing social tension and polarization, which the government tries to palliate by expanding an inefficient public sector to maintain employment. The result is only to precipitate a final crisis of business confidence, and an economic collapse. The trade unions mobilize for the demand of complete socialization of the means of production. The regime responds with police attacks on demonstrations. The workers of the capital riposte with the formation of their own organ of popular sovereignty, the Committee of Public Safety—in effect, an English Soviet, which organizes and requisitions food supplies in London amidst increasing shortages. Confronted with this threat to its monopoly of legitimacy, the government proclaims a state of siege and rings the city with troops—unleashing their fire-power in direct armed repression against the next major demonstration. The resultant massacre produces a wave of revulsion among even intermediate classes against the government, as jurors refuse to convict those arrested by it. Banned by the regime, the Committee of Public Safety soon reemerges stronger than ever, under more militant leadership, and presses further measures for the improvement of the condition of labour on the employers. The economy spirals downwards again, and the middle strata now rally back to the established order in fear of their own ruin. A new and more vigorously reactionary government is elected: the workers' deputies secede from Parliament and join the Committee of Public Safety. The Cabinet then arrests the members of the Committee. The next morning England awakes to a complete General Strike. The only means of communication to operate are socialist newspapers. The State appears temporarily paralyzed, as even wealthy youths start looting. Finding itself in a sudden void, the government releases the Committee of Public Safety and negotiates a temporary truce with it—legitimating its existence for the first time, under a more innocuous title. This formalization of two rival powers, far from securing a return to calm, sets the stage for civil war. Extreme right vigilante groups now form among the possessing classes, whose armed squads garrison industrial installations and harry the streets. Guerrilla fighting spreads across the country. The government then throws in the regular army on the side of the squads to crush working-class resistance. As the culminating struggle explodes, the majority of rank-and-file soldiers deserts to the revolutionary cause, while their officers lead the camp of counter-revolution. After a prolonged conflict, combining civilian resistance and military combat, the forces of socialism triumph.

The care and depth of thought that Morris devoted to the nature of a computable revolutionary process in Britain—with its dialectic of social reforms and economic crisis, political moves and counter-moves by capitalist and popular centres of sovereignty, brusque pauses and accelerations in mass mobilization, oscillations by intermediate forces, military actions unleashed within and outside the State apparatus—represents an extraordinary *theoretical* feat, in historical retrospect. There is nothing like it in any other national literature of the time or since. Written in 1890, it marks the climax of Morris's reflections on the transition to socialism in the Socialist League. Little over a month after the final installment of *News from Nowhere* was published in *Commonweal*, Morris abandoned the League, now captured by anarchist opponents. The organizational failure of the League, the rise of strikes in the coalfields, and the first electoral successes of the ILP in 1892, led to a change in perspective. He now renounced the parliamentary abstentionism which had been the most striking weakness of his positions hitherto. But in doing so his strategic views were henceforward subject to a new oscillation: successive texts or statements reveal shifting emphases and insights, without ever achieving stable synthesis. In unpublished lecture notes probably drafted in 1892, he wrote: 'The sordid squabble of an election is unpleasant enough for a straightforward man to deal in: yet I cannot fail to see that it is necessary somehow to get hold of the machine which has at its back the executive power of the country, however that may be done. And that the organization and labour which will be necessary to effect that by means of the ballot box will—to say the least of it—be little indeed compared with what would be necessary to effect it by open revolt; besides that the change would be done more completely and with less chance, indeed with no chance of counter-revolution'.[11] Here he brought his

11. 'Communism' (notes for second lecture), British Museum Add. Mss. 45333. His confidence in the final clause waned within the space of the same text. After saying that he thought 'what is called violence will never be needed', he immediately subjoined: 'unless indeed the reactionists were to refuse the decision of the ballot-box and to try the matter by arms', before concluding weakly that he was 'pretty sure they could not attempt' to do so 'by the time things had gone so far as that'.

customary clarity and sharpness of formulation to a classic social-democratic conception: the notion of 'getting hold of the machine which has at its back the executive power of the country'—as if the administrative and repressive apparatus of the capitalist State were a neutral instrument to be utilized by whatever majority prevailed in the representative apparatus of Parliament. In an article for the ILP in January 1894, he wrote similarly: 'The workers have started to claim new conditions of life which they can only obtain at the expense of the possessing classes; and they must therefore *force* their claims on the latter. The means by which they will attempt this are not doubtful. To speak plainly, there are only two methods of bringing the necessary force to bear: open armed insurrection on the one hand; the use of the vote, to get hold of the executive, on the other. Of the first method they are not even thinking; but the second they are growing more determined to use day by day, and it is practically the only direct means. And it must be said that, if they are defeated in their attempt, it means the present defeat of Socialism: though its ultimate defeat is impossible.'[12] The simplified antithesis of arms versus votes, again, expressed with signal directness what was to be a constant theme of later reformist discourse—one which his own projections in *News from Nowhere* had so effectively undermined. In part, the rejection of the former reflected a necessary repudiation of the anarchist dementia of the 90s. In an interview with the SDF paper *Justice* in the same month, describing anarchism as 'a social disease caused by the evil conditions of society', he remarked that 'here in England, at any rate, it would be simply madness to attempt anything like an insurrection.' He went on to repeat the notion that 'whatever may be said of other countries, we have here a body, in our Parliament, at the back of which lies the whole executive power of the nation. What we have to do, it seems to me, is to get control of that body, and then we have that executive power at our back.' On the other hand the same text, which marked his final rapprochement with an SDF concerned to present his views in the most

---

12. 'What is Our Present Business as Socialists?', *Labour Prophet*, III, no. 25, January 1894: Thompson cites this text in a section under the rubric of 'Mature Theory' (WM, p. 610). Elsewhere in the same article, Morris's memory of the English working class of the 1880s is of interest: 'They seemed incapable of conceiving any better state of society than that which allowed them to live in a condition of inferiority, in return for keeping that society alive by their labour. They did not even understand that they were a class, but practically accepted the position assigned to them by the well-to-do, of their being the fortuitous dregs of industry successful in competition for riches.'

moderate light, also contains a contrary and much more complex appreciation of possible strategic *combinations* for the overthrow of capitalism in Britain. After stressing the need to create 'a strong party', which 'would have complete control' over its 'delegates' in parliament, he went on to envisage a socialist government utilizing electoral legitimacy to cover popular revolt and divide or paralyze the forces of repression deployed against it. 'You cannot start with revolt—you must lead up to it, and exhaust other means first. I do not agree that you should abstain from any act merely on the grounds that it would precipitate civil war, even though the result of the civil war were problematical, so long as the initial act was justifiable. But with the tremendous power of modern armies, it is essential that everything should be done to legalize revolt. As we have seen, the soldiers will fire upon the people without hesitation so long as there is no doubt as to the legality of their doing so. Men do not fight well with halters round their necks, and that is what a revolt now would mean. We must try and gain a position to legalize revolt—to get at the butt end of the machine-gun and the rifle, and then force is much less likely to be necessary and much more sure to be successful.'[13] This order of battle—*via* votes *to* arms—is much closer to the conceptions of *News from Nowhere*, modified by the abandonment of abstentionism. It is echoed in the prediction in *Socialism—Its Growth and Outcome*, written with Bax in 1893, that 'armed revolt or civil war may be an *incident* of the struggle, and in some form or another probably will be, especially in the latter phases of the revolution'.[14] On the eve of his death in 1895, Morris reiterated once again his intransigent hostility of principle to reformism: 'To the Socialist the aim is not the improvement of condition but the *change in position* of the working-classes'.[15] The reformist road might well be taken by the working class in the immediate future, but it would eventually have to 'repudiate this demi-semi-Socialism', if the conflict between capital and labour was to be historically settled. In his final lecture-notes of March 1895, while still reiterating his hopes of a parliamentary majority, he expressed more forcibly than ever his conviction that communism could not be achieved without the profoundest social convulsions. The painless panaceas of today remained alien to him to the

13. 'A Socialist Poet on Bombs and Anarchism. An Interview with William Morris', *Justice*, January 27, 1894.
14. *Socialism—Its Growth and Outcome*, p. 285.
15. 'Improvement of Condition—or Change in Position?', May Day No, *Justice*, 1895.

end: 'I believe that the very upward movement of labour, the consciousness among working men that they should be citizens and not machines,
will have to be paid for like all other good things, and that the price will be
no light one. I have thought the matter up and down and in and out, and I
cannot for the life of me see how the great change which we long for can
come otherwise than by disturbance and suffering of some kind'—'can
that combat be fought out, again I say, without loss and suffering? Plainly
speaking I *know* that it cannot.'[16]

The repertoire of possible scenarios for the conquest of power by the
working class canvassed by Morris—including at one time or another:
straightforward insurrection by the masses, involuntary precipitation of
civil war by a reformist administration, creation of organs of dual power
counterposed to parliament, use of an electoral majority to command a
passive state machine, armed revolt as eventual outcome of prolonged
civil deadlock, and governmental coverage legitimating a popular rising—had no equal anywhere in Europe in his day, and few after it.
Nothing comparable to it can be found in Engels, Plekhanov, Labriola or
Kautsky.[17] Morris, too, was more consistently and trenchantly
revolutionary in his explorations than any of these contemporaries. The
inventiveness and attack of his strategic imagination is not the least part
of his greatness. Yet although the evidence for it can be found open and
displayed in *William Morris—from Romantic to Revolutionary*, it seems
scarcely registered by Thompson. The book contains no real pause for
reflection on Morris's successive attempts to tackle the problem of
capitalist state power, no serious discussion of the different means he
advocated for overthrowing it. What is the explanation of this paradox?

16. 'What We have to Look For', British Museum Add. Mss. 45333.
17. Nor was there any other socialist thinker in the 19th century who foresaw so
accurately the potential stabilization of a welfare capitalism in the 20th century. This
aspect of Morris's thought is much better known, thanks to the work of both Thompson
and Williams. It is worth registering here, however, one significant theme in it that has
been little noted—Morris's repeated warning that the development of capitalism would
not necessarily lead to the social *polarization* that Marx had predicted in *Capital* and
Engels generally assumed after him. In 1886 already Morris expressed his foreboding at
'the creation of a new middle class made out of the working class and at their expense; the
raising, in short, of a new army against the attack of the disinherited' (*Signs of Change*, p.
44). A year later, he predicted that the effect of reformism would be to 'give various opportunities to the reactionists for widening the basis of monopoly by creating a fresh middle-
class under the present one, and so staving off the day of the great change' ('The Policy of
Abstention', p. 451).

The answer should probably be sought at two different levels. In one sense, Thompson's relative lack of interest in this dimension of Morris's work can be taken as the obverse of his interest in Morris's utopianism. The moralist loomed much larger than the strategist for him when he wrote the book in the 50s, and had virtually effaced the latter altogether by the late 70s. This reading of Morris was consistent with Thompson's deepest political preoccupations throughout his career. These were *original* concerns, which went against the stream of Communist writing at the time *William Morris* was published. It was much more unusual, and to Thompson must have seemed more important, to foreground Morris's contribution to the morality than to the strategy of socialism. To that basic option he has remained true ever since. The abuse committed by my rejoinder to him over a decade ago was to reduce the profound continuity of this pursuit of a communist morality to a mere 'moralism'. But a real contrast between his direction and ours existed—a *legitimate* one: we were persistently more interested in questions of socialist strategy. Because of this, we ultimately moved towards different views of the structure of the bourgeois State and the rupture involved in a socialist revolution against it. To understand this divergence, it is necessary to look at the formation and evolution of Thompson's political outlook more closely.

By the time *William Morris* was written, the Communist Party of Great Britain had already adopted the first edition of *The British Road to Socialism*. Personally vetted by Stalin, this document expunged all mention of the classical tenets of the Third International. The 'dictatorship of the proletariat' disappeared without explanation or trace. Institutions of dual power—soviets or workers' councils—vanished. Not a line alluded to the necessity of 'smashing' the permanent administrative and repressive apparatus of the capitalist state. The very notion of 'proletarian democracy' was banished. On the contrary, the party programme now declared: 'The enemies of Communism accuse the Communist Party of aiming to introduce soviet power in Britain and abolish Parliament. This is a slanderous misrepresentation of our policy'. The true objective of the CPGB was to 'transform capitalist democracy into a real people's democracy, transforming Parliament, the product of Britain's historic struggle for democracy, into the democratic instrument of the will of the vast majority of her people'. Far from losing importance, Parliament would gain it in this prospect. Rejecting 'all those theories which declare national sovereignty out of date', *The British Road* called for 'the unity of all true patriots to defend British national interests and independence', and announced that the party strove 'to restore to the British Parliament its exclusive sovereign right to control the country's financial, economic and military policy' and 'the command of the British Armed Forces to British commanders'.[18]

By May 1956, the Executive Committee of the Party could proudly claim: 'Ours was the first Communist Party outside the socialist countries to put forward a programme for the peaceful transition to socialism through the establishment of a broad popular alliance, election of a people's government and the transformation of Parliament and the State.'[19] A decade later, the third edition of *The British Road* once again pledged the party's belief that 'socialism can be achieved in Britain, not without prolonged and serious effort, but by peaceful means and without armed struggle.' The condition for its advent lay in popular aspiration. 'Such a peaceful, democratic advance can, in the Communist Party's view, be achieved in Britain if the great majority of the people desire it.' The national road to socialism would be paved by 'continuous use and development of the traditional democratic means of struggle' in England: the most important of these, the document reiterated, was Parliament, 'the supreme organ of representative power'. Advance towards socialism should not be precipitate, but gradual: a whole stage of 'anti-monopoly alliance' should supervene before socialism itself could be on the agenda.[20] Eventually a parliamentary majority would legislate socialist measures, supported by a mass movement outside parliament, within the framework of the constitution. Such were the official perspectives developed by the CPGB from the early 50s onwards; in successive drafts the very word 'revolution' scarcely ever figures.[21] Inwardly, many older

---

18. *The British Road to Socialism*, London 1951, pp. 14, 10, 11. For Stalin's approval, or inspiration, of the document, see now the useful article by Andrew Chester, 'Uneven Development: Communist Strategy from the 1940s to the 1970s', *Marxism Today*, September 1979.

19. 'The Lessons of the Twentieth Congress of the CPSU', Resolution of the Executive Committee of the Communist Party, *World News*, 19 May, 1956.

20. *The British Road to Socialism*, London 1968, pp. 6, 17, 24-25, 48. For a thorough critique of this edition, see Bill Warren, 'The British Road to Socialism', *New Left Review* 63, September-October 1970.

21. In this respect, the 1978 edition—a more sophisticated and substantial document—marks a conspicuous change, no doubt reflecting the pressures exerted by the growth of a revolutionary left outside the CP in the 70s.

cadres of the party probably did not resign themselves immediately to the discreet idiom of *The British Road*, with its calculated vagueness about the nature of the capitalist state, its bland equation of democratic with peaceful advance, its studious avoidance of any evocation of different class forms of sovereignty. But already many other members no doubt perceived the document primarily as a token of welcome distance from Soviet or East European models of government, and were content not to inquire further into it. Certainly it is striking that amidst all the furore of 1956, none of the contending forces in the party appears seriously to have questioned this part of its heritage.[22]

It can now be seen why Thompson's study of Morris might well have passed rather lightly over his strategic thought, even independently of the fact that its author's major preoccupations in any case lay elsewhere. For Morris's political legacy in this area was in many ways a distinctly uncomfortable one for a loyal Communist by 1955.[23] It spoke all too clearly and directly of matters which the party now deemed best forgotten or unsaid: dual power, popular risings, military repression, civil war. Even his 'parliamentarist' dicta were awkwardly round and plain to an officialdom systematically addicted to periphrasis, euphemism, evasion. The whole *language* of Morris's strategic pronouncements, always crisp and firm, was radically incompatible with the flaccid ambiguities of latter-day bureaucratic vocabulary. Thompson was far too scrupulous a historian not to furnish the actual record of Morris's politics, and too good a writer to have any truck with the idiom of the functionary. But whether he dissented in any major sense from the strategic discourse and prospect of his party is impossible to tell. There is no evidence of it in *William Morris* itself. On the other hand, the original version of the book contains a number of passages that recall the militant

22. In *The Reasoner*, Thompson's only reference to *The British Road* was a reservation to the effect that it was still insufficiently national: 'I would ask whether we are fully satisfied that our policy can truthfully be called *The British Road to Socialism*: or whether certain passages in it might not better be entitled *The Russian Road to Socialism, Done into English*? Certainly I hope that the "formulations" about "people's democracy" will be re-examined in this light.' See 'Reply to George Matthews', no. 1, July 1956, p. 13. The phrases in question were, in fact, dropped a few weeks later by the party leadership: see J.R. Campbell, initiating discussion of the new draft of *The British Road*, in *World News*, 22 September 1956. There was no echo of them in the second edition adopted in 1958.
23. Introducing a selection of *The Political Writings of William Morris* in 1973, A.L. Morton could still tell his readers that: 'Their author was little of a political theorist' (London, p. 11). Symptomatically, not one of the texts by Morris discussed above is included in this volume.

temper of the time, whatever the formal auspices of *The British Road*, and which have—significantly, or otherwise—been omitted from the revised edition. Above all, the first *William Morris* was informed by a fierce polemic against *reformism*, that is notably mitigated in the second. Denunciations of the 'moral degeneration of reformism'—its 'complacency, its "good intentions", its pious phrases, its blind eye to imperialism, exploitation and war'[24]—have generally been dropped, perhaps as over-heated. So too has the attack on Labour Party appropriation of Morris's name, for which Attlee was castigated—along with all 'those who spoke of Morris's influence as being "British", or "empirical", or "humanitarian",' and whose purpose was 'to distract attention from Morris's real principles, the real sources of his moral indignation—his understanding of the class struggle, his hatred of imperialism and war'.[25] Morris's 'feeling that the bourgeois myth of parliamentary democracy had taken on its most insidious and hypocritical forms in Britain'[26] is also no longer to be found—possibly because the formulation does not square particularly well with later definitions of the peculiarities of the English. In fact, the essay of that name strikes a very different note about reformism: there it is the 'truly astronomic sum of human capital that has been invested in the strategy of piecemeal reform'[27] and the 'evident returns' it has secured, which find the major emphasis. The decrease in hostility to the Labour Party is obvious by the mid-60s. But it should not be exaggerated in the period that actually followed the publication of *William Morris* itself.

For when the New Left was formed in the late 50s, and Thompson could develop a political position on the transition to socialism freely and publicly, he distinguished himself by his insistence on the need to understand this transition as a 'revolution'—a word at that time out of favour among many of its spokesmen. As he noted, the use of the term drew on him a suspect reputation for 'apocalyptic' thinking in circles

24. *William Morris*, 1955 edition, p. 502.
25. *William Morris*, 1955 edition, p. 739. Thompson writes in the revised edition that he has taken out lines like these 'not because I apologize for them in 1955 but because they are not relevant in 1976' (p. 812)—leaving an unresolved ambiguity as to whether their lack of relevance is due merely to the dating of references to Attlee, or rather to alteration of conditions under Wilson and Callaghan. Are there no contemporary examples of the same treatment of Morris within the Labour Party of today?
26. *William Morris*, 1955 edition, p. 545.
27. PT, p. 71.

with a less Communist formation within the New Left. It is worth recalling his presentation of what he intended by the notion. 'In his early propagandist years', he remarked in an article entitled 'Revolution' in 1960, 'Morris thought somewhat naively of an insurrectionary revolution, on the model of the Paris Commune', whereas by 1893 'he had come to envisage the final conquest of power as taking place by parliamentary means'.[28] But 'his concept of the revolutionary transition was little changed', since 'it was not the necessity of a *violent* revolution upon which Morris was insisting, but the necessity for a critical conflict in every area of life at the point of transition'. This remarkably vague formulation is given some, although far from clinching, specification in the argument that follows. Dismissing the opposite notions of 'evolution' and 'cataclysmic revolution' as roads to socialism in Britain, Thompson contended that 'it is possible to look forward to a peaceful revolution in Britain, with far greater continuity in social life and in institutional forms, than would have seemed likely even twenty years ago', because 'socialist *potential* has been enlarged, and socialist forms, however imperfect, have grown up within capitalism'—as capitalist forms once grew up within feudalism. What then would such a revolution amount to, as a political process? The equilibrium between capitalist and countervailing powers within present society 'could be heaved *forward*, by popular pressures of great intensity, to the point where the powers of democracy cease to be countervailing and become the active dynamic of society in their own right. This is revolution.'[29] If so, one might be tempted to comment, it seems anodyne enough to be accepted by an enlightened bourgeois. Elsewhere, 'the historical watershed between "last stage" capitalism and democratic socialism' is defined as 'the point at which the socialist potential is liberated, the public sector assumes the dominant role, subordinating the private to its command, and over a very great area of life the priorities of need over-rule those of profit'[30] Nothing so harsh as expropriation is even mentioned; while the State is ignored altogether. How is the watershed so defined to be reached? Essentially by 'unrelenting reformist pressures in many fields, which are designed to reach a revolutionary culmination.' What form will such a climax take? 'The point of breakthrough is not a narrow political concept: it will entail

28. 'Revolution', NLR 3, May-June 1960, p. 4.
29. 'Revolution', p. 7.
30. 'Revolution', pp. 7-8.

a confrontation, throughout society, between two systems, two ways of life. In this confrontation, political consciousness will become heightened: every direct and devious influence will be brought to the defence of property rights; the people will be forced by events to exert their whole political and industrial strength.' But what, it may be asked, will the people do with their strength? Thompson's reply is the nearest he gives us to a concrete delineation of his conception of a British revolution. 'It involves the breaking-up of some institutions (and the House of Lords, Sandhurst, Aldermaston, the Stock Exchange, the press monopolies and the National Debt are among those which suggest themselves), the transformation and modifications of others (including the House of Commons and the nationalized boards), and the transfer of new functions to yet others (town councils, consumers' councils, trades councils, shop stewards committees, and the rest).' [31] Of this it could be said that virtually all the measures enumerated are compatible with the maintenance of capitalist relations of production and the preservation of the bourgeois state. Most parliamentary democracies have no hereditary chamber, few have nuclear weapons, some have no press monopolies, and one or two capitalist economies even lack stock exchanges, while many have more democratic legislative assemblies and less elitist staff colleges. Thompson, however, does not press his particulars here, for he holds that there is something more important than them: 'The *form* of a revolution may depend upon forms of power; but, in the last analysis, its *content* depends upon the consciousness and will of the people.' [32] Institutions are in the end of less moment than impulses or ideas.

The political conceptions set out in 'Revolution' nearly 20 years ago are of twofold significance. On the one hand, their degree of continuity with the main strategic perspectives of the CPGB from the mid-50s onwards is unmistakable. In a more humanized language, with greater stress on democratic 'self-activity' from below, but also a less definite fate reserved for private capital, many of the same fundamental assertions—and evasions—reappear. Not only will the transition to socialism probably be peaceful, with greater institutional continuity with capitalism than was once believed, because of the advances of the labour movement. 'The focus of political power' also remains 'Parliament', which must however be 'transformed' in the course of the transition. The agents of

31. 'Revolution', p. 8.
32. 'Revolution', p. 8.

social change are the 'people', its adversaries the 'monopolists'. For 'it is the business of socialists to draw the line', in Thompson's words, 'between the monopolists and the people'.[33] The major difference between the two conceptions, in the early 60s, lay in the lack of credibility of the CP's attachment to the advanced democracy it urged on the country, while it retained the discretionary rule of an iron bureaucracy in its own ranks. No one, by contrast, could doubt the sincerity of Thompson's commitments. These, moreover, were to prove lasting. For Thompson has shown the greatest consistency and fidelity in his conception of a transition to socialism in Britain. In 1961, he defended it once more at length in 'Revolution Again'. 'The historical concept of revolution', he wrote, 'is not one of *this* change in "structure", or *that* moment of "transition", nor need it be one of cataclysmic crisis and violence. It is a concept of historical *process*, whereby democratic pressures can no longer be contained within the capitalist system; at some point a crisis is precipitated which leads on to a chain of inter-related crises which result in profound changes in class and social relationships and in institutions—"transition" of power in the epochal sense'.[34] He returned to it, with a variation, in 'The Peculiarities of the English' in 1965, envisaging either 'a more or less constitutional political party, based on the class institutions, with a very clearly articulated socialist strategy, whose cumulative reforms bring the country to a critical point of class equilibrium, from which a rapid revolutionary transition is pressed through'—or (more obscurely) 'further far-reaching changes in the sociological composition of the groups making up the historical class, which entail the break-up of the old class institutions and value-system, and the creation of new ones.'[35] The collective text of the *May-Day Manifesto* in 1968 is not attributable to Thompson alone, and contains no plea for a revolutionary transition in his sense—in this respect being closer to mainstream New Left opinion of the previous decade. But the

33. 'Revolution', p. 8. The phrase is an echo from Morris, with a significant difference. What Morris wrote was: 'Our business is to help make the people conscious of this great antagonism between the people and constitutionalism'—for 'we are responsible for the enunciation of socialist principles and for the consequences which may flow from their general acceptance, whatever they may be. This responsibility no socialist can shake off by declarations against physical force and in favour of constitutional methods of agitation; we are attacking the Constitution with the very beginnings, the mere lispings of Socialism.' *Signs of Change*, pp. 53, 51.
34. 'Revolution Again', NLR 6, November-December 1960, p. 30.
35. PT, pp. 71-72.

underlying argument of key passages is not dissimilar. 'It is only at the level of unthinking repetition that the choice between "revolution", in its traditional sense of a violent capture of state power, and "evolution", in its traditional sense of the inevitability of gradual change towards socialist forms, can survive. These are not, and have not for some time been, available socialist strategies, in societies of this kind.'[36] The same section of the *Manifesto* declares: 'We would very willingly admit the power and the importance of the House of Commons if it would show some signs of political action in general terms, as opposed to what it takes to be significant in its own terms. We can conceive, and would like to see, a House of Commons embattled against organized private power or established interests; fighting a popular cause against arbitrary authority or secret decision.' It goes on, 'We are told we have parliamentary government, but all we can say is that we would like to see some.'[37] What that 'all' excludes is the very notion of alternative institutions of *proletarian* democracy—communes, soviets or councils—embodying a new and insurgent sovereignty, held not only by Marx and Lenin, but as we have seen by Morris too.

In the 70s, Thompson has made clear his distance from the revival of more classical conceptions of socialist revolution in the Marxist tradition. In 1975, he saw 'a time of unparalleled socialist opportunity' in Britain, if only the nation did not enter the EEC—where 'British Labour will cast away its one incomparable historical asset (a united movement) in anxious negotiations with its fragmented and ideologically embittered counterparts'. For in England 'one can glimpse, as an outside chance, the possibility that we could effect here a peaceful transition—for the first time in the world—to a democratic socialist society. I mean that we could do this in the next five years, not in the next century'—'the opportunity is there within the logic of our own past itinerary. The lines of British culture still run vigorously towards the point of change where our traditions and organizations cease to be defensive and become affirmative forces: the country becomes our own.'[38] Within rather less than five years, these euphoric prospects had given way to the cataclysmic visions of *The Poverty of Theory*. But the underlying political stance remained consistent. The Preface to *The Poverty of Theory* speaks of the May

36. *May-Day Manifesto*, London 1968, p. 152.
37. *May-Day Manifesto*, pp. 147-148, 148.
38. *Sunday Times*, April 27, 1975.

Revolt in France and industrial turbulence in England appearing 'to offer the impatient very much more rapid routes to something called "revolution" '.[39] In his Afternote to the same volume, he condemns Althusser's critique of the PCF on virtually every ground save one: its tacit acceptance of the party's *strategy*, as distinct from organization and tactics—a strategy Althusser has described as that of a 'peaceful and democratic transition to socialism'.[40] Thompson's comments on Eurocommunism in the text itself, while disputing the credentials of the PCF (if not the PCI) leadership to advocate such a road, indicate no great divergence with the route itself. Most recently of all, he has re-stated in an interview all the major elements of his long-standing position. The way forward towards socialism is to fight for reforms until a 'watershed' moment is reached, when the interests of the people and the interests of capital confront each other in 'a moment of intense awareness'. This would not necessarily be 'a revolution in the way people commonly envisage it', however, because a peaceful transition is both more desirable and historically more frequent.[41]

It would not be appropriate to reiterate in detail here the strategic conceptions of the transition to socialism for which the present NLR has stood. It will be sufficient to note the major differences. For us, a socialist revolution means something harder and more precise: the dissolution of the existing capitalist state, the expropriation of the possessing classes from the means of production, and the construction of a new type of state and economic order, in which the associated producers can for the first time exercise direct control over their working lives and direct power over their political government. That change will not occur without a fundamental economic crisis, either determined by the prior contradictions of capitalist development itself, or by the inevitable dislocations induced by the very attempt to alter the mechanisms of accumulation in a market economy. When it impends, the primary locus of bourgeois class power will redeploy towards the repressive rather than the representative apparatuses of the capitalist state. These apparatuses must be broken as

39. PT, p. i.
40. 'On The Twenty-Second Congress of the French Communist Party', NLR 104, July-August 1977, p. 14.
41. 'Recovering the Libertarian Tradition', *The Leveller*, no. 22, January 1979, p. 22. Thompson remarks that he is no longer sure that 'the classic revolution is such a good thing'.

organized institutions for any revolutionary transfer of power to occur. This can be achieved only by the creation of organs of socialist democracy, mobilizing a popular force capable of undermining the unity of the coercive machinery of the established state, and cancelling the legitimacy of its parliamentary machinery—whether or not constitutional government is in the hands of parties of the Left, itself a contingency neither impossible nor inevitable. The emergence of such forms of a second power, incarnating the sovereignty of a proletarian democracy alternative and antagonistic to that of bourgeois democracy, must be the long-term strategic goal of the socialist movement. Its short-term political practice should consciously seek to link the immediate demands of the working class to this ultimate objective by the formulation of transitional goals calculated to unbalance the established order, and to weld together all oppressed groups and strata against it. The political advent of a situation of dual power, accompanied by the onset of economic crisis, permits no gradual resolution. When the unity of the bourgeois state and the reproduction of the capitalist economy are ruptured, the ensuing social upheaval must rapidly and fatally pit revolution and counter-revolution against each other in a violent convulsion. In such a conflict, capital will always command a mass basis beyond a handful of monopolists. In this end-game situation, socialists will seek to avoid a conclusion by arms, but will not sow illusions as to the probability of a resort to them. Capitalism did not triumph in any major advanced country in the world today without armed conflict or civil war, whether in England, France, Germany, Italy, Japan or the United States. Yet the economic transition from feudalism to capitalism is only from one form of private property to another. Is it conceivable that the much greater historical change involved in the transition from private to collective property, necessitating an expropriation of power and wealth far more drastic, will assume less lacerating political forms? Likewise, if the successive passages from antiquity to feudalism to capitalism produced epochal changes in types of regime and representation—from ancient assemblies to mediaeval estates to bourgeois parliaments, not to speak of imperial, absolutist and fascist states—is it possible that the passage to socialism, which has already thrown up workers' councils as well as bureaucratic states, will not do so in the future as well?

The tradition to which these conceptions belong is broadly speaking that of Lenin and Trotsky, Luxemburg and Gramsci. It was on the basis of such principles that the Third International was founded, in rejection of the theory and practice of the Second International, and that the Fourth International was founded as the Third started to retrace its steps from them in the epoch of the Popular Fronts. Today, the parties that are the heirs of the Third International in Europe espouse policies increasingly convergent with those of the parties of the classical epoch of the Second International, in the first two decades of this century. The continuity of the political ideas of Kautsky and Bauer with those of Berlinguer and Carrillo on the road to socialism in Western Europe is now virtually complete. Thompson's conceptions are a libertarian version of this alternative line of descent. Its most influential expression today, of course, are the doctrines of Eurocommunism. To draw a clear demarcation between these two theoretical lineages is not to foreclose comradely debate between them. In fact, nothing is more important than that close and critical exchange should develop among their respective partisans, in a climate free of anathema or contempt. Neither position is free from certain central problems, whose common root is the absence of any successful transition to socialism at all in the advanced capitalist countries to date. The critical weakness of the first is its difficulty in demonstrating the plausibility of counter-institutions of dual power arising within consolidated parliamentary democracies: all the examples of soviets or councils so far have emerged out of disintegrating autocracies (Russia, Hungary, Austria), defeated military regimes (Germany), ascendant or overturned fascist states (Spain, Portugal). Conversely, the neuralgic zone of the second is its difficulty in providing any convincing account of the possibility of a gradual dismantling in social peace of a capitalist state constructed for class war, or a meliorist transformation of a market economy into its historical opposite: all examples of reforming governments to date have either simply adapted to the capitalist state and economy, changing their own nature and goals more than those of the society over which they preside (England, Norway, Sweden, West Germany, Austria), or if they proved serious in their intentions have been brutally beaten down by military force (Chile). No socialist has any call for political complacency about their stock of strategic notions today. Thompson shares positions with his adversaries Althusser and Poulantzas, not to speak of Hirst and Hindess, within a broad spectrum that now stretches from Eurocommunism to left Social Democracy. The great majority of the Marxist intelligentsia in the West has rallied to these perspectives of late, and much creative work has been done from their standpoint. Nicos Poulantzas's *State, Power, Socialism* and Geoffrey Hodgson's *Socialism and Parliamentary Democracy* are the two most intelligent and original expositions of this new consensus, just as Ernest Mandel's *From Stalinism to Eurocommunism* is the most effective critique of it, while Massimo Salvadori's *Karl Kautsky and the Socialist Revolution* provides the best historical background to the contemporary controversy between the two viewpoints. Polemic in this field, natural and inevitable within the ranks of the Left, should always be tempered by awareness that all strategic conceptions of the transition to socialism inherently contain arguments of a *probabilistic* type. For theory may estimate, but only the practice of the future will ascertain, the limits of variation of the political and social structures of the present, whether of capital or of labour. There can be no axiomatics of revolutionary change, in the strong sense. The real terrain of arbitration between the two opposing conceptions which confront each other today is *historical*—not speculation on an unknowable future, but examination of a known past. It is on that ground, the firm earth of the historian on which every Marxist should keep their feet, that evidence points to the greater cogency and realism of the tradition of Lenin and Trotsky.

The major need in Europe today is for fraternal and responsible debate between differing views of these fundamental issues. Having set out the general terms of the contrast between Thompson and ourselves, a few comments may be ventured on the evolution of particular emphases within Thompson's overall position, as a token of the sort of discussion possible where differences are registered and respected. For a new set of themes has emerged in his writing in the late 70s, which is of the greatest interest. The starting-point for them is to be found in the powerful conclusion to *Whigs and Hunters*. There Thompson develops three main arguments. Firstly, he criticizes the view that law in 18th century English society was merely an economic instrument in the hands of the possessing classes. Although this was indeed one of its functions, as his own study of the Black Acts demonstrates, it was far more, and more complex, than this. It was also the primary ideological means of ruling-class legitimation, in an age when religion was falling into relative desuetude. But its very 'hegemonic' capacity depended on the credibility of legal rules and procedures as a system of justice to the dominated classes: and this in turn imposed objective limits and restraints on its manipulability by the dominant classes. To be socially effective, English law could not be mere fraud—force by another name. The dialectical result was that 'in certain limited areas' the law could become 'a genuine forum within which certain kinds of class conflict were fought out'[42]—even on occasion leading to setbacks for the government in the courts, as in the case of Wilkes, which simultaneously inhibited the administrative power and heightened the juridical hegemony of the ruling order. Thompson's account of this dialectic is of exemplary subtlety and insight, and should be accepted by every Marxist.

His second thesis is an extrapolation from the first. Thompson insists 'upon the obvious point, which some modern Marxists have overlooked, that there is a difference between arbitrary power and the rule of law.'[43] But this point is far less obvious than he seems to suppose. For, as we have seen earlier, some of the most sweeping despotisms in history have promulgated and enforced comprehensive legal systems. A tyranny can perfectly well rule *by law*: its own laws. The Mongol Empire is a famous case in point. The great Yasa of Genghis Khan stipulated juridical equality of all before the provisions of its code.[44] The exigencies of any imperial administration, indeed, have an inbuilt tendency to generate extensive legal codification. What Thompson has done is to conflate the historically very specific—and unusual—case of English law in the 18th century with law in general. The very phrase 'rule of law', archetypal islander idiom, tells its own story. For 'law' never 'rules'—to imagine that it could is to reify social relations in a classic formalist fallacy. The conceptual slide that has occurred in Thompson's text becomes plain in the next sentence, where he writes: 'The rule of law itself, the imposing of effective inhibitions upon power and the defence of the citizen from power's all-intrusive claims, seem to me to be an unqualified human good.'[45] The real meaning of the phrase as he uses it is

---

42. WH, p. 265.
43. WH, p. 266.
44. For an account of the Yasa, see George Vernadsky, *The Mongols and Russia*, New Haven 1953, pp. 99-110.
45. WH, p. 266. This specification contrasts in turn with that of Douglas Hay, whose three criteria for the 'rule of law' are fixed offences, firm rules of evidence, and learned and honest judges: *Albion's Fatal Tree*, p. 23. Hay is generally less seized of the role of juries than Thompson. The different usages of the term are an index of its malleable indeterminacy. Thompson has shown more awareness of its variant meanings and authoritarian usages in his latest writings, without ceasing to appeal to it as a normative ideal: see 'Trial by Jury', *New Society*, November 29, 1979.

something quite different, in other words: what is actually intended is much closer to 'civil liberties'. The distinction is not a nugatory one. For it reminds us immediately of the dangers of speaking of law as a homogeneous unity. This reflection is directly germane to Thompson's third thesis.

In the 16th and 17th centuries, he argues, law in England was 'less an instrument of class power than a central arena of conflict'.[46] In the course of prolonged struggles, the law had been changed. 'Inherited by the 18th century gentry, this changed law was, literally, central to their whole purchase upon power and upon the means of life. Take law away, and the royal prerogative, or the presumption of the aristocracy, might flood back upon their properties and their lives; take law away and the string which tied together their lands and their marriages would fall apart.' But at the same time, 'it was inherent in the very nature of the medium which they had selected for their own self-defence that it could not be reserved for the exclusive use only of their own class. The law, in its forms and traditions, entailed principles of equity and universality which, perforce, had to be extended to all sorts and degrees of men.'[47] The 'immense capital of human struggles over the two previous centuries' was thus 'passed down as a legacy to the 18th century, where it gave rise to a vision, in the minds of some men, of an ideal aspiration towards universal values of law'— even while 'the oligarchs and the great gentry were content to be subject to the rule of law only because this law was serviceable and afforded to their hegemony the rhetoric of legitimacy'.[48] But 'when the struggles of 1790-1832 signalled that this equilibrium had changed, the rulers of England were faced with alarming alternatives'. What were these? 'They could either dispense with the rule of law, dismantle their elaborate constitutional structures, countermand their own rhetoric and exercise power by force; or they could submit to their own rules and surrender their hegemony.' After taking some hesitant steps in the direction of repression, from the campaign against Paine in the 1790s to the Six Acts of 1820, they eventually took the second course. 'In the end, rather than shatter their own self-image and repudiate 150 years of constitutional legality, they surrendered to the law. In this surrender they threw

46. WH, p. 264.
47. WH, p. 264.
48. WH, p. 269.

retrospective light back on the history of their class, and retrieved for it something of its honour.'[49]

Whigs and Hunters closes on this elegiac note. Is it one we should ratify? The answer, I think, is no. For what Thompson has done here is to amalgamate very different juridical rules and processes into a generic and hypostatized construct, 'the rule of law'. To begin with, any legal code needs to be divided into its civil, criminal and constitutional provisions. These constitute distinct sectors of law, which may be quite dissimilar or even contradictory in tenor. Roman imperial law is a famous example: an autocratic constitutional system of sovereignty, presiding over a perfected and egalitarian civil law for the citizenry, underpinned by a savagely punitive criminal law for the underclasses. The legacy of struggle by the English gentry in the 17th century, to which Thompson refers, concerned essentially constitutional law. The primary arsenal of expropriation at the disposal of the same class in the 18th century lay in civil law, by far the most voluminous region of English jurisprudence. The outright repression of the Black Acts was an extension of criminal law. At the same time, of course, the legal *procedures* for these variant substantive codes were unified in certain common practices and institutions: in England, trial by jury was far the most important, if not the most universal. To run all this together in a single rhetorical rubric as 'the rule of law' is historically and politically quite misleading. The crucial error to which it leads can be seen in Thompson's final description of the Reform Crisis of 1832: 'rather than repudiate 150 years of constitutional legality, they surrendered to the law'. Here the genuinely positive and popular 'inheritance of struggle' for the achievement of *civil liberties* is elided without further ado into the mystifications of 'constitutional legality'—for which Paine, for one, had nothing but contempt. In fact, of course, the dominant classes of 1832 did not 'surrender' at all, but successfully negotiated their own survival in a new political bloc, and they did so not at the behest of the 'law', but under the threat of revolutionary upheaval from below. It should not be necessary to make these points here, since no one has formulated them more definitely than Thompson himself in the past. What has gone wrong at the end of *Whigs and Hunters* can best be seen, in fact, by looking at the declension of the three successive judgements of 1832 to be found in his major works. In

49. WH, p. 269.

William Morris (first edition), he wrote: 'The vision of 1789 was finally trampled under foot in the prudent Reform Bill of 1832. "Liberty, Equality, Fraternity"—all were disregarded.'[50] In *The Making of the English Working Class*, his formula for the Reform Bill was scarcely less trenchant: 'Blood compromised with gold to keep out the claims of *egalité*.'[51] In *Whigs and Hunters*, the pact of blood and gold has disappeared. Now the counter-revolutionary arrangements of 1832 throw a softening 'retrospective light' on the history of the ruling class, and 'retrieve something of its honour'!

Does this sequence signify a movement to the right by Thompson? At first sight it might seem plausible to think so. But the theoretical logic at work is more complex and more interesting, I think. Allowance must, of course, be made for the histrionic temptations of a final strophe in a book of this sort. Beyond these, however, what is really at issue in the conclusion to *Whigs and Hunters* is an underlying conception of the State. We can see this if we look at the group of essays written in late 1978-1979, all of which are concerned with a single set of problems: the growth in the power of the security apparatuses of the British State, the decline in the protections afforded by the law against their incursions, the default of parliamentary control over either process.[52] Written with passion and authority, they represent perhaps the most effective *political intervention* by any socialist writer in England in recent years—forcing to public attention, by sheer eloquence and learning, processes otherwise neglected or unobserved on the margins of conventional consciousness. The whole British Left is in debt to their moral and intellectual energy. In them, Thompson now invokes an abstract 'rule of law' as a defence of popular liberties less than specific legal institutions—above all, the jury system. Rightly attacking the indifference of the Left to the abolition of the need for unanimous verdicts by a Labour government, at the instigation of the police, and denouncing the rise in screening procedures, operated by the police, he insists on the very ancient origins of the jury as an institution, which go back to the pre-feudal epoch in England, and have nothing to do with bourgeois liberalism as such. Asserting its indispensable value as a 'stubbornly maintained democratic

50. *William Morris*, 1955 edition, p. 45.
51. MEWC, p. 902.
52. A collection of them is now promised for 1980, under the title *Writing by Candlelight*.

practice', he remarks: 'I would like to think of the jury system as a linger-
ing paradigm of an alternative mode of participatory self-government, a
nucleus around which analogous modes might grow in our town halls,
factories and streets.'[53]

This radical perspective reminds us of the role of the jury system in
other countries and times—in classical Greece, for example, where it was
the cornerstone of Athenian democracy. But to recollect this example, far
more advanced than that of our Anglo-Saxon forebears, is also to notice
what is missing from Thompson's list. There is no equivalent of the
Assembly in it: Parliament remains in place. For a further theme of these
essays is a lament for Parliament as bewitched—or rather literally 'black-
mailed'—into passive submission to the erosion of civic freedoms by the
security services. Thompson etches a compelling portrait of these
agencies in Britain today—'some of the most secretive and arrogant
"servants" (in practice often *masters*) among modern states', whose
'operations are distinguished by their invisibility and lack of accountabi-
lity'.[54] His explanation of their growth, however, is less persuasive.
Essentially, he attributes it to the cumulative effect of two world wars
(which accustomed the population to uniforms and talk of national
interest), the re-import of imperialist ideology at home, and the influence
of McCarthyism during the Cold War.[55] All told, these have generated a
climate of 'authoritarian statism', which has allowed the power and
pretensions of the security apparatuses to grow alarmingly since the 50s.
Today, the 'nerve of libertarian outrage' needs to be awakened again, and
a concerted campaign fought for the reform of the Official Secrets Act,
the passing of a Freedom of Information Act, the establishment of
civilian controls on the police, and the exposure of illegitimate acts by the
security forces.

Here some reservations impose themselves. The explanation offered
for the expansion of internal surveillance in recent decades is too *ad hoc* to
be convincing. The reasons for this growth are not so much to be found in
a sequence of fortuitous conjunctures, still less in the nebula of 'statism',
as in a structural change in the objective position of the British ruling
class and its State. Ever since the Second World War, that class has been

53. *Introduction* to *Review of Security and the State 1978*, compiled by State Research,
London 1978, p. xiii.
54. *Introduction*, pp. i, iii.
55. *Introduction*, pp. v, vi.

in a historical sense profoundly *on the defensive*—its economy one of the weakest links within a world capitalist system that has itself lost control of over a third of the planet, and is under constant siege in the peripheries of its empire of exploitation. Inevitably, obsessive fears have increasingly pervaded the established order in Britain, leading to a multiplication of the technology and manpower of its repressive machinery. There is little surprising in this. The actual practices of domestic espionage and provocation have probably altered less, and their efficacy has possibly even decreased. For all the scandals of recent years, there have been no operations with the same national political reach as, say, those of Oliver the Spy or the Zinoviev Letter. Probably the most significant change for the future has been the increased role of the regular army in 'low-intensity operations', which Thompson, treating the crisis in Northern Ireland essentially as an intra-Irish conflict, tends to overlook.[56] More important than this, however, is the role putatively allocated to Parliament in his analysis. Confronted with the fact that Parliament has signally failed 'to fight a popular cause against arbitrary authority and secret decision' that he had envisaged for it in the 60s, Thompson motivates its unaccountable silence by the threat of blackmail under which Labour Ministers and MPs allegedly lie from the dossiers on their private and public lives of the Special Branch. 'I know of no historical precedent for this', he writes.[57] Hinting that Wilson himself may have been forced to resign because of obscure menaces emanating from the recesses of MI5, he conjectures that schemes for a 'right-wing take-over' in the form of an authoritarian National Government are being hatched within the security services, armed forces and police: indeed 'my sense of politics suggests that the take-over is already under way'.[58]

This picture is altogether too melodramatic. The image of a Parliamentary Labour Party cowering before the files of the security agencies is quite unconvincing—the notion of ambitious political

---

56. 'Whatever aggravations have been afforded by British politics and by the British military presence, the source of the malaise is not to be found in contemporary "British imperialism" but in a historic conflict within Ireland itself, and *within the Irish working class*': *Introduction*, p. xiii. Rightly condemning the Provisional IRA, Thompson wrongly commits a simplifying *petitio principii* here. The obvious question, for a historian above all, is posed by a recombination of his terms: what is the 'historic source' of the 'conflict' within Ireland?

57. 'The Secret State within the State', *New Statesman*, 10 November 1978.

58. Ibid.

conspiracies brewing among colonels and detective-inspectors scarcely less so. The Labour Party pursues its policies in Parliament not under sinister compulsion, but by its own unembarrassed volition: there is no major incompatibility between its ordinary objectives and those of the police systems over which its Ministers routinely preside. The English Parliament is not a bastion of popular liberties against the state, temporarily deactivated, but an essential and integral part *of* the British capitalist state. So long as it retains its representative legitimacy within a market economy, there is no need for repressive plot or putsch by the security forces that flank it. The fashionable locution, 'statism', now bandied about on the Left, obscures these relationships. Logically, it has status only in anarchist parlance. Thompson is certainly no anarchist. In fact, if his diagnosis of the growth in the power of the security organs in Britain is too extreme, his proposals for dismantling it can be faulted for being, on the contrary, too modest. The set of reforms he advocates are vital and feasible immediate demands for campaigning today. But they do not constitute either an intermediate or a long-term programme of objectives for a *socialist* movement. Such a perspective is still missing from Thompson's interventions. The prospect that is offered instead remains, for all its urgency and eloquence, a defensive one. 'We should certainly campaign for a Freedom of Information Act. The campaign will have educative value. It might secure small gains, and for historians, significant ones. But we should be under no illusions about it; whatever act is passed, our public servants will find a way around it.'[59] Elsewhere, Thompson accepts the maintenance of the major existing security apparatuses themselves, asking only for their wings to be clipped. 'If I had the power', he writes, 'I would close down the Special Patrol Group at once, as well as many of the activities of the Special Branch and of MI5.'[60] Why should we be content with merely limiting the 'activities' of these forces? It is their structure and personnel which are irreconcilable with a socialist democracy.

Thompson would perhaps on reflection agree. The concessions being made here are not ones of principle, but of perspective. What they express is a confinement of the *horizon* of political struggle in Britain to what Thompson predicts will 'for the next 30 years' be 'democratic

59. *Introduction*, p. xvii.
60. 'On the New Issue of Postage Stamps', *New Society*, 8 November 1979.

practice and control of a very powerful State machine'.[61] There is an element of admirable sobriety in this. But there is also a risk. For if 'democratic practice' is separated so completely from 'socialist struggle' in analytic prospect and in articulate demand, then 'libertarian' campaigns could imperceptibly revert to 'liberal' politics. That danger dogs any discourse which pits a new 'statism' against traditional 'freedoms'. The conception of liberty involved is always a negative one—the protection *from* the State extolled by Berlin and so many liberal philosophers. It is no accident that the ideology of the present Conservative regime itself is clamorously 'anti-statist'. The fight for the preservation of civil liberties will only be truly successful if it is capable of *advancing* them beyond the threshold of the liberal opposition between State and individual, towards the point where the emergence of *another kind of State*—not just safeguards against the existing State—is their logical and practical terminus. For this *transitional demands*, linking immediate to ultimate, democratic to socialist, goals are essential. The full potential of the political issues of democracy raised by Thompson can only be realized by persistent and public demonstration of their convergence in socialism. Radical libertarian campaigns in the present are not to be won with continuist appeals to a constitutional past, but by credible programmes for a common future finally emancipated from it.[62] With this we come full circle, to the need for a revival of the faculties of moral and political imagination—what was traditionally called utopian thought—on the Left today. No one has done more to bring this need home to us all than Edward Thompson. The *connections* between the two positives of his recent writing, defence of civil liberties and illustration of utopian virtues, are where collective work is now most wanting, and most necessary.

61. 'Recovering the Libertarian Tradition', p. 21.
62. The appropriate correction to Thompson's reiterated appeals to the British Constitution, in his recent articles for *New Society* (see especially 'Trial by Jury', with citation from Burke), was written by himself a decade ago, reflecting on the lessons of the struggle over secret surveillance at Warwick University. *Mutatis mutandis*, its argument is eminently applicable to the wider scale on which he has now raised the same issues. 'The logic of the whole conflict leads not just to a defensive position (of establishing traditional safeguards for "academic freedom") but must lead on to a positive and far-reaching reconstruction of the university's self-government and of its relations to the community. We have forced matters to a point where we must demand a *more* democratic constitution than any existing university enjoys, or nothing—and perhaps something very much worse than nothing—will have been won.' *Warwick University Limited*, p. 159.

The divisions between Thompson and *New Left Review*, I have argued, rooted in different formations, can best be seen as contrasted emphases on morality and strategy. Thompson himself has acknowledged generously enough, on one occasion, that 'the nub of the question' was 'an emphasis on culture' as against 'a re-emphasis on power'.[63] Neither of these was ever absolute. I have tried to show that Thompson has always had his own conception of the paths to power; while NLR has pursued its own concerns with patterns of culture, on which I have not dwelt here, but which can readily be traced in articles and works it has published. But undeniably the distribution of stress has been very different. There is no question here of comparing the merits of the results. Thompson's work as a historian is, simply, incomparable. What rather needs to be said is that the Left as a whole, in Britain as elsewhere, *benefits* rather than suffers from a diversity of interests and outlooks. No one writer, or group of writers, can hope to encompass all the facets needed for a living socialist culture. A certain one-sidedness is inherent in all intellectual production as such: the important thing is that there should be many sides. A division of labour in this sense is inevitable within the thought of any significant Left, and should be welcomed rather than deplored. In fact, the dominant emphases in the writing of the 'old' and 'new' levies of the New Left should be complementary rather than conflictual ones. Strategy without morality is a machiavellian calculus, of no interest or use to a real socialist movement. Stalinism did indeed reduce Marxism to that, power without value, in its time: men like Rakosi or Zachariadis are the malignant mementoes of it. Morality without strategy, a humane socialism equipped only with an ethic against a hostile world, is doomed to needless tragedy: a nobility without force leads to disaster, as the names of Dubcek and Allende remind us. Thompson's formula for William Morris furnishes the fitting synthesis: what revolutionary socialism above all needs today is *moral realism*—with *equal* stress on each of the terms. For that kind of synthesis to start to emerge, here or anywhere, initial divisions of labour on the Left must connect into eventual forms of active cooperation. Silence and distance render this impossible. Thompson's work is haunted by political or intellectual junctures that failed to occur—historical rendez-vous that were missed, to our enduring loss: romantic poets and radical workers at the start of the 19th century,

63. 'Interview with E.P. Thompson', p. 17.

Engels and Morris at the end of it, libertarian and labour movements today. It is in mind of those greater examples that this essay has in part been written, to avoid at least a lesser one. Debate across the whole range of Thompson's ideas is here intended as some surety against it. So far, our contrasting contributions to a common socialist culture have in many ways each involved restatements or criticisms of classical inheritances, whether values imagined by Morris or Caudwell, or strategies devised by Luxemburg or Gramsci, more than innovative advance into unknown terrain. The reasons for that are not hard to seek: the absence of a truly mass and truly revolutionary movement in England, as elsewhere in the West, has fixed the perimeter of all possible thought in this period. But the example of Morris himself, who did not exactly live at a high tide in the history of the British working class, shows how much can still be done in what appear to be adverse conditions. It would be good to leave old quarrels behind, and to explore new problems together.

Bibliography

Below is a select list of Edward Thompson's writings, arranged in some sort of order for exploration by readers who may be relatively new to his work as a whole. The list is by no means exhaustive, excluding—among others—all newspaper articles, unsigned editorials or other matter in journals. The categories into which it is divided are inevitably arbitrary and overlapping to some extent. Political 'essays' are distinguished from 'articles', for example, by reason of length rather than importance. The nine last items included under the latter rubric will, indeed, be collected and published in a book, *Writing by Candlelight*, in early 1980. A volume of the longer political essays is also promised by Merlin Press, under the title *Reasoning*. A volume of the historical essays on 18th century England will eventually be published as *Customs in Common*. Two texts of especial interest, not covered in the survey of Thompson's work above, are 'Disenchantment or Default?', which discusses the pattern and significance of Wordsworth's and Coleridge's responses to social and political changes in the 1790s and afterwards, and—in related key—the recent 'Comment' in the *Stand* symposium on 'Common Values', which also draws parallels between the last decade of the 18th century and the present. Finally, space has precluded here any allusion to the historical reviews of which Thompson is such a master, a number of which are listed at the end. It is very much to be hoped that these, which include some wonderful writing, will one day be gathered together too. A critical stringency of the order they bring to bear on authorities such as Stone, Thomas or Lévi-Strauss ('Rough Music') must make any critic of Thompson's own work trepid.

Books

William Morris – Romantic to Revolutionary	1955 (revised 1977)
The Making of the English Working Class	1963 (Penguin 1968)
Whigs and Hunters	1975
The Poverty of Theory and Other Essays	1978

Works Edited

*There is a Spirit in Europe**	1947
The Railway – An Adventure in Construction	1948
Out of Apathy	1960
May Day Manifesto†	1967
Warwick University Limited	1970
The Unknown Mayhew‡	1971
Family and Inheritance – Rural Society in Western Europe 1200-1800§	1976

Brochures

The Fascist Threat to Britain	1947
The Fight for a Free Press	1952
The Communism of William Morris	1965

Political Essays

Socialism and the Intellectuals	*Universities and Left Review,* no. 1, Spring 1957
Socialism and the Intellectuals – A Reply	*Universities and Left Review,* no. 2, Summer 1957.
Socialist Humanism	*The New Reasoner,* no. 1, Summer 1957.
Agency and Choice	*The New Reasoner,* no. 5, Summer 1958
Nato, Neutralism and Survival	*Universities and Left Review,* no. 4, Summer 1958
Commitment in Politics	*Universities and Left Review,* no. 6, Spring 1959
The New Left	*The New Reasoner,* no. 9, Summer 1959

*jointly edited with T.J. Thompson
†jointly edited with Stuart Hall and Raymond Williams
‡jointly edited with Eileen Yeo
§jointly edited with Jack Goody and Joan Thirsk

A Psessay in Ephology	*The New Reasoner*, no. 10, Autumn 1959
Revolution	*New Left Review*, no. 3, May-June 1960
Revolution Again	*New Left Review*, no. 6, November-December 1960
The Long Revolution	*New Left Review* 9-10-11, May-June, July-August, September-October 1961
An Open Letter to Leszek Kolakowski	*The Socialist Register 1973*
Caudwell	*The Socialist Register 1977*
Introduction	*Review of Security and the State 1978*

Political Articles

Comments on a People's Culture	*Our Time*, October 1947
The Murder of William Morris	*Arena*, vol. II, no. 7, April-May 1951
William Morris and the Moral Issues Today	*Arena*, vol. II, no. 8, June-July 1951
Winter Wheat in Omsk	*World News*, 30 June, 1956
Reply to George Matthews	*The Reasoner*, no. 1, July 1956
Through the Smoke of Budapest	*The Reasoner*, no. 3, November 1956
The Business University	*New Society*, 19 February 1970
A Report on Lord Radcliffe	*New Society*, 30 April 1970
Sir, Writing by Candlelight	*New Society*, 24 December 1970
Yesterday's Mannikin	*New Society*, 29 July 1971
A Special Case	*New Society*, 24 February 1972
A Question of Manners	*New Society*, 11 July 1974
The State and Its Enemies	*New Society*, 19 October 1978
The State within the State	*New Statesman*, 10 November 1978
On the New Issue of Postage Stamps	*New Society*, 8 November 1979
Law and Order and the Police	*New Society*, 15 November 1979
The Rule of the Judges	*New Society*, 22 November 1979
Trial by Jury	*New Society*, 29 November 1979
Anarchy and Culture	*New Society*, 6 December 1979
The End of an Episode?	*New Society*, 13 December 1979
An Alternative to Doomsday	*New Statesman*, 21-28 December 1979

Interviews

An Interview with E.P. Thompson	*Radical History Review*, III, 4, Fall 1976
Recovering the Libertarian Tradition	*The Leveller*, no. 22, January 1979

Poems

On the Liberation of Seoul

Arena, vol. II, no. 6, February-March 1951

Homage to Salvador Allende

Spokesman Broadsheet, 30 September 1973

Criticism

Poetry's Not so Easy
A New Poet
Comment—on 'Common Values?
  An Argument'

Our Time, June 1947
Our Time, June 1949
Stand, vol. 20, no. 2, 1979

Historical Essays

Homage to Tom Maguire

Asa Briggs and John Saville, ed., *Essays in Labour History*, London 1960

The Peculiarities of the English
Time, Work-Discipline and
  Industrial Capitalism
Disenchantment or Default?
  A Lay Sermon

The Socialist Register 1965
Past and Present, no. 38, 1967

Conor Cruise O'Brien and William Dean Vanich, ed., *Power and Consciousness*, New York 1969

The Moral Economy of the English
  Crowd in the 18th Century
Rough Music: Le Charivari Anglais
Patrician Society, Plebeian Culture

Past and Present, no. 50, 1971

Annales ESC, March-April 1972
Journal of Social History, Summer 1974

The Grid of Inheritance

Family and Inheritance—Rural Society in Western Europe, Cambridge 1976

Folklore, Anthropology and Social
  History
Eighteenth-Century English Society:
  Class Struggle without Class?

Indian Historical Review, vol. 3, no. 2, January 1978
Social History, vol. 3, no. 2, May 1978

Historical Reviews

of:

R.J. White, *Waterloo to Peterloo*, and Donald Read, *Peterloo*

'God and King and Law', *New Reasoner*, no. 3, Winter 1957-1958

Peter Laslett, *The World We Have Lost*

'The Book of Numbers', *Times Literary Supplement*, December 1965*

Alan Macfarlane, *The Family Life of Ralph Josselin*, and Keith Thomas, *Religion and the Decline of Magic*

'Anthropology and the Discipline of Historical Context', *Midland History*, Spring 1972

Peter Laslett (ed), *Household and Family in Past Time*

'Under the Same Roof-Tree', *Times Literary Supplement*, 4 May 1973*

John Foster, *Class Struggle and the Industrial Revolution*

'Testing Class Struggle', *Times Higher Educational Supplement*, 8 March 1974

Raymond Williams, *The Country and the City*

'A Nice Place to Visit', *New York Review of Books*, 6 February 1975

Lawrence Stone, *The Family, Sex and Marriage in England 1500-1800*

'Happy Families', *New Society*, 8 September 1977

George Rudé, *Protest and Punishment*

'Sold like a Sheep for £1', *New Society*, 14 December 1978

*Unsigned, but attribution unmistakable.

Index

The name of E.P. Thompson has been omitted from the index.